b29574559

iWork®

FOR

DUMMIES®

2ND EDITION

iWork® FOR DUMMIES® 2ND EDITION

by Jesse Feiler

WILEY

John Wiley & Sons, Inc.

iWork® For Dummies,® 2nd Edition

Published by
John Wiley & Sons, Inc.
111 River Street
Hoboken, NJ 07030-5774
www.wiley.com

For general information on our other products and services, please contact our Customer Care Department within the U.S. at 877-762-2974, outside the U.S. at 317-572-3993, or fax 317-572-4002.

For technical support, please visit www.wiley.com/techsupport.

Wiley publishes in a variety of print and electronic formats and by print-on-demand. Some material included with standard print versions of this book may not be included in e-books or in print-on-demand. If this book refers to media such as a CD or DVD that is not included in the version you purchased, you may download this material at http://booksupport.wiley.com. For more information about Wiley products, visit www.wiley.com.

Library of Congress Control Number: 2012934493

ISBN 978-0-470-77020-7 (pbk); ISBN 978-1-118-22094-8 (ePDF); ISBN 978-1-118-23471-6 (ePub); ISBN 978-1-118-25923-8 (eMobi)

Manufactured in the United States of America

10 9 8 7 6 5 4 3 2 1

WILEY

About the Author

Jesse Feiler has been a user of Macs and Mac software since the beginning in 1984. Through his consulting company, North Country Consulting (`www.northcountryconsulting.com`), he provides services to small businesses and nonprofits, with an emphasis on FileMaker and OS X. He is also the author of the MinutesMachine app for managing meetings.

Active in the community, he has served on a variety of nonprofit boards and projects primarily in community development, the arts, and public libraries. The New York State Association of Library Boards honored him with an award for "exemplary service and dedication to libraries" in part for his role in bringing public access Internet to small rural libraries in upstate New York.

Jesse has written extensively on OS X (and its precursor, Rhapsody), FileMaker, and Apple technologies, such as Core Data and Objective-C, as well as mobile devices and tools, such as Drupal. He lives in Plattsburgh, New York with a rescued greyhound, Rex, who has been absolutely no help on this (or any other) book.

Author's Acknowledgments

Many people have helped bring this book together. First of all, my agent, Carole Jelen, at Waterside Productions, provided her usual valuable insight and suggestions. Colleagues and clients at North Country Consulting put in their comments and suggestions about the book and the features they use most in the iWork applications.

Kelly Ewing, project editor, has been an enormous help as we've struggled through the complexities of capitalization of technical terms (a constantly moving target). Dennis Cohen has provided invaluable technical assistance. Thanks also to Laura Bowman, the proofreader.

In addition to the names of those listed on the Publisher's Acknowledgments page, my thanks to the Apple technical documentation staff, who have maintained their usual high standard of documentation for developers, making it easy to see how the software is put together.

Publisher's Acknowledgments

We're proud of this book; please send us your comments at http://dummies.custhelp.com. For other comments, please contact our Customer Care Department within the U.S. at 877-762-2974, outside the U.S. at 317-572-3993, or fax 317-572-4002.

Some of the people who helped bring this book to market include the following:

Acquisitions and Editorial

Project Editor: Kelly Ewing

Acquisitions Editor: Kyle Looper

Technical Editor: Dennis Cohen

Editorial Manager: Jodi Jensen

Editorial Assistant: Amanda Graham

Sr. Editorial Assistant: Cherie Case

Cover Photo: © iStockphoto.com / René Mansi

Cartoons: Rich Tennant (www.the5thwave.com)

Composition Services

Project Coordinator: Katherine Crocker

Layout and Graphics: Corrie Niehaus, Lavonne Roberts

Proofreaders: Laura Bowman, Lauren Mandelbaum

Indexer: Sherry Massey

Publishing and Editorial for Technology Dummies

    Richard Swadley, Vice President and Executive Group Publisher

    Andy Cummings, Vice President and Publisher

    Mary Bednarek, Executive Acquisitions Director

    Mary C. Corder, Editorial Director

Publishing for Consumer Dummies

    Kathleen Nebenhaus, Vice President and Executive Publisher

Composition Services

    Debbie Stailey, Director of Composition Services

Contents at a Glance

Table of Contents

Introduction

iWork For Dummies addresses the basics of all six iWork apps — Pages, Keynote, and Presentations on Mac and iOS (iPhone, iPad, and iPod touch). It then delves into the specifics of each app. Tools such as page layouts, charts and tables, and slide presentations can show up in any iWork application. This reflects the way people work, although it doesn't often reflect the way in which other office products have been built. If you're used to another office suite, some of this may be disorienting. Everyone knows that tables and charts are part of spreadsheets, page layout tools are part of word processing, and slide shows are for presentations.

As is often the case with things that "everyone knows," this approach is often wrong. You can easily find an office suite in which a word processor can be used to build charts and tables. While spreadsheets can also be used to build charts and tables, the commands and the results can be quite different.

In iWork, the basic commands for page layout, charts and tables, and graphic objects are the same for all iWork applications. Some expanded options and features are added for specific applications. For example, you use the same basic tools to create and edit charts and tables in all three applications, but Numbers, which is the spreadsheet application, has added features for charts and tables beyond those available in Pages and Keynote.

About This Book

This book is written for people like you who want to get the most out of iWork, whether it's on a Mac or an iOS device. If you're new to the Mac or to the world of iOS devices, take a few moments to review the basics as described in the documentation that comes with your Mac or iOS device, as well as the tutorials and information on http://support.apple.com.

You can start here in the Introduction and read straight through to the end of the book if you want. You can also jump around so that you focus on chapters that are relevant to what it is you want to do at a given moment.

You'll find numbered lists of steps you can use to accomplish specific tasks. You may want to step through them even if you're not going to be using that particular functionality immediately. There's nothing like getting your hands on the iWork apps to understand how the apps and their interfaces work.

Finally, if you come away from this part of the book thinking that there's really only one iWork application with a variety of options, you won't be far wrong. A major feature of iWork and its applications is that there's only one program to understand.

Conventions Used in This Book

Most of the conventions with regard to spelling and capitalization that are used in this book are the conventions used in the Apple documentation for iWork. Here are a few additional conventions for you to know about:

- The Command key to the left (and, on some keyboards, also to the right) of the spacebar is represented by 🍎. On some keyboards, it's also labeled Command, and it may have an Apple logo or a ⌘ on it.
- Web addresses and code that you may type is shown `like this`.

How This Book Is Organized

iWork For Dummies has five parts.

Part I: Introducing iWork

In Part I, I provide an overview of iWork, as well as the commands and techniques you can use for any of the iWork apps. Here's where you find out how to create charts and tables and how to create and adjust shapes, text boxes, graphics, and other media in any of the iWork apps. Also in Part I, you see how to use the menus, toolbar, and inspectors that are available in each iWork for Mac app. With iWork for iOS, you have no menus or inspectors, and you have a different toolbar from that in the iWork for Mac apps. I describe all these interface elements in Part I.

Part II: Turning the Page with Pages

In Part II, you find out about Pages, the word-processing component of iWork. On a Mac, Pages is actually two applications in one: a standard word-processing application (much like Microsoft Word) and a page layout application (think Quark XPress or InDesign). The functionality of both types of documents is available in a single document style in iOS.

Part III: Counting on Numbers

Part III describes Numbers, the spreadsheet application, and the newest component of iWork. For a long time, spreadsheets were the domain of people who worked only with numbers, but studies showed that many users didn't use all (or even many) of the features built into their spreadsheets. The folks at Apple have thought long and hard about spreadsheets, charts, and tables, and Numbers is the result.

Part IV: Presenting Keynote

In Part IV, I describe Keynote, the tool for presentations. As Apple has focused more and more on media (everything from iTunes and the iOS devices to iLife, iMovie, and iPhoto), the components of successful presentations have been available to all users on all Macs. Keynote has been a matter of pulling all those tools and features together into a simple-to-use presentation tool. In so doing, Keynote has redefined people's expectations for presentation software. In Part IV, you see how to create slides, work with transitions, and integrate your own media with your presentations. The tools that let you see the next slide and your notes on one display while a large projection screen displays your slides for your audience are among the most powerful available on any platform.

Part V: The Part of Tens

Part V is an overview of tips and techniques that apply to all three iWork applications.

Icons Used in This Book

Throughout the margin of this book, you see little pictures that highlight information for you.

This icon identifies things to remember. If you want to highlight the text with a colored marker, feel free to do so.

This is not a developer book, but sometimes if you know how parts of the applications have evolved, it can help you understand how to use those applications better. This information is separated from the main text so that you can decide for yourself whether or not to use it.

This icon provides shortcuts and hints for improving your iWork documents and streamlining your work process.

It's really hard to make a major mistake on the Mac: Almost every command is undoable, and Mac developers use the built-in undo mechanism to encourage people to experiment with new commands and features. Still, this icon warns you of the few times when you have to be careful.

Where to Download the Example Files

I use two lengthy documents as examples (one is a Pages document and the other is a Numbers document). If you want to download them and experiment for yourself, go to my website at `http://northcountryconsulting.com` or `www.dummies.com/go/iworkfd` and look for Downloads.

Where to Go from Here

Occasionally, we have updates to our technology books. If this book does have technical updates, they will be posted at

`www.dummies.com/go/iworkfdupdates.`

In addition, example files and updates are also posted to my own website: `http://northcountryconsulting.com.`

Part I
Introducing iWork

The 5th Wave   By Rich Tennant

"Look-what if we just increase the size of the charts?"

In this part . . .

*i*Work's three apps — Pages for word processing and page layout, Numbers for spreadsheets, and Keynote for presentations — let you create very different kinds of documents. But the iWork infrastructure means that each one of those documents can use common features. You add shapes, tables, or charts to Pages in basically the same way you add them to Keynote. iWork has broken down artificial barriers so that you do the same things in the same way in all iWork applications.

With the launch of iWork for iOS in 2011, those three apps are joined by companions that run on your mobile iOS devices. You can transfer documents from one operating system to another while leaving your documents relatively untouched. (There are some formatting features that do not convert.) And with the release of iCloud, your iWork documents can be synchronized automatically across your device; they can also be shared with others through iWork.com.

This part provides an introduction to iWork and to these common interface elements and to working in iWork — manipulating fonts, colors, and shapes; using the toolbar at the top of every iWork window; and taking advantage of the powerful inspectors.

Chapter 1

Starting Out with iWork

In This Chapter

▶ Leaving the past behind

▶ Using iWork everywhere

▶ Working in iCloud

▶ Taking advantage of iWork timesavers

*W*ord processing and spreadsheet applications are among the most widely used software products on personal computers; presentation software is a close runner-up. Having started from scratch on the hardware side and then the operating system side, people at Apple started dreaming about what they could do if they were to start from scratch to write modern versions of word-processing, spreadsheet, and presentation programs. They knew they'd have to follow their recent advertising campaign theme: *Think Different.*

Freed from supporting older operating systems or from foregoing features that couldn't be implemented on Windows, they began to dream about how good those programs could be if they could start over.

So they did.

Meanwhile, other folks at Apple were thinking about mobile devices. Considering the fact that cellphones in the early 2000s sported the processor performance and memory capabilities of the computers on which the early versions of Mac OS X had been written, they wondered what they could do if they rethought computers in the mobile world.

And they did that, too.

Welcome to iWork.

Working Everywhere

iWork now fits into a world centered on you: your ideas, data, and documents; your desktop and mobile devices; and your life on the web. iWork and its components run in all these environments; they can share data (many times automatically) so that you don't have to worry about synchronizing them yourself. Here are the platforms on which iWork can run:

- ✔ **Mac OS X:** The Macintosh computer is where it all started. Today, any Mac model can run iWork. You can buy some of them with iWork pre-installed, or you can add it to a new computer using build-to-order options during the online ordering process. If you choose to buy from an Apple Store, you may also be able to choose a custom installation of iWork.

- ✔ **iOS:** This is the operating system for iPad, iPhone, and iPod touch. iWork runs on each of them, and you can move your iWork docs back and forth among your iOS devices.

This means that whether you use a Mac and whether you prefer a desktop computer or an iPad, there's an iWork app for you. Furthermore, you can take advantage of two important sharing mechanisms for your iWork docs:

- ✔ **iCloud:** Apple's Internet-based service allows you to share your data among your devices. If you have an iCloud account, you can synchronize your calendars, address book, reminders, documents, and data across all of your devices. (The upcoming section "Flying through iCloud" shows you how to set up iCloud.) iCloud is built into iOS 5 and later and Mac OS X 10.7 (Lion) and later. If you don't have it with one of these operating systems, check out www.apple.com for details on how you can upgrade your devices to the newest operating system.

- ✔ **iWork.com:** iWork.com lets you share your iWork documents with other people. You can upload them to iWork.com, publish them, or distribute them to selected people. They can download the documents in standard formats that are compatible with products such as Microsoft Word.

The biggest difference between iCloud and iWork.com is that iCloud is designed so that your data, documents, music, appointments, and so on are all *synchronized* to your various iOS devices, Macs, and PCs while iWork.com is designed to let you *share* your documents with *other* people. (Although you can share iWork documents with PCs in formats compatible with PC apps, the iWork apps do not run on PCs.)

I assume that you already have iWork installed on one or more devices: iPad, iPod touch, iPhone, or Mac. If you need more assistance with installations, go to www.apple.com/support/software. If you need assistance with purchases, go to http://store.apple.com or click or tap the App Store on your iPhone, iPad, iPod touch, or Mac.

That last sentence was a bit of a mouthful! From now on, here are some shortcuts. Unless otherwise noted, iPhone means iPhone and iPod touch. iOS device means iPhone, iPad, or iPod touch. And iWork app means an app for iWork on any of the supported devices (Mac or iOS) unless the app is designated specifically for one such as Pages for iOS or Keynote for Mac. Also note that screenshots may show the same data in different devices. If there are important differences, I point them out. The point for you to remember is that you can move your documents from one platform to another and pick up where you left off in most cases.

Flying through iCloud

You need an iCloud account to use Apple's iCloud services. Synchronization of your music, videos, books, data, documents, appointments, address book, and so on is built into iOS and Mac OS X. All you have to do is create an iCloud account if you don't have one and then set your computer to use it.

When you set up a new Mac, you're guided through the process of creating an account for yourself. That account is where all your documents and data will be stored. By default, you're automatically logged into your account, so you may not even notice it. However, you can go to Apple⊳System Preferences to create new accounts. Each person on the Mac will have a separate account.

Here's how you set up iCloud on a Mac:

1. **Log into iCloud the first time you use your Mac (or the first time you use a new account on your Mac), as shown in Figure 1-1.**

   If you add a new account on your Mac, the first time that person logs into their account, they will be guided through the sequence shown here. Each user account can have its own iCloud account, and an iCloud account can be shared by several users.

2. **Click Sign In or, if you don't have an iCloud account, click Create an Apple ID.**

   If you've purchased anything from iTunes, you have an Apple ID. You may also have one if you have purchased any of a variety of other services through Apple. If you're not sure, click Forgot Password? and you'll be guided not only through a lost password recovery procedure but also through the process of possibly locating an existing Apple ID.

   After you sign in, you see some of the features of iCloud, as shown in Figure 1-2. Select the ones you want to use. You can also create an iCloud account on its own without using the iCloud features shown in Figure 1-2. You might do this if you want to manage your contacts outside of iCloud but do not want to enable iCloud for sharing documents. (Note that, over time, this sequence may change as new features are added.)

Figure 1-1:
Log into
your iCloud
account the
first time.

Figure 1-2:
Explore
iCloud
features.

You're notified that iCloud is set up (see Figure 1-3).

3. **If you want to adjust your settings (including turning iCloud off or on), use System Preferences in the Apple menu, as shown in Figure 1-4.**

Figure 1-3:
Your iCloud account is set up and activated.

Figure 1-4:
Use System Preference to adjust iCloud settings.

4. **Click the iCloud icon and adjust the iCloud settings, as shown in Figure 1-5.**

Figure 1-5:
Adjust your
iCloud
settings.

 You definitely want Documents & Data on to use iWork. Mail & Notes, Contacts, and Calendars set up synchronization with your mobile devices as well as Macs and PCs that also are set up for this iCloud account.

5. When you're finished, just close the window.

Using iWork.com

The public beta version of iWork.com is a new way of sharing your iWork documents as you work on them. It differs from iCloud in that iWork.com is designed for collaboration with other people rather than synchronization among your own devices.

Want to work with two colleagues on a presentation? No big deal: Start by uploading your Keynote document to iWork.com. Then a friend can download it and make changes in the document as a Microsoft PowerPoint document. Back it goes to the Internet, and someone else can download it in yet another format. This is an example of the technology called *cloud computing* that is also behind iCloud. It's also an example of people being able to work together on their own terms. You don't have to get together and decide which presentation (or spreadsheet or word-processing) application you'll all use.

The Share menu lets you send documents from Keynote, Numbers, and Pages via e-mail; you can also export documents in industry-standard formats.

iWork.com adds another way of collaborating on a document. You can post an iWork document to your iWork.com area, where it is visible to you and to people you invite to view it. Those people can then add notes and comments to the documents on the web.

You can download documents from iWork.com in a variety of formats. This makes two types of interactions possible:

- ✔ **Comments and notes on iWork documents:** You can add comments to specific parts of iWork documents (a section of text, for example); you can also add notes to the document as a whole (rather than to a specific part of it). As a result, a number of people can work together on a document.

- ✔ **Multiple revisions to iWork documents:** You can download the documents to your own computer in a variety of formats. Many of these formats include the comments that you and others have added. Once a document is downloaded, you can modify it and add more comments that describe the modifications.

Logging on to iWork.com

There are slight differences on OS X and iOS when you log on to iWork.com. In both cases, you're asked to log on the first time you try to access iWork. com. For many people, this means the first time you choose to share a document or to look at your shared documents. If you aren't asked to log on, then your logon information has been saved. (There is a logout command you can use in these cases if you want to switch user IDs.)

Logging on to iWork.com on OS X

When you're using an iWork app, the Share menu allows you to log on to iWork.com, as shown in Figure 1-6. If you're logged in, you use this menu to log out. (Sign In will be replaced by Sign Out when you're logged in.)

Figure 1-6:
Use the
Share menu.

Share via iWork.com...
Show Shared Documents
Sign In...

Send via Mail ▶
Send to iWeb ▶

Export...

If you need to create a new Apple ID, see Figure 1-1 earlier in this chapter.

If you're using a computer in a public area (such as a public library), it makes sense to log out from any private areas that you're using so that the next person using the computer doesn't have access to your data.

Logging on to iWork.com on iOS

Instead of a Share menu on Mac OS X, on iOS you use Tools (the wrench at the right of the toolbar) and tap Share and Print, as shown at the right of Figure 1-7.

Figure 1-7: Access iWork.com from iOS.

Just as on OS X, if you need to log on, you're asked to do so, as shown in Figure 1-8.

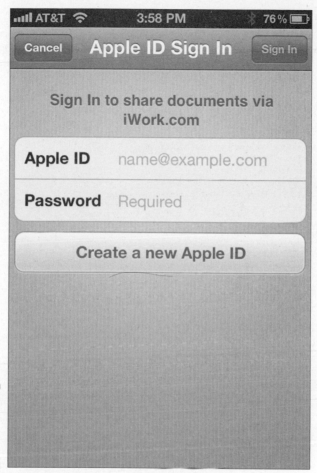

Figure 1-8:
Sign in to
iWork.com
on iOS.

Sharing documents with iWork.com

There are also minor differences in sharing on OS X and iWork.com. However, remember that you're accessing the same remote site (in the cloud), so the differences are just in the interfaces.

Sharing documents from OS X

On OS X, choose Share➪Share via iWork.com to share an open iWork document. You're prompted to specify the ways in which the document can be downloaded, and you're also prompted to supply an e-mail address for your colleague (see Figure 1-9). You can also set options as to whether people can annotate the document.

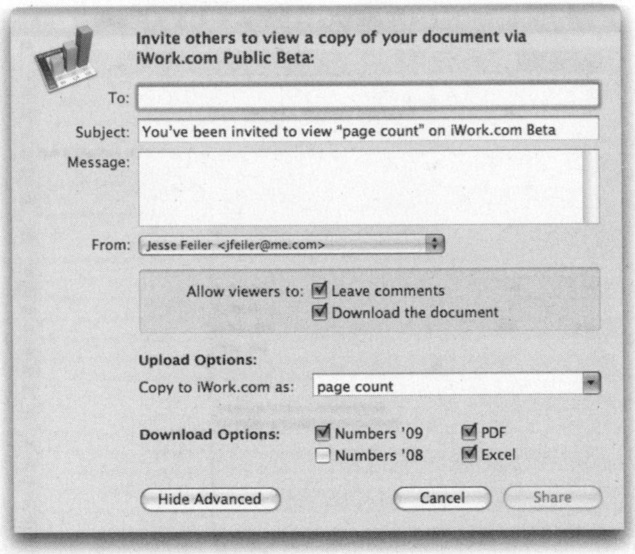

Figure 1-9: Prepare documents for sharing on iWork.com.

Invite others to view a copy of your document via iWork.com Public Beta:

To:

Subject: You've been invited to view "page count" on iWork.com Beta

Message:

From: Jesse Feiler <jfeiler@me.com>

Allow viewers to: ☑ Leave comments
☑ Download the document

Upload Options:
Copy to iWork.com as: page count

Download Options: ☑ Numbers '09 ☑ PDF
☐ Numbers '08 ☑ Excel

Hide Advanced   Cancel   Share

Sharing documents with iWork.com on iOS

On iOS, the process consists of presenting you with an e-mail to be sent to an address you specify. You can add more than one address, and you can write a message, as shown in Figure 1-10, on an iPhone.

Figure 1-10:
Share documents from an iPhone.

Tap the *i* at the right to set the options that, on OS X, are set as you see in Figure 1-9. The iPad version is shown in Figure 1-11.

Figure 1-11:
Set iWork.
com sharing
options on
iPad.

Viewing your shared documents

Viewing shared documents consists of processes on OS X and iOS.

Viewing shared documents from OS X

After you've logged on, you can choose Share⇨Show Shared Documents
to open the browser window shown in Figure 1-12. (iWork uses the default
browser for your computer, and you must have an Internet connection to
view your shared documents.)

In constructing the Share menu, the iWork application you're using will take
note of whether or not you're logged on. In addition, it may post information
about notes or changes that have been made, as shown in Figure 1-13.

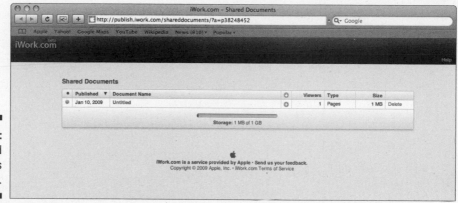

Figure 1-12:
View shared
documents
in a browser.

Figure 1-13:
The Share
menu
provides
summary
information
changes
to shared
documents.

You can download your shared iWork documents from iWork.com. Use the Download menu at the right to choose a download format, as shown in Figure 1-14. You'll find the appropriate iWork format, but you usually also find cross-platform formats, such as PDFs, and Microsoft Office formats, such as PowerPoint, Excel, and Word.

In general, changes and comments appear in all formats; document notes on the iWork document itself generally appear only if you download the document as an iWork document.

In the case of complex documents, you may want to save copies of the downloaded files before you make changes to them.

Figure 1-14:
Download
your shared
iWork docu-
ment in the
format you
want to use.

Inviting People to View Shared Documents

You can add individuals to the list of people who can share a document. Click Add at the right of the window shown in Figure 1-15. Enter the name and e-mail address for the new person.

As you can see in Figure 1-16, you're given a link that you can send to that person; the link lets the person view the document.

Figure 1-15:
Invite new
people to
share your
documents.

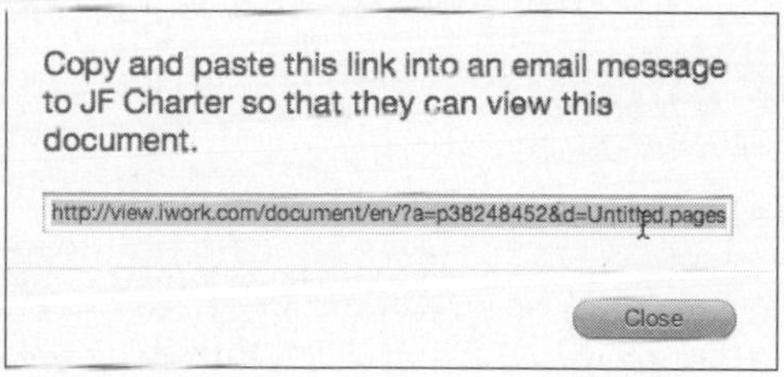

Copy and paste this link into an email message
to JF Charter so that they can view this
document.

http://view.iwork.com/document/en/?a=p38248452&d=Untitled.pages

Close

Figure 1-16:
Get the link
to send
to your
colleague.

If you ever want to see the link again, select the triangle next to the person's name and e-mail address, as shown in Figure 1-17. You can then send it to a colleague who has lost the link.

Figure 1-17:
You can
always
retrieve
the link.

Adding Document Notes

Someone who is invited to view your document and make changes can add document notes to it. When logged on to iWork.com, he simply needs to click Add at the right of the window to add a document note. It will be appropriately identified and time-stamped, as shown in Figure 1-18.

Document notes are downloaded when you download a document as an iWork document, but they're not always downloaded when you download the document in another format. You don't have to worry about document notes being visible on iWork.com; as you can see in Figure 1-19, they're added to a chronological list.

Adding Comments to Document Objects

You can select an element of an iWork document and add a comment to it. Follow these simple steps:

1. **Select the object to annotate.**

   You can select text, a text box, or anything else that's selectable in your iWork document. Figure 1-20 shows part of the For Sale banner selected for annotation.

Figure 1-20: Select the object to annotate.

2. **Click Add Comment at the top of the window, as shown in Figure 1-21.**

3. **Type the comment.**

   The comment is identified with your name and is time-stamped automatically. As shown in Figure 1-21, you can reply to a comment from someone else, and they can reply to a comment from you. (It's called working together.)

Figure 1-21:
Click Add
Comment.

Living the Suite Life

A suite of applications provides a collection of applications that can work together. For example:

- ✔ **Adobe Creative Suite** combines graphics-oriented applications, video, and desktop publishing, such as Photoshop, InDesign, Illustrator, and Acrobat. There are various configurations of Adobe Creative Suite with differing combinations of these and other products.

- ✔ **Apple iLife** combines iPhoto, iTunes, iMovie, iWeb, iDVD, and GarageBand.

- ✔ **Microsoft Office** is a suite of applications that comes in a variety of flavors: On Mac OS X, it normally includes Microsoft Office, Microsoft Excel, and Microsoft PowerPoint. On Windows, Microsoft Office has further variations, some of which include Microsoft Access (a database).

Sometimes, a suite of applications is sold as a package; other times, each application is sold separately. After being a single product for a number of years, you can now buy the iWork apps individually.

Whether you look at each app individually or the big picture of the iWork suite, here's how iWork fits into the picture.

Official business

iWork is an *office suite,* like Microsoft Office. Office suites provide applications that are, well, office oriented. An office suite usually includes at least

- A *word-processing* application, such as Microsoft Word or iWork's Pages
- A *spreadsheet* application, such as Microsoft Excel or iWork's Numbers
- A *presentation* application, such as Microsoft PowerPoint or iWork's Keynote

One of the coolest advantages of iWork is that major features, not just small operations such as changing a font or selecting a color, are available in the same way in all its applications. You really have only one program to learn when you're using iWork.

One piece at a time

A lot of technical trickery is in the background, but you *use* iWork through three applications that are similar to Microsoft Office applications (but way cooler, I think).

Pages

For many people, word processing is the core of an office suite. In fact, many people don't get beyond it. You can create two types of word-processing documents with iWork for Mac:

- **Standard word-processing documents,** in which the text flows from page to page as needed (for example, add a paragraph on page three, and the bottom of page three flows onto the top of page four automatically). In general, the automatic flowing of word-processing documents is used for documents that will be read in the way in which letters and memos are read.

- **Page layout documents,** which have the type of structure you see in newspapers and magazines. Articles don't just flow one after the other. Instead, an article on page one may be continued on page four while another article on page one may be continued on page eight. Also, objects such as photos are often placed in a specific position on a page, and they don't move as text is added or deleted.

With Pages for iPad and iPhone, this distinction is not made, but the functionality is there anyway. iWork provides you with a variety of sophisticated tools to create your Pages documents. These include advanced font handling, color, tables, and charts, as well as the ability to place QuickTime movies and hypertext links in your Pages documents. Of course, printed versions of those documents won't support QuickTime movies or hypertext links, but they will be active when you look at the document on a computer screen, your iPhone, or iPad.

Apple starts you off with a variety of templates for various documents. Figure 1-22 shows you the templates available for newsletters in the Page Layout set of templates.

Figure 1-22: Choose a template as a starting point.

If you choose one of the templates, it opens in Pages. You see in later chapters how to explore that document, but here's a sneak preview. A Pages pop-up menu in the interface shows you the template's pages, as shown in Figure 1-23.

You can customize the templates and the pages as you see fit. But before you do so, take the time to look at what you have in front of you. It isn't just a matter of nicely formatted pages. In addition, the specific pages in each template (they're different in each template) should give you ideas not just for laying out and constructing your document but also for the types of information you should consider for different types of documents.

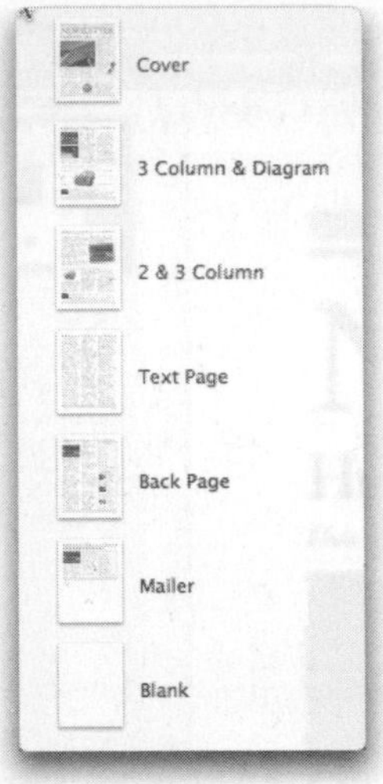

Figure 1-23:
Explore
the pages
within the
template.

For example, the Program template from the Brochures set of templates has a page laid out already for mailing information. Had you thought of putting mailing information on your brochure? Maybe you did, and maybe you didn't — but Pages did.

Numbers

Spreadsheet programs let you enter data in rows and columns. One of their main features is that you can also enter formulas. That way, if you have a column listing your grocery expenditures for a week, for example, the addition of another bill will cause the column's total to be recalculated. Spreadsheets are about data (usually numbers) and fast calculation updates.

You probably think you know what a spreadsheet looks like, but take a look at the Numbers document in Figure 1-24. This is a Numbers document based on the Numbers Home Improvement template. A single document can have a number of *sheets* (like sheets in a Microsoft Excel workbook). But there the similarity ends. A Numbers sheet can contain a variety of objects: zero or more tables (traditional spreadsheets), zero or more charts, as well as other iWork objects, such as graphics, text boxes, movies, and audio. In Figure 1-24, the sheet is shown with a table, a chart, and a picture.

A *comment* is attached to the table. All iWork applications support comments, although each has its own method of displaying them. Sometimes they look like those colored notes you stick on memos and refrigerator doors.

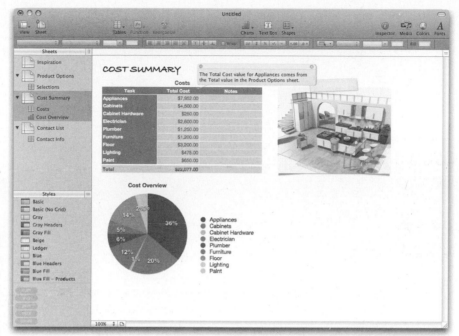

Figure 1-24:
Numbers is
more than a
spreadsheet
application.

Keynote

It's only been a few thousand years since people starting giving presentations. Call them lectures, classes, sermons, or sales pitches, they're all pretty much the same: Someone stands in front of a large or small group of people and explains, teaches, or informs them. Sometimes, the presentation has multimedia elements: slides in an architecture class, music in a history lecture about a composer, and movies in a talk about "My Summer Vacation."

The Keynote authoring and presentation tools are unsurpassed, but it doesn't stop there. Take a look at Figure 1-25 to see the variety of export formats available in Keynote. When you're preparing a Keynote presentation, you're simultaneously authoring a QuickTime movie, a Flash animation, HTML, or even a DVD. All you have to do is click one extra button to start the export process. (Not all of these run on all platforms. For example, Flash doesn't run on iOS.)

Keynote was the original iWork application. Built by Apple engineers for MacWorld keynote speeches delivered by Steve Jobs, Keynote has been refined over the years to the powerful tool it is today.

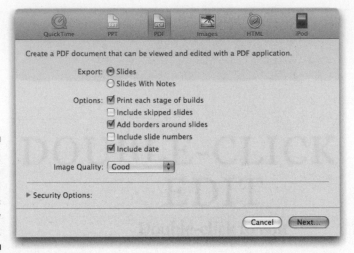

Figure 1-25:
Keynote exports presentations in a variety of formats.

The Big Difference

You can do similar things with various office suites, but the big difference with iWork comes from two aspects of iWork that are hallmarks of Apple's approach to software development:

- ✔ **It's all about communication.** From the beginning of the Mac, the people at Apple have focused not merely on raw computing power but also on how that power and technology can be used to help people communicate.

- ✔ **Do it once, do it right, and reuse it.** Apple's pioneering use of scripting languages (AppleScript primarily) helped people turn the Macs into devices that could learn, as in "watch what I do and then do it automatically."

Perhaps the clearest indication of where Apple's values lie came in its recent corporate name change: It's now Apple, not Apple Computer. Computers are a means to an end.

It's all about communication

For decades, people have been hailing the advent of the paperless office, but the flood of paper has only increased. When you think about what people are trying to do with all that paper, you realize that it's not about automating the production of documents — it's about communicating. That's what iWork is about — helping you communicate as effectively and easily as possible. Apple has provided elegant interfaces and sophisticated designs for your communications, but this isn't done for decoration. The focus is communication.

If you don't think it's all about communication, take a look back at Figure 1-24, which shows Numbers in action. In the upper left, you can see a recognizable table (or part of a spreadsheet). There's a pie chart and an image showing how the items in the spreadsheet could look if used together. If you think spreadsheets aren't about communication, think about how many spreadsheets you've seen that look like this one. (If the number is zero, don't be alarmed: Not everyone in the world uses iWork . . . yet.)

As you explore iWork, don't be dazzled by the wide variety of communication tools. The most effective communication is the clearest. If you want someone to understand how to change the toner cartridge in a photocopy machine, a movie might be the best tool. If you want to explain the structure of an organization, a static diagram might be the clearest representation. And remember the many documents that have changed the world through their words alone.

Look at the iWork communication tools not as a challenge in which you must use them all; instead, look at them as a wonderful array of tools from which you can select the most appropriate ones for any task. Too much of anything — graphics, movies, or even words — is counterproductive.

For every iWork document, ask yourself these questions:

 ✔ What am I trying to say?
 ✔ Who am I trying to say it to?

After you can answer those two questions, you're ready to go.

Do it once, do it right, and reuse it

iWork has a variety of tools that save you time by letting you easily reuse work you've done already. Not only can you reuse your own work, but you can also reuse the work of other people.

Customizing with themes and templates

The iWork applications have a variety of tools for reuse; the chief ones are themes and templates:

✔ **Themes (Keynote):** A *theme* allows only certain types of modifications. The limits on what you can change mean that an application that supports themes knows the basics about what to expect. You can switch from one theme to another without compromising your data. For example, when you select a Keynote theme, you select a size for all its slides. You cannot change the size for an individual slide. This use of themes is supported with Keynote and with other applications, such as Bento and iMovie.

✔ **Templates (Pages and Numbers):** A *template* is a document that's ready for you to modify with your own data and formatting. It has formatting set for you that you can then customize. It may have placeholders for text and images that you later insert; it may have text and images that will be used without change in your documents. After you change a margin in a template, for example, your new margin is used in documents you create from that modified template.

All iWork for Mac applications support themes or templates and allow you to save a document as a theme or a template. If you choose to modify a theme or a template, you can then resave it as a theme or a template of your own. Figure 1-26 shows how easy it is to create your own theme in Keynote with a simple command. Design the presentation you want to reuse and then choose Save Theme. When you want to reuse it, use the Choose Theme command.

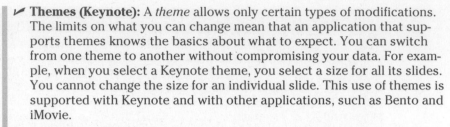

Figure 1-26: Create your own theme in Keynote.

The iWork applications ship with themes and templates ready for you to use (see Figure 1-27). These are worth exploring even if you plan to start from scratch because you can find ideas in all the themes and templates that you can use in your own ways. Apple has built on the real-life experiences of iWork users. The themes and templates may remind you of features or issues that you haven't thought of.

Figure 1-27:
Use the
iWork
themes and
templates.

Reusing parts of documents

All iWork applications let you create parts of your documents that you can reuse. These reusable parts can be

- ✓ **Sections** in Pages word-processing documents
- ✓ **Pages** in Pages page layout documents
- ✓ **Master slides** in Keynote
- ✓ **Sheets or tables** in Numbers

To break down a project to a manageable size, look for the intermediate size parts that you can work on. For example, if you're part of a committee of 10 people working on a 200-page planning document for a company, a community, or an event, where do you begin? If you just start writing, you're likely to be at the task a long time. Very long. Try to break down the task. What are the logical components? These will probably become chapters.

If you're working on a budget for your school, you may soon be looking at hundreds of rows and hundreds of columns. Use Numbers tables to divide and conquer. Instead of budgeting expenses for the Language Arts department in five columns, make Language Arts into its own small table. Numbers makes it easy to integrate many small tables into a large whole.

Whether a Pages document, a Numbers project, or a Keynote presentation, if you make the components about one page in length, you almost always have an easier-to-understand document.

Sharing styles

A *style* is a collection of attributes, such as fonts, typefaces, colors, and number formatting. You set up a style and give it a name, and then you can reuse it throughout your document. Common styles have names, such as Header, Subheader, Address, or Footnote. Using styles means you can set one attribute — the *style* — rather than individually setting the various parts of the style.

If you use styles, you can change an attribute of the style so that it's changed in every occurrence of the style.

iWork supports styles in all its applications.

Letting your Mac do the work

Mac OS X and iWork support scripting of applications. (Scripting is not available on iOS.) The two primary tools for scripting are AppleScript and Automator. With a script, your work is automated. You start the script, and it runs. You can either write scripts or use the Record feature in ScriptEditor so that your actions are captured automatically into a script.

Scripts are particularly useful for the following:

- ✔ **Repeated tasks:** If you have a task that needs to be carried out several times with only slight variations, AppleScript is your savior. For example, you can write a script that retrieves text and images from a FileMaker database and places them in a Pages document to automatically produce a catalog.

- ✔ **Complex tasks:** One of the challenges of complex tasks is remembering all the steps and sequences. AppleScript can remember them for you. You may not save time, but a script does the task the same way every time.

- ✔ **Integration tasks:** AppleScript excels at integrating applications and their data. For example, a FileMaker/Pages script would communicate with FileMaker to retrieve some data, switch to Pages to place it, switch back to FileMaker to get some more data, and so on.

Chapter 2

Working Effectively with iWork

In This Chapter

▶ Getting to know the common interface elements on iOS and on iPad

▶ Working with iWork documents

▶ Using iCloud

*F*rom the very beginning, what has set iWork apart from other office suites has been the consistency of its interface. You adjust fonts, colors, images, and text the same way in Pages, Numbers, or Keynote. Partly because the interface is so consistent, people have started experimenting — for example, by placing images in spreadsheets and tables in presentations.

iWork on iPhone, iPod touch, and iPad (the iOS devices) all offer the same consistent interface from OS X, so how you use iWork for each of the apps on each of the operating systems is fundamentally the same.

Any differences that do exist are usually due to a basic feature of the device on which you are running. I discuss the most important distinction — using iWork menus on OS X — in the following chapter. iOS devices lack menus, so the menu system is a Mac-only interface. But the underlying functionality is very much the same on both OS X and iOS.

This chapter introduces you to the common iWork tools and the interface elements on OS X and iOS that let you access those tools.

Many of the commands in the user interface let you manipulate objects: text, graphics, shapes, table cells, and the like. The way that you manipulate similar objects is the same across the iWork applications, but what is often different is how you create the objects. Creating a text box in Pages, Numbers, and Keynote are *similar* processes, but the process of manipulating the newly created text box is almost *exactly* the same in each application. If you're primarily interested in creating objects, you may want to explore the chapters that are specific to Pages, Numbers, and Keynote first. However, if you're interested in manipulating them, this chapter is your key. Depending on your specific needs, you may want to switch back and forth between chapters.

Exploring the Mac iWork Window

In addition to the presence of a menu bar on iWork for Mac, perhaps the biggest interface difference has to do with the iWork windows. Yes, that's windows plural. You probably don't really pay attention to the fact that you can move around and resize windows on Macs and PCs because you're used to it. On iOS devices, the screen is essentially a window. You can move to another screen or window, but you can't resize them and move them around. It's one at a time.

The iWork window that is the basis for all the iWork for Mac apps is flexible and customizable and has a lot of functionality. The more limited space available for the iOS devices means that it doesn't have room for many of the features found on iWork for Mac. The most important features are implemented in different ways on iOS than they are on Mac. Other features — the "power user" features — remain in the Mac versions. Most of the time, if you add these features to an iWork document, you can move the document back and forth using iCloud so that you can continue to work on it on all your devices whenever you feel like it. In some cases, moving a document to an iOS device may remove a few features, but don't worry: iWork always tells you what's going on.

The format bar, located just below the toolbar, is a common interface element. However, its components are sufficiently different for each of the iWork applications, so it is described in the context of each specific application rather than in this chapter.

The iWork window

Figure 2-1 shows you the bare bones of an iWork window, with a report template in Pages. What stays the same for all iWork apps is the outer frame: the title bar at the top with the close, minimize, and zoom buttons at the upper left; the bottom frame with (from left) a pop-up menu to set the zoom factor for the window, the page information, and up- and down-arrows to move to the next or previous page. (If there is no next or previous page, the appropriate arrow appears dimmed.) At the right, the scrolling tools common to many Mac windows are provided. Finally, in the lower right, the resize corner lets you resize (and reshape) the window.

With the release of OS X 10.7 (Lion) in 2011, window behavior has new features on OS X. Specifically, you can have scroll bars behave as they do in these figures, but you also have the choice to have them appear based on the device you are using. With a trackpad, the option is for scroll bars to appear only if you move the pointer over them. (This is basically the behavior of scroll bars on iOS devices — they appear only when you tap in the area of the scroll bar.) In addition, you can drag windows from any side. You can turn the new behavior on and off in File⇨System Preferences in the General pane using the Show Scroll Bars radio buttons. And if you really want to show off, you can let your friends know that the scroll bar is the entire mechanism, while the thing that you drag is a *scroller* that moves along the scroll bar.

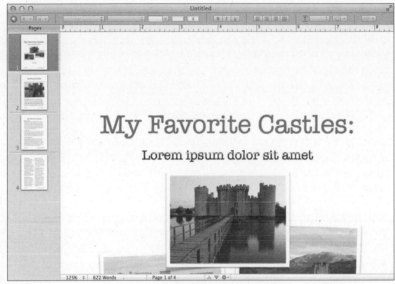

Figure 2-1:
A bare-bones iWork window.

The iWork toolbar on OS X

For a number of years, commands from the menu bar have been moving into individual windows in a section at the top called a *toolbar*. Each iWork application has its own toolbar, but some basics apply to all of them. You can show or hide the toolbar using option-command-T or View⇨Show/Hide Toolbar. Figure 2-2 shows the Pages toolbar. (Compare it with Figure 2-1.)

TIP

The gray background of the toolbar behaves just like the background of the window's title bar. You can drag the window by clicking anywhere in that gray background.

If the window isn't wide enough to show the toolbar, the icons at the right are shown (text only) just beyond the right side of the toolbar when you click the double arrow shown at the right in Figure 2-3.

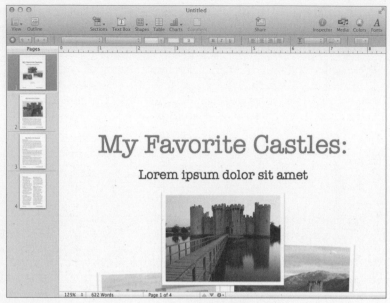

Figure 2-2:
Show the
toolbar.

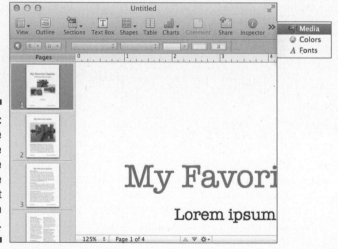

Figure 2-3:
Click the
double
arrow at the
right to see
icons that
don't fit on
the toolbar.

Some toolbar icons have small downward-pointing arrows that bring up a menu of choices. Usually, the choices are visual, as shown in Figure 2-4, but sometimes the choice is a traditional menu with text commands.

Some toolbar icons have a plus symbol at the upper left, as shown in Figure 2-5. These icons add something to the document: another page, another table, or whatever the icon indicates. In the case of Pages, these icons can represent a specific type of page to add based on the chosen template. As you see in Figure 2-5, you can choose to add a blank page or a page with eight or ten new labels.

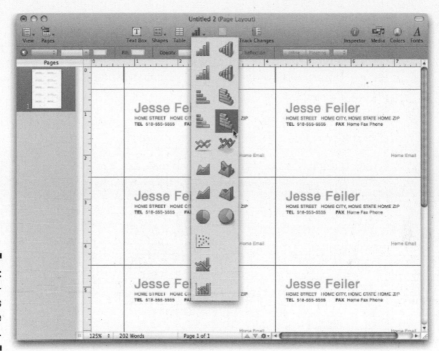

Figure 2-4:
Some tool-
bar icons
have
submenus.

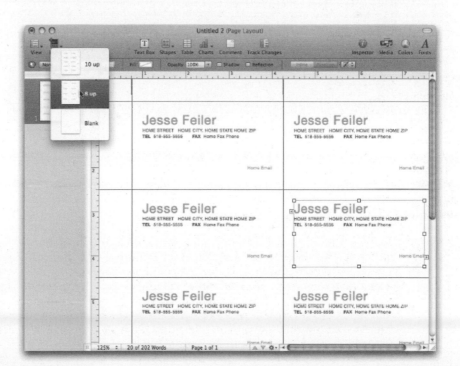

Figure 2-5:
Some icons
let you add
objects to
the current
document.

Exploring iWork for iOS

On iOS (iPhone, iPad, and iPod touch), you have only the single screen view — no separate windows. The interface is different, but you can do many of the same things you do on your Mac.

Toolbars appear at the top of the iWork screen on iOS, as shown in Figure 2-6. (iOS toolbars look different from Mac toolbars.)

There actually are two types of iWork toolbars. The one shown in Figure 2-6 lets you manage all of your iWork documents for whatever app you're running. The other one lets you manage the specific document that you're working on.

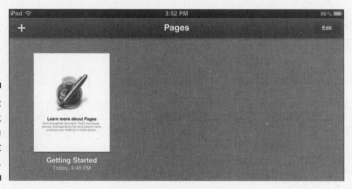

Figure 2-6: iOS iWork apps have a toolbar at the top.

Managing documents with the toolbar

The document management toolbar, shown in Figure 2-6, has the name of the app in the center and the Edit button at the right along with the + at the left.

The + lets you create new documents, as described in the upcoming section "Managing your iWork documents on iOS."

When you tap Edit, your document icons start to jiggle — just as on the Home screen of your iPad or iPhone. (And, just as on the Home screen, tap and hold a document icon, and you enter Edit mode automatically.)

Drag a document onto another one to create a folder, as shown in Figure 2-7. (Yes, this, too, is just the way things work elsewhere on iOS.)

These buttons are now enabled

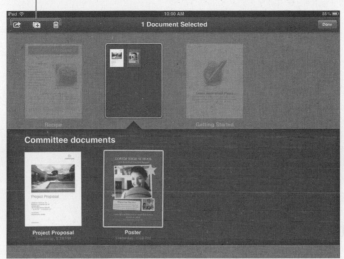

Figure 2-7:
You can
drag a doc-
ument onto
another one
to create a
folder.

Tap in the folder name, and the keyboard slides up so that you can rename the folder.

You can drag a document out of the folder and back to the documents screen. When you remove the last document from a folder, the folder disappears.

When you're finished organizing your documents, tap Done to make them stop jiggling.

Working with a toolbar for a single document

When you're working on a single document, you have a different toolbar, as you can see in Figure 2-8. (This toolbar is from Keynote rather than Pages; you soon see the reason.)

On the far-left side of the toolbar, the Documents button lets you see all your Pages, Numbers, or Keynote documents, depending on which app you're working with. Next to Documents is the Undo button. (It's the same as the Edit⇨Undo command you may have on OS X for iWork and most other apps.) In the center of the window is the document's name.

Info   Automate

Animation

Insert   Tools

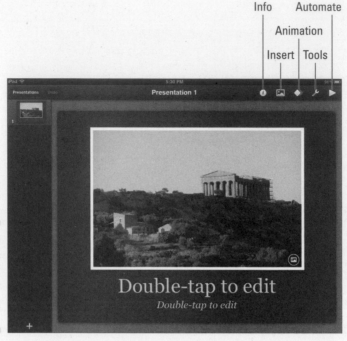

Figure 2-8:
Work with
a single
document's
toolbar in
Keynote.

At the right of the iWork toolbar are four or five buttons:

- ✔ **Info:** Provides information and choices about the current selection in the document. From here, you may choose a style, a list format, or a layout (alignment, columns, and line spacing) for a selected paragraph. If nothing is selected, this button is dimmed.

- ✔ **Insert:** Lets you insert images from your photo albums on iPad or iPhone. If you want to insert a photo into your iWork document, add it to your album by taking the photo or synchronizing it in iTunes.

- ✔ **Animation:** Used to add an animation to slide transitions. This double-diamond button (refer to Figure 2-8) appears only in Keynote.

- ✔ **Tools:** The wrench opens a popover containing tools that are based on the document as a whole rather than on the current selection within the document. Figure 2-9 shows the tools for a Pages document.

Both Share and Print and Settings have disclosure triangles that let you drill down one more level. Figure 2-10 shows the Share and Print options.

Figure 2-9: Tools for a Pages document.

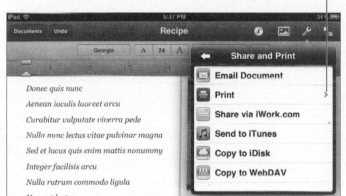

Figure 2-10: Sharing documents.

You can use the left-pointing arrow in the popover to return to the tools.

The Settings are shown in Figure 2-11. Note that Word Count has been turned on; it appears at the bottom of the document.

✔ **Full-screen:** The double arrows expand the document to fill your iPad screen, hiding the toolbar and other features. Tap in the full-screen document to return to the editable view with the toolbar.

Keynote also has an Automate button to the right of the Tools button. (Refer to Figure 2-8.) Tapping the Automate button begins playing your presentation.

Word Count is displayed here

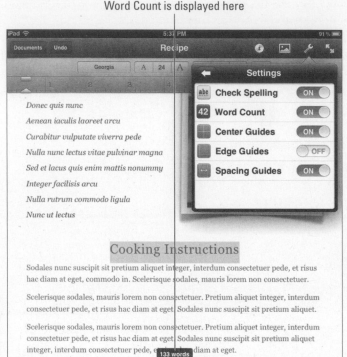

Figure 2-11:
Adjusting
settings.

The ruler that you may have seen in Pages is used by its word-processing features. Similar tools at the top of the screen are used in Numbers and Keynote, depending on what you're trying to do.

Another interface element that you encounter from time to time is known as a *modal view*. Think of a modal view as a dialog that appears on top of the screen (sometimes covering all of it) with the background appearing to be slightly dimmed. Often, a button in the upper-right corner (usually with a blue background) lets you accept the information in the view. Sometimes, a modal view presents you with a choice — buttons appear in both the upper-right and upper-left corners. In these instances, tap the button that represents the action you want to take.

Using popovers

An important interface element in the Pages document shown previously in Figure 2-9 is a *popover*. Common to all iWork apps, the popover resembles the dialog in OS X and other operating systems but is redesigned for iOS. This list describes three actions you can take with a popover:

- ✔ **Recognize the purpose of the popover.** Each popover includes an arrow that points to the button that opened it.

- ✔ **Dismiss the popover.** If you want to dismiss the popover (the equivalent of the Close or Cancel button on your Mac), tap anywhere outside the popover.

- ✔ **Make a selection on the popover.** When you tap a choice in a popover, it's carried out, and the popover closes automatically.

Managing iWork Documents

I talk about some of the tools for managing documents earlier in this chapter. In this section, you can see them all together. You can perform four basic functions:

- ✔ **Create a document from a template**. You usually have a blank template to use if you really want to start from scratch, but the templates provide a lot of guidance as you build your documents.

- ✔ **Delete a document.** When you're finished with a document, you don't have to keep it around, and you can delete it.

- ✔ **Duplicate a document.** This command makes an exact copy of a document on your device. (The duplicated document may be shared with your other iCloud devices automatically.) This behavior takes place on your device.

- ✔ **Copy a document into your documents area.** This means that you can copy a document from iCloud, a WebDAV server, or iTunes. In that way it differs from duplicating a document on your device. You can't edit documents in these shared locations; you copy them to your Mac or iOS device and work on them there.

In addition to these functions, you can use iWork.com to share your iWork documents with other people.

Managing your iWork documents on OS X

On OS X, you manage your iWork documents in exactly the same way you manage any other documents. You use the New, Open, and Save commands in the iWork apps. You use the Finder to move your files around and to organize them into folders. (You can also do that when you're creating a document.)

Managing your iWork documents on iOS

The data for your iWork documents is stored in files on your iOS device, possibly on your Mac or PC, and also sometimes on shared *WebDAV* (Web-based Authoring and Versioning, used for collaboration and managing of files on the web) servers and on iWork.com, if you choose. (You can find more on iWork.com in "Managing your iWork documents on iWork.com," later in this chapter.")

You can store iWork files on a PC, but iWork runs on only iOS and OS X. You can easily convert your iWork files to the comparable Microsoft Office file types so that you can work on them on a PC in that format.

One feature that makes iWork for iOS successful is that the iWork team has made it easy for you to move documents around and work on them in whatever environment you want, from your desktop to a mobile device, such as your iPhone or iPad (or iPod touch).

What matters is that you can get to your documents, read and write them, and share them with people. It's also critical that you can get to documents that other people share with you without either one of you having to jump through hoops.

Deep down inside the iOS operating system are files and folders, but most of the time, you manipulate them indirectly through apps. When it comes to apps, the files and folders are in a special area reserved only for that app. (This area is called a *sandbox.*) Some apps, such as the iWork apps, can read files from servers, such as iDisk and WebDAV; if you select one of those files, it's copied into the appropriate place on your device for you to work on it.

The storage areas for files are kept separate for each app. If you install Pages and then remove it from your iPad, your Pages documents disappear along with the Pages app. Before uninstalling any app, make certain that you have backed up any files you have created.

Copying a file into an iWork for iOS app

If you have a file on your Mac or on a server (an iDisk or WebDAV server), you can copy it into an iWork app to work on it there. Of course, the document needs to be saved as one of these compatible file types:

- **Numbers:** `.numbers`, `.xls`, `.xlsx`
- **Keynote:** `.key`, `.ppt`, `.pptx`
- **Pages:** `.pages`, `.doc`, `.docx`

These are the primary document types. You can import other files, such as JPEG image files, by adding them to your iPhoto library, music files in iTunes, and so on.

1. **From your documents page (Documents, Spreadsheets, or Presentations), tap + at the left end of the toolbar.**

2. **For iDisk or a WebDAV server, log in with your password.**

   You have no login for iTunes because your account ID is stored and your device is paired with only one computer.

3. **Select the file you want.**

   As you can see in Figure 2-12, you can navigate folders. Files that are dimmed out aren't compatible with the app you're running. In Figure 2-12, the only file that you can copy is a Keynote presentation because it's the Keynote document. The file will be copied into your documents (Presentations, Spreadsheets, or Documents, depending on its type).

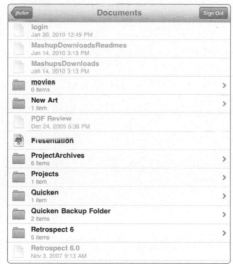

Figure 2-12: Select the file to copy.

4. **You're warned if any errors occur (see Figure 2-13).**

   The most common errors are caused by opening a document created in another application or an earlier version of an app; these errors can include missing fonts, resizing of slides in Keynote, and the use of unsupported features. Wherever possible (almost always), the app works around these issues.

5. **Correct any errors and then get to work.**

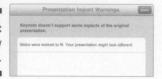

Figure 2-13:
Review any
errors.

Copying a file from an iWork for iPad app

You've copied a file from another place onto your iOS device, and now you're ready to reverse the process. To share a file you've created in iWork on your iOS device, follow these steps:

1. **In the documents screen, tap Edit at the right end of the toolbar.**

2. **Tap the document you want to copy.**

   As you see in Figure 2-14, the three buttons at the left of the toolbar are now enabled.

These buttons are now enabled

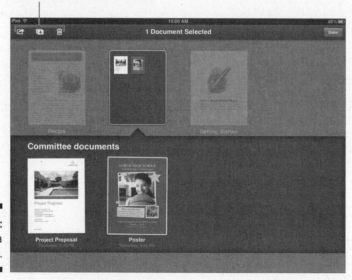

Figure 2-14:
Copy a
document.

The right button lets you move the selected document to the Trash. The middle button lets you make a duplicate of the document. The far left button is the one you want: It lets you copy the document to a new location.

3. **Tap the Export button.**

   The popover shown in Figure 2-15 opens.

Figure 2-15:
Export a file.

You see that in addition to moving files to iTunes, iDisk, and WebDAV, you can e-mail a file and share it on iWork.com. (iWork.com is described in the "Managing Your iWork documents on iWork.com" section, in this chapter.) You can choose the export format, so although iWork apps run only on Mac and iOS, you can export documents in PDF or Microsoft Office formats and send them to your Windows-using friends.

4. **Select the Apps tab from the group of tabs running across the top of the pane.**

5. **Scroll down to the bottom of the pane and select the iWork app you're interested in.**

   The documents on your iPad for that app are shown.

6. **Select the document you want and click Save To.**

7. **Choose the folder and the name you want to use for the saved file.**

   The file is moved to your computer.

Moving files to your iOS device from your computer

The process for moving files from your computer to your iOS device is similar to the process described in the previous section. To copy files from your computer to your iOS, follow these steps:

1. **Connect your iOS device to the computer from which the files are to be moved.**

   You can use a cable or a Wi-Fi connection if you selected that option. You can use a Mac or PC, but you must have installed iTunes on it.

2. **Find your iOS device under the Devices section of the Source List (see Figure 2-16) and click it.**

3. **Select the Apps tab from the group of tabs running across the top of the pane.**

4. **Scroll down to the bottom of the pane and select the iWork app you're interested in.**

   The documents on your iOS device for that app are listed.

5. **Click Add in the lower-right portion of the window.**

   Alternatively, you can also simply drag the document icon from the Finder or Windows Explorer window into the file list area.

6. **When prompted, select the file on your computer's disk.**

   When you select a file, it's moved to the list of files in iTunes and usually moves immediately to your iOS device. If it doesn't move immediately, click Sync.

Locate your device here

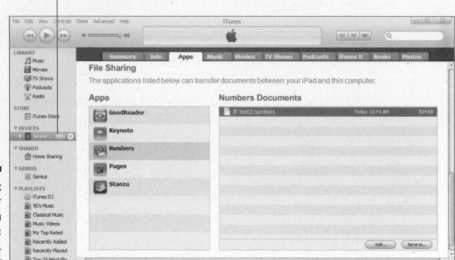

Figure 2-16:
Find your
device on
your Mac
or PC.

Managing your iWork documents on iCloud

iCloud is integrated into iWork on iOS 5 and OS X 10.7 (Lion) and subsequent versions. The first time you use an iWork app for iOS, you're prompted to use the iCloud option (see Chapter 1). You can turn this option on and off in the future if you want by using Settings.

When you use iCloud with iWork for iOS apps, iCloud documents appear in your document's display (that is, the screen you get to using Documents, Presentations, or Spreadsheets at the left of the main toolbar). After you've enabled iCloud, documents you create in an iWork for iOS app automatically synchronize with iCloud.

When you use iCloud with OS X, things are a little different. Instead of the automatic integration you see on iOS 5 and later, on OS X, the integration is through your browser (normally Safari on OS X and iOS).

Logging into iCloud on OS X

The first time you visit icloud.com with Safari, you're invited to learn more or sign in (see Figure 2-17).

Figure 2-17: Visit iCloud for the first time.

If you choose to sign in, you're prompted for your ID, as shown in Figure 2-18.

As you can see, you can choose from the various iCloud services, including iWork. The specific services may vary with your account. Click iWork to move to the iWork iCloud hub, shown in Figure 2-19.

Figure 2-18:
Log in to
iCloud.

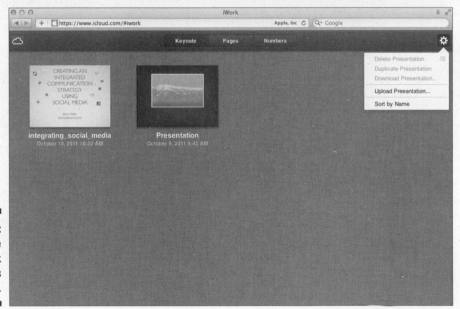

Figure 2-19:
Manage
your iWork
documents
on iCloud.

As you see in Figure 2-19, a toolbar appears at the top of the window. Click the cloud at the top left to return to iCloud. Use the controls in the center of the window to see your iCloud documents for the various iWork apps. Figure 2-19 shows Keynote documents.

Actions (the gear wheel at the top right) lets you work with a selected document or add more documents to iCloud. In Figure 2-19, the delete, download, and duplicate actions are disabled because no document is selected.

Uploading a document to iCloud on OS X

Here's how to upload a document to iCloud on OS X:

1. **Choose Upload Document, as shown in Figure 2-20, to upload a document.**

   Select the correct app in the toolbar — Pages, Numbers, or Keynote.

2. **Select the document from the sheet shown in Figure 2-21.**

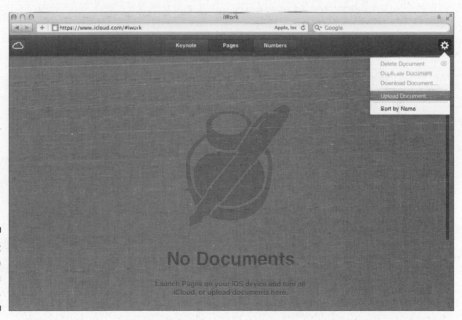

Figure 2-20: Choose to upload a document.

Figure 2-21:
Select the
document to
upload.

You're notified as the document is uploading (see Figure 2-22).

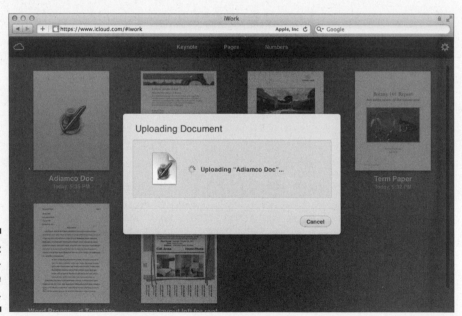

Figure 2-22:
The docu-
ment will be
uploaded.

Downloading a document from iCloud on OS X

To download a document from iCloud on OS X, select the app you want to work with at the top of the window and then select the document to download. Then choose the format you want to use, as shown in Figure 2-23. This lets you use a variety of apps and programs; you can also easily send the files to people who don't use iWork (if you happen to know any of them).

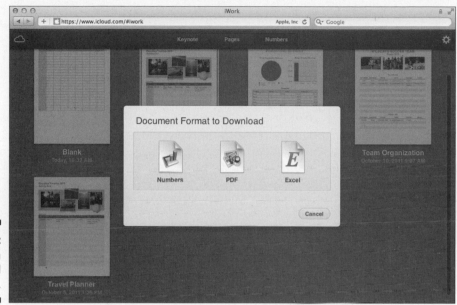

Figure 2-23:
Choose a
download
format.

Managing your iWork documents on iWork.com

iWork.com lets you work together with other people and lets devices such as iPads, iPhones, Macs, PCs, and iWork.com work together. (You can even throw other, browser-equipped smartphones into the mix. Some rumors indicate that iPhone isn't the only smartphone in existence.)

Want to work with two colleagues on a presentation? No problem: Start by uploading your Keynote document to iWork.com on the Internet. Then a friend can download the document and make changes in it as a Microsoft PowerPoint document. Back it goes to iWork.com, and someone else can download it in another, different format. This example illustrates the *cloud computing* process. When working in the cloud, people can work together on their own terms. They don't have to get together and decide which presentation (or spreadsheet or word-processing) application they'll all use. That said, there certainly are a number of features that are unique to specific apps; these may not convert well. Fortunately, these tend to be features that are not used by many people.

You can share your iWork documents with people using other cloud services, such as Google Docs.

You can download documents from iWork.com in a variety of formats. Downloading documents means that you can take two types of actions:

- ✔ **Add comments and notes to iWork documents.** You can add comments to specific parts of iWork documents (a section of text, for example). You can also add notes to the document as a whole (rather than to a specific part of it). As a result, a number of people can work together on a document.

- ✔ **Track multiple revisions to iWork documents.** You can download the documents to your own computer in a variety of formats. Many of these formats preserve the comments that you and others have added. After you've downloaded a document, you can modify it and add more comments describing your modifications.

All these actions are made possible by the iWork.com site; the actual sharing of documents is handled by your web browser and iWork software. Here's the division of labor:

- ✔ **Upload to iWork.com:** This is done from your iWork software: from the Share menu on OS X and from your documents screen (refer to Figure 2-21).

- ✔ **Download from iWork.com:** You download by connecting to iWork.com with your browser and logging in with your iWork.com ID and password. This process works with a browser that can run on OS X, your iPad, your iPhone or iPod touch, and Windows (among other operating systems). If you can run a browser and if your device and its operating system support downloading via browsers, you can receive a shared file. You can find a list of supported browsers at `www.apple.com/iwork/iwork-dot-com`.

After you've downloaded an iWork file, you can get to work. Even if iWork doesn't run on your computer, you may have another application that does run and can read the standard formats (including the Microsoft Office formats). That means you can edit downloaded iWork documents using Microsoft Office on Windows or OS X or by using Google Docs on any platform it runs on.

iWork.com is designed to be the bridge across various platforms and formats so that you can share your iWork documents. You may want to share your documents with yourself as you switch from your iPad to your Mac or to Windows. For that reason, the following sections show how to log on to iWork.com from iWork on OS X as well as iPad.

Sharing a document on iWork.com

You need an Apple ID to log on to iWork.com. If you've used MobileMe or you now use iCloud, you have an Apple ID. If you've purchased items from iTunes or an App Store, you have an Apple ID. If you use iChat, you have an Apple ID.

And if you've activated an iPhone or iPad, you also have an Apple ID. If you're not certain whether you have an Apple ID (or if you want to create a new one), log on to `https://appleid.apple.com/cgi-bin/WebObjects/ MyAppleId.woa`.

You log in to iWork.com to upload (share) documents and retrieve documents. (See the next section on how to log on to retrieve documents.) To share a document on iWork.com:

1. **Open the document you want to share in the appropriate iWork for iPad app.**

2. **On your documents screen, share it via iWork.com (refer to Figure 2-21).**

3. **If prompted, log in as shown in Figure 2-24.**

4. **Address the e-mail to the person (or several people) you want notified of the file.**

   You can type a message, if you want (see Figure 2-25).

5. **If you want, tap Sharing Options at the right to change the default sharing settings, as shown in Figure 2-26.**

Figure 2-24: Log in to iWork.com.

Figure 2-25: Let people know that the document is ready to be shared.

Figure 2-26:
Change the
Sharing
options, if
you want.

You're done. The file is uploaded, and your e-mail is sent.

Accessing shared documents on iWork.com

Your message, together with a download link, is delivered to all the addressees you have listed. People only have to click the link in the e-mail. A recipi-
ent who has an iWork.com account has more options. If you have an iWork.
com account, you can access shared documents by following these steps:

1. **Choose whether or not to view your shared files, as shown in
   Figure 2-27.**

Figure 2-27:
Download
the file.

2. **If the Sharing Options permit, the Download button lets people download the file in various formats.**

   Tapping anywhere in the box downloads the native iWork version of the
   document.

Chapter 3

Managing the iWork for Mac Menus and Toolbars

In This Chapter

▶ Using the basic menus

▶ Speeding up things with shortcut menus

▶ Saving time with toolbars

The menu and toolbar systems for iWork provide a great deal of standardization so that each iWork app functions in very much the same way. This chapter provides an introduction to the menus and toolbars.

I don't cover common OS X menu commands, such as Save, Quit, Cut/Copy/Paste, and Undo/Redo, in this chapter.

The Application Menu in Pages, Numbers, and Keynote

The Application menu is where you set preferences (which can be different for each application). This menu is also where you find the About command, shown in Figure 3-1, which shows the version information.

You can show or hide all application windows. (This applies to all Mac applications, including the iWork applications.) You can also show all application windows.

The Application menu is also where you can register your software or try it out before you buy it. And, at the end of the menu, you find the Quit command.

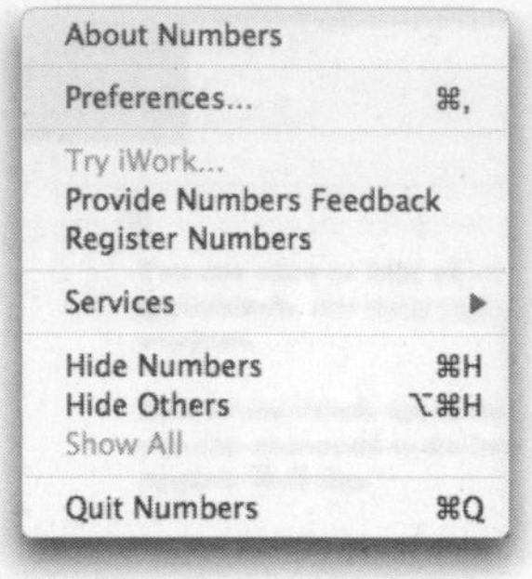

About Numbers	
Preferences...	⌘,
Try iWork...	
Provide Numbers Feedback	
Register Numbers	
Services	▶
Hide Numbers	⌘H
Hide Others	⌥⌘H
Show All	
Quit Numbers	⌘Q

Figure 3-1:
Set prefer-
ences in the
Application
menu.

The File Menu

The File menu, shown in Figure 3-2, has the basic commands to create and open documents (including reopening recent documents) as well as print them. All are standard commands for most File menus. In iWork applications, two sets of special menu commands relate to themes and templates. You can use built-in templates for Numbers and Pages documents; when you create a new document from one of these, formatting, colors, and fonts are predetermined to give your document the best appearance. When it comes to colors in charts or tables, an iWork application coordinates those with the palette of colors in the template you have chosen.

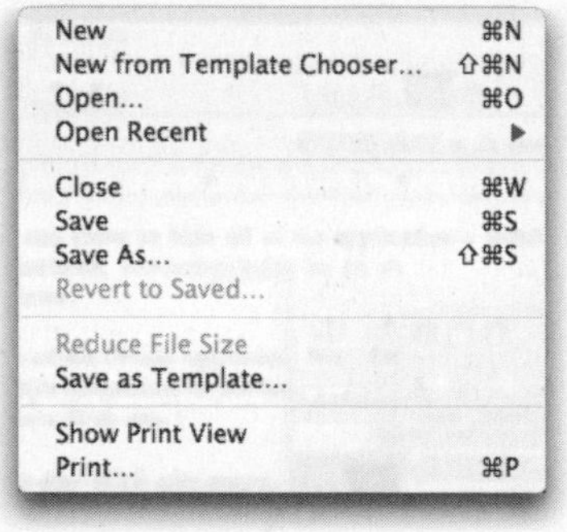

New	⌘N
New from Template Chooser...	⇧⌘N
Open...	⌘O
Open Recent	▶
Close	⌘W
Save	⌘S
Save As...	⇧⌘S
Revert to Saved...	
Reduce File Size	
Save as Template...	
Show Print View	
Print...	⌘P

Figure 3-2:
The File
menu.

Toward the bottom of the File menu for Numbers and Pages is a command to save the current document as a template. All the settings are saved in this template so that you can easily create a document based on it.

A *template* is a collection of settings that you can apply to a new iWork document when you create it. You can modify those settings as you see fit, and you can save the modified template.

In the case of Keynote, instead of templates, you have *themes.* The difference between themes and templates is that you can reapply a theme to a document as you are editing it. This is possible with a highly structured document such as a Keynote presentation. (It's also possible with a Bento library and in iPhoto, iMovie, and iDVD.) Because the document's structure is strict, Keynote knows where all the elements are, and it can always reformat slides and bullet items when you apply a new theme.

The Edit Menu

Like all Edit menus in Mac OS X, an iWork application's Edit menu combines the standard Undo and Redo commands as well as commands for Select, Copy, and Paste, as shown in Figure 3-3. Writing tools such as Find and Spelling are available to enhance your text; there's more on the Find and Spelling tools in Chapter 23.

Figure 3-3:
The Edit menu lets you use the standard cut-and-paste commands.

One of the important commands in the Edit menu is the Paste and Match Style command. This command pastes selected text in the document, but it picks up the current style of the location where the text is pasted. As a result, the pasted text fits right in.

The Insert Menu

The Insert menu lets you insert files and objects into your iWork document. You can insert the following types of objects into any iWork document:

- Comments
- Text boxes
- Shapes
- Charts
- Tables
- Functions (such as sums)

The fact that these items are all available in menu commands and on the toolbar is a great feature of iWork.

You use the Insert⇨Choose command to open a standard Open File dialog so that you can select a file to insert into your iWork document at the current insertion point or inside a selected object. The types of files that are available depend on the iWork application and the selected object. In general, when you want to insert a file into an iWork document, the Choose command is the command you want.

You can also insert a file into an iWork document by dragging it from a Finder window to the appropriate location in the document. Each iWork application has additional objects to insert.

The Slide Menu (Keynote)

The Slide menu lets you manage slides in a presentation. You often manage slides by using the buttons in the Keynote window and dragging slides in the Slides pane, as shown in Figure 3-4.

You can reorder slides and move them into a hierarchical structure by dragging them to the right or left. You can also use commands in the Slide menu to manage them.

Figure 3-4:
Rearrange
Keynote
slides.

The Table Menu (Numbers)

You use the Table menu to manage Numbers tables. As you can see from Figure 3-5, you can use many commands to add or change rows and columns.

You can also use triangles in the frame of rows and columns to invoke relevant row and column commands, as shown in Figure 3-6. Whether you use the Table menu or the commands in the table frame, the basic procedure is the same: Select a row or column and then use the appropriate command to modify it.

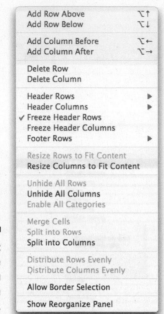

Figure 3-5:
Use the
Table menu
to modify a
table.

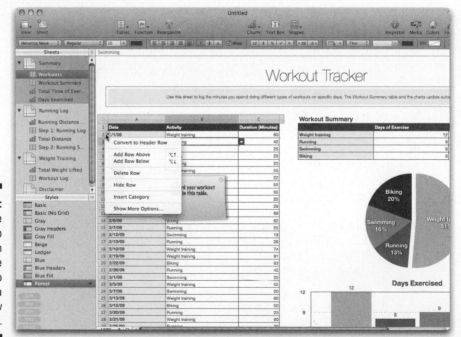

Figure 3-6:
Use triangle
pop-up
menus in
the table
frame to
modify a
single row
or column.

The Format Menu

The Format menu gives you commands for working with fonts and text. In fact, you find a variety of ways to accomplish the same goal in the Format menu.

Formatting fonts with menu commands

The Format➪Font submenu and its submenus give you a lot of control, but not as much as the Fonts window, which I describe in Chapter 4. Figure 3-7 shows the Format➪Font submenu structure and its Kern submenu.

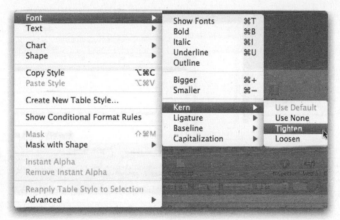

Figure 3-7: Adjust kerning.

You can switch back and forth between the menu commands and the Fonts window.

The first part of the Font menu covers the basics, such as italics (and covers them with less precision than the Fonts window). But then you start to see the differences:

✔ Instead of setting a font size, you can select some text and make it bigger or smaller until it looks right to you. Use the keyboard shortcuts to change font size quickly: ⌘++ (plus) to make selected text larger and ⌘+–(minus) to make it smaller.

✔ You can tighten or loosen *kerning* (the horizontal spacing between characters). You don't have to set specific values.

Formatting text with menu commands

You can use the Format⇨Font submenu to set alignment or justification. *Alignment* refers to the way the text in a paragraph is set: It can be aligned left (with a flush left margin, like in this book), aligned right (with a flush right margin), or centered. Fully justified text is aligned flush at both margins.

The Arrange Menu

All the iWork apps allow you to place objects on a page (or sheet, in the case of Numbers). You can organize and arrange these objects so that they make sense and look good. One key to this process is the Arrange menu, which is shown in Figure 3-8.

Bring Forward	⌥⇧⌘F
Bring to Front	⇧⌘F
Send Backward	⌥⇧⌘B
Send to Back	⇧⌘B
Send Objects to Background	
Make Background Objects Selectable	
Bring Background Objects to Front	
Align Objects ▶	Left
Distribute Objects ▶	Center
	Right
Flip Horizontally	Top
Flip Vertically	Middle
	Bottom
Lock	⌘L
Unlock	⌥⌘L
Group	⌥⌘G
Ungroup	⌥⇧⌘G

Figure 3-8:
Use the
Arrange
menu.

You can create long sections of text and large tables of numbers, but most of the time, you're better off focusing on smaller units: a paragraph or two, a table of a few rows and columns, or a short sequence of slides that presents a concept.

You may find that the simplest way to start to arrange a page (or sheet or slide) is to place the components you want to use on the page. Figure 3-9 shows a page where I've started an arrangement.

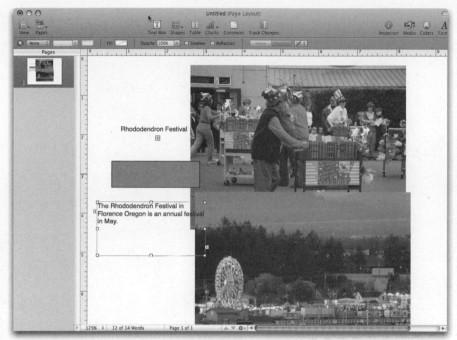

Figure 3-9:
Begin to
arrange
your
content.

You can arrange content in many ways. Most of the time, it's a matter of trial and error as you experiment to see what works best. Here's a sequence of steps you can try:

1. **Resize the objects.**

   If you're using images and objects from various sources, they're likely to be different sizes. Resize them so that they're basically the same size, with the more important ones (the title, for example) a bit larger.

2. **Bring objects forward or backward.**

   The Ferris wheel photo in Figure 3-9 has plenty of sky. It covers up part of the book cart. If you select the book cart image, you can choose Arrange⇨Bring Forward to place the book cart in front of the sky so that the details of the cart are more visible, as shown in Figure 3-10.

3. **Create a title.**

   Figure 3-9 also contains a text box ("Rhododendron Festival") and a colored shape designed as its background. Together, they'll make a good title. (This combination of shape and text box is a common iWork technique.) Select the text box and the shape and then choose Arrange⇨Align Objects⇨Middle. The result is shown in Figure 3-11. (Note that, at this point, all you see of the title is the plus icon at the bottom of the text. You'll fix that shortly.)

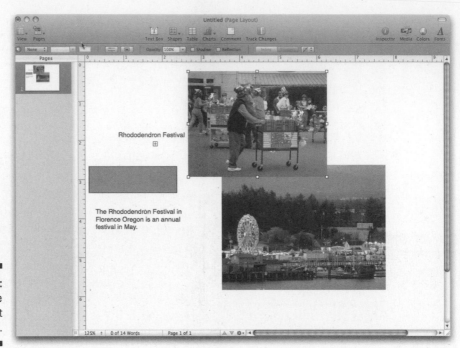

Figure 3-10:
Move the
book cart
forward.

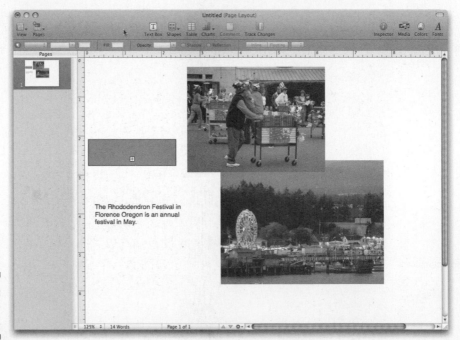

Figure 3-11:
Start to cre-
ate a title.

Aligning two objects in the middle aligns them in the vertical middle. To totally align two objects, follow up the middle alignment with center alignment, which aligns them horizontally. You usually need both commands (middle and center) to properly align objects on top of one another.

4. Create a text box.

Another text box is shown in Figure 3-11. Unlike the Rhododendron Festival text box that will become a title with a colored background, this second text box will stand on its own without a special background. You can see the beginning of this second text box with the text, "The Rhododendron Festival in Florence, Oregon, is a special event in May."

5. Move the shape backward.

As you can see in Figure 3-11, the Rhododendron Festival text box is visible only with its handles. That's because it's behind the colored shape. Select the shape and choose Arrange⇨Send to Back. The shape moves back, and the text is now visible, as shown in Figure 3-12.

6. Correct the alignment.

Something is a bit wrong with the spacing in Figure 3-12. This is common as you move objects around and resize them. Sometimes the correction is a matter of trial and error; other times, you can see what the problem is immediately.

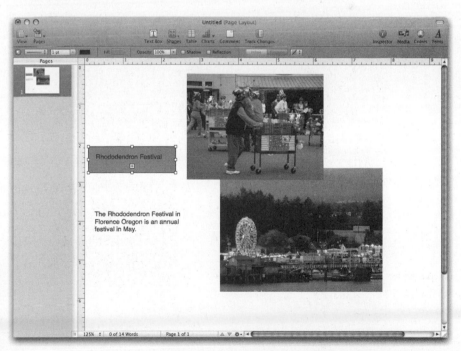

Figure 3-12:
Move the shape backward.

A simple way of correcting these types of alignment issues is to click in the text and display the format bar. Figure 3-13 shows the problem: The title text is aligned left; it will look better if it's aligned in the center. This issue is common (and easily solved): Just click the Align Center button, which is immediately to the right of the Align Left button.

These are the little tweaks that make the difference between an elegant document and one that doesn't quite cut the mustard.

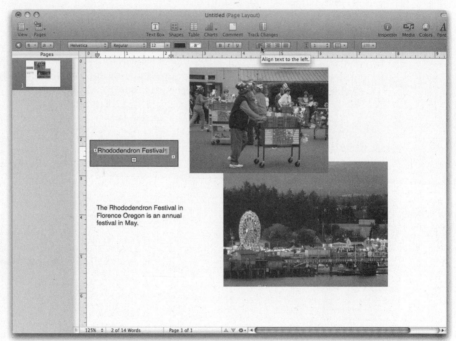

Figure 3-13:
Change
the text
alignment.

The View Menu

The View menu lets you show or hide parts of an iWork window. The View pop-up menu on the toolbar provides the same functionality. Each app has its own features; they're described in the relevant chapters for each app.

The Play Menu (Keynote)

You use the Play menu, shown in Figure 3-14, to control how a Keynote slide show is played. There's more information on this topic in Chapter 19.

Figure 3-14:
Use the
Play menu
for Keynote
presenta-
tions.

The Window Menu

The Window menu is a standard part of OS X. You use it to minimize the current window (which you can also do with the yellow minimize button in the upper-left corner of the window). You can also maximize the window, just as you do with the green button at the upper left of the window.

The Window menu lists all the application's windows. You can choose Window⇨Bring All to Front to bring all of an application's windows forward. You can also choose Pages/Keynote/Numbers⇨Hide Others so that no other windows are visible on the screen.

The Share Menu

The Share menu lets you share documents on the web and with users in other formats. There's more on the Share menu in Chapter 22.

Working with Shortcuts

The iWork menus group commands by their basic functions, such as editing, inserting, and formatting. The menu commands are generally static. Some are disabled if they don't make sense for the selected objects, but generally their names and their order remain static. (The exceptions are toggle commands such as Show Inspector/Hide Inspector; depending on whether an inspector is shown, one command or the other is shown in the menu.)

Sometimes you aren't certain exactly what you want to do, but you know what you want to do it to. Shortcut menus (sometimes called contextual menus) come to the rescue.

To access a shortcut menu, select one or more objects in an iWork window and then hold down the Control key while you press the mouse button. (On multitouch trackpads, a two-fingered tap works, while on a mouse with two buttons, a right-click works.) A shortcut menu pops up next to the object. This shortcut menu assembles all menu commands from the various iWork menus that are relevant to the object. Most of the disabled commands in the menu bar are excluded from the shortcut menu, so you wind up with just the commands you can actually use on the selected object. Occasionally, some commands in the shortcut menu are disabled, but they're the exception rather than the rule.

Figure 3-15 shows a shortcut menu in Numbers when a spreadsheet cell is selected. Commands relevant to the cell and to its column or row, as well as the standard editing commands, are all in one place.

Figure 3-15: Use shortcut menus to save time.

Looking at the Toolbar

Along with menus, toolbars are an integral part of the OS X user interface. Although each app's toolbar is different, the overall behavior of the toolbar (where it is and how to show, hide, and customize it) is managed by Mac OS X.

Figure 3-16 shows an iWork toolbar for Keynote. Every toolbar button causes an immediate action that is visible in the document. The buttons on the toolbar perform commands; sometimes these commands are also available on the menu.

In the default view, the buttons have both text and an icon. When you customize the toolbar, you can change the default view so that only the text or only the icon is shown. For example, Figure 3-17 shows a Pages toolbar with only text on the toolbar buttons.

Figure 3-16:
Use the
toolbar
for fast
access to
commands.

Figure 3-17:
You can
have text-
only toolbar
buttons.

Many toolbar buttons add an object to the document. In Figure 3-16, the New button adds a slide (because this is the Keynote toolbar), and the Text Box, Table, and Comment buttons add a text box, table, and comment, respectively.

The icons for toolbar buttons often have small variants in their images. Most common is the downward-pointing arrow, which brings up a pop-up menu for that toolbar button. In Figure 3-16, menus are available for View, Themes, Masters, Shapes, Charts, and Smart Builds.

Often the menu for a toolbar button lets you add a particular type of object to the document (a specific type of shape, for example). Other times, the menu lets you choose from various options. Figure 3-18 is the menu for the View button in Keynote; you can use the menu to choose which parts of the window to show or hide. The View button contains the same commands as the View menu.

Figure 3-18: Select parts of the window to show or hide with the View button.

You can customize the toolbar, but the default toolbar has a consistency across the iWork applications:

- ✔ **The toolbar buttons on the left side:** The left side of each app's toolbar provides application-specific toolbar buttons:

    • **Numbers:** The first toolbar buttons at the left display the Numbers View menu and add a sheet to your Numbers document.

- ✔ **Keynote:** The first toolbar buttons in Keynote create a new slide and play your presentation. Next, pop-up toolbar buttons let you choose views, themes, and slide masters.

    • **Pages:** The first toolbar buttons in Pages are the View menu and the Sections menu, which lets you insert a new section in your Pages word-processing document. For page layout documents, the Pages View menu is accompanied by a Pages menu that lets you add page layout pages.

    • **The toolbar buttons in the center:** All buttons in the center of the toolbar add objects to the current document. For Pages and Keynote, these toolbar buttons let you add text boxes, shapes, tables, charts, and comments; you can also turn track changes on and off. In Numbers, you can add tables, insert functions, and reorganize (sort) your data.

    • **The toolbar buttons on the right side:** The buttons to the right of the toolbar open other windows or dialogs. In Figure 3-16, they open the Inspector window, Color Picker, and Font panel. This chapter focuses on the default set of toolbar buttons. Because you can customize the toolbar, you may have other buttons in your toolbar.

Using the Toolbar View Button to Customize the Window

Toward the left of each iWork toolbar is a View button that displays a pop-up menu. (The Keynote View pop-up menu was shown in Figure 3-18.) You can use the menu to show or hide parts of your iWork window, such as rulers, the format bar, or comments. Each window can have its own settings, which are preserved with the document.

You can show or hide three areas of the window for any iWork app:

✔ **Rulers:** Rulers appear around the main part of the window to help you position objects precisely. You can adjust the settings for rulers in each application's Preferences dialog.

✔ **Format bar:** Located just below the toolbar, the format bar lets you format text and other objects.

✔ **Left pane:** Located on the side of an iWork window, the left pane contains program-specific information. You can click any image in the left pane to select it or to navigate to it in the main part of the window. In Keynote, the pane can contain images of master slides as well as slides. In Pages, the pane can contain page thumbnails or a search box. In Numbers, the pane can contain sheets and tables. The View menu identifies the individual items in the left pane (such as master slides); the left pane itself is not shown in the View menu.

✔ **Main window:** Other options in the View menu control what is shown in the main part of the window, such as presenter notes (Keynote), invisible characters (Pages), and a formula list (Numbers).

If you aren't certain what a certain interface element is called, experiment with showing and hiding the various items in the View menu. As soon as you find the command that hides or shows the element you're interested in, you will find its name.

Including Comments

You can add comments to your iWork documents by clicking the Comment button on the toolbar or by choosing Insert⇨Comment. You can then show or hide those comments using the View button on the toolbar or the View menu.

Customizing the Toolbar

You can customize toolbars, as shown in Figure 3-19. You open the dialog shown in Figure 3-19 by choosing View➪Customize Toolbar or by Ctrl-clicking (or right-clicking) anywhere on the toolbar to bring up the contextual menu for the toolbar, from which you can choose the Customize Toolbar command.

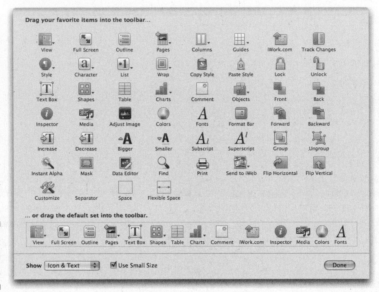

Figure 3-19:
Customize your toolbar.

When you drag icons into or out of the toolbar, the existing icons will move aside (or move together) as necessary. Notice that you have some special icons, such as the spaces at the bottom of the set of icons. You can use those or *separators* (vertical lines) to organize your toolbar. In the lower left, you can choose icons and text, text only, or icons only as well as the size of the icons. It's your toolbar, so make it comfortable to use.

You can also Ctrl-click the toolbar button to cycle through two sizes of text only and two sizes of icons only as well as the combination of text and icons. (This behavior applies only to pre-Mac OS X Lion.)

All toolbars on Mac OS X have one additional feature: You can always move the default icons as a single group by dragging them from the bottom of the customization dialog.

Chapter 4

Using Text and Text Boxes

In This Chapter

▶ Using text boxes to display text

▶ Working with fonts, alignment, and spacing

▶ Moving beyond text with text boxes

*i*Work text boxes are objects that you place on a page and that can contain text. They can appear in any iWork app documents. You can use a text box to highlight a small section of text with special formatting. On OS X, you can use a text box to display part of a lengthy run of text that may continue in another text box on the same or another page. Text boxes can also contain objects, such as graphics, shapes, and charts. Their handling of text flow distinguishes them from other objects in iWork.

This chapter shows you the various permutations and uses of text boxes.

Creating a Simple Text Box

The easiest way to start learning about text boxes is to create one and work with it. Experiment with a document that has a good deal of text in it to see the results of inserting a text box and adjusting its settings.

The text box created in this section is actually a *floating text box*. By default, all text boxes you create are floating text boxes; also, they're the only kind of text box you can create in a page layout document. The other kind of text box, an *inline text box,* is described in the following section. You can only place it in a word-processing document.

You can create a simple text box by clicking the Text Box icon on the toolbar. Figure 4-1 shows how you can create a text box in Pages for Mac.

About the text in this chapter

Demonstrating how Pages handles text sometimes requires a lot of text. Formatting the text at the top of a For Sale flyer requires a mere seven letters and one space. In some ways, that's trivial. Many of the tools and techniques you use to format *For Sale* are the same that you use to format a hundred pages or more of text, but when you deal with a large text document, some special problems (and solutions) arise.

To demonstrate some of the issues involved in large documents, this chapter sometimes uses text from *The Pickwick Papers* by Charles Dickens. With about 300,000 words, the novel is just under 800 pages long in a standard paperback edition or when displayed in Courier 12. That's enough text to demonstrate text-handling capabilities in Pages. And it's one of the greatest and funniest novels ever written.

You can download the Pages word-processing text from the author's website as described in the Introduction.

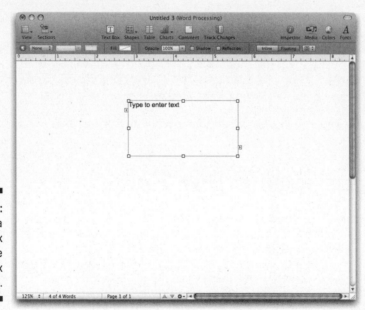

Figure 4-1:
Create a
text box
with the
Text Box
icon in OS X.

Figure 4-2 shows how you can create a text box in Numbers for iPhone. Because of the smaller screen, you need to tap Insert (the mountain view) and then T for text. The text box is created, as shown in Figure 4-2.

With Keynote for iPad, you can also create a text box, as shown in Figure 4-3. After you create a text box, it behaves the same way with each app.

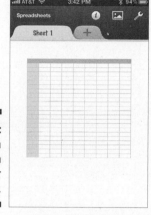
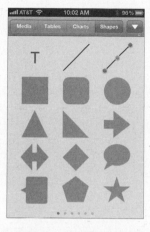
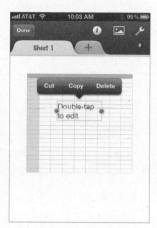

Figure 4-2: Create a text box in Numbers for iPhone.

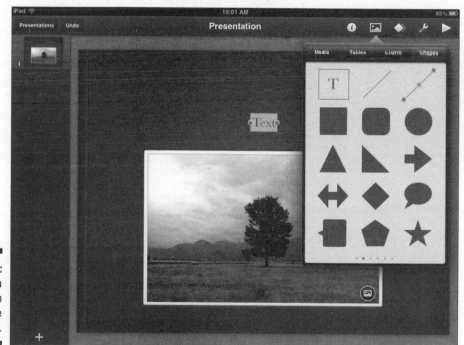

Figure 4-3: Create a text box in Keynote for iPad.

You can resize or reshape the text box with any of the handles. You can also drag it around by clicking and dragging the interior of the box. If you double-click or double-tap in the text box, you can type text or paste it in the text box.

Position the text box where you want it on the page. If text is behind it, the text that's already on the page flows around the box, if needed.

The text box contains text, but the box itself behaves like a shape. This means you can customize your text box using two sets of tools. Figure 4-4 shows a text box with text that is centered horizontally and vertically. The text box itself has a line border and a background gradient as well as a shadow.

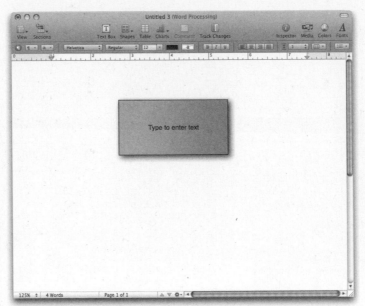

Figure 4-4:
Customize your text box.

Configuring a Text Box

There are two types of settings for a text box: You can configure the box itself, and you can configure the text within it. On both OS X and iOS, it's easy to keep track of what you're configuring even though the interfaces are basically the same. If you select a text box (that is, you click or tap in the text box to reveal its resizing handles), the settings you adjust apply to the text box and all the text within it. If you select some of the text within the text box, your settings apply only to that text.

Modifying a text box on OS X

You can modify text and a text box with the following two inspectors on OS X:

✔ **Text inspector:** Select some or all of the text in the text box or the text box itself and style it with Text inspector. The Text inspector settings are shown in Figure 4-5.

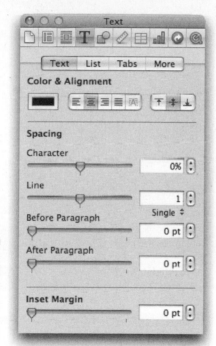

Figure 4-5:
Change the
text settings
with Text
inspector.

✔ **Graphic inspector:** You can set the fill, stroke, and opacity for the text box using Graphic inspector. Use the Stroke setting to show the border of the box and select the Shadow check box if you want to add a shadow. The Graphic inspector settings are shown in Figure 4-6.

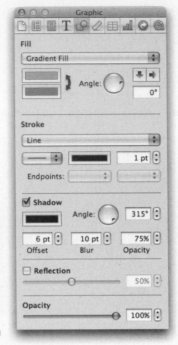

Figure 4-6:
Change the
text box
settings with
Graphic
inspector.

Modifying a text box on iOS

On iPhone and iPad, use the Info popover, shown in Figure 4-7, to modify
the text box itself. Select the text box with a single tap and then tap the info
button at the right of the toolbar.

If you see the resizing handles on the frame of the text box, it means you're
setting values for the text box and all the text within it.

There are three tabs at the top of the popover: Style, Text, and Arrange. The
first one, Style, is selected in Figure 4-7. Note that, at the bottom of the popover when Style is selected, you can move to Style Options, as shown at the
bottom of Figure 4-7.

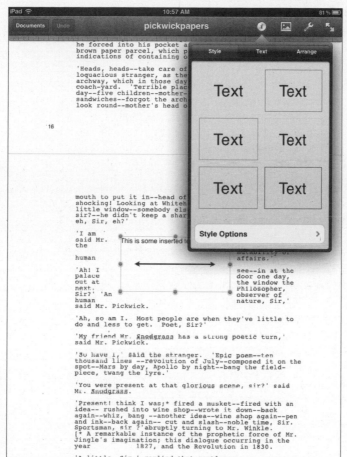

Figure 4-7:
Modify a
text box
on iOS X.

Style options, shown in Figure 4-8, has three tabs at the top: Fill, Border, and Effects. The Effects tab is shown in Figure 4-8.

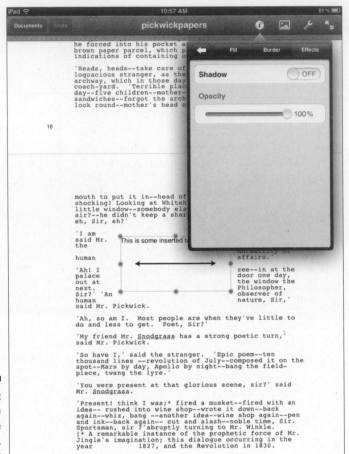

Figure 4-8:
Use
the Style
Effects tab.

If you tap the Text tab at the top of Figure 4-7, you can experiment with the Text tab shown in Figure 4-9. Remember that with the text box itself selected, your settings affect all of the text within the box. (The following section shows you how to work on selected text within the text box.)

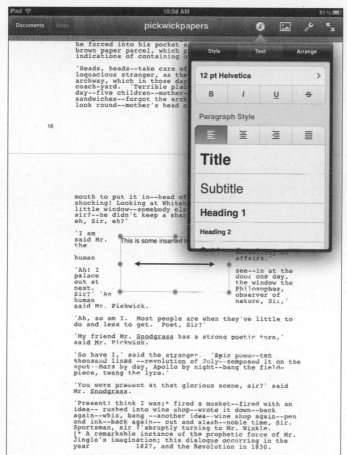

Figure 4-9:
Use the Text
settings.

Finally, the Arrange tab, shown in Figure 4-10, lets you set columns, the relative position of the text box back-to-front in the context of other objects and shapes, as well as the way text in the document (or other text boxes) wraps around this text box. That is the topic of the following section.

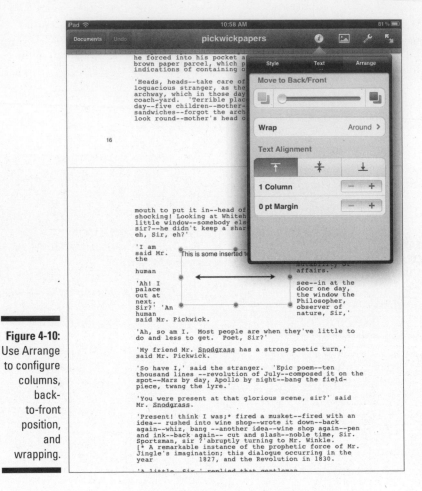

Figure 4-10:
Use Arrange
to configure
columns,
back-
to-front
position,
and
wrapping.

Working with Fonts and Text

In common with some other apps, the iWork apps let you format text using *styles*. A style is a collection of settings, such as font, font size, font color, line spacing, tab stops, and more. Often, styles are given meaningful names, such as title, intro paragraph, *excerpt* [that's the fancy name for a quote that is indented rather than set off with quotation marks], and the like. Some apps (including Pages) differentiate between *character styles* and *paragraph styles*. iWork lets you use the Edit menu or, on iOS, selection buttons to copy and paste styles. When you copy or paste a style, the style and its formatting are used to format whatever text you paste the style onto.

When you're working with text, it helps to remember that the iWork programs (like many other programs today) separate text — the words — from the formatting of that text. For that reason, this section focuses on the formatting and not the typing or pasting of text into your document.

Working with fonts and text on OS X

All iWork for Mac apps use the Fonts window to provide the greatest amount of control over text fonts. The menus have font commands, but for the greatest control, the Fonts window is what you'll want to use.

You can override your basic font settings for individual paragraphs, sentences, or even individual characters. Use the Fonts window to set the font for the whole document and then modify sections as needed by selecting them and returning to the Fonts window.

The Fonts window is part of Mac OS X; it's used in many applications, not just iWork.

Selecting fonts

Setting a font and its size is the most basic thing you do with fonts:

1. **Select the text you want to change.**

   If you want to set fonts for text before you type, click the insertion point where you want to begin typing. If the document is new, the pointer is automatically positioned at the beginning of the document.

   If you've selected text in your iWork document, you see it change as you work in the Fonts window.

2. **Open the Fonts window by clicking the Font button on the toolbar or by choosing Format⇨Font⇨Show Fonts.**

   The Fonts window is shown in Figure 4-11.

3. **Select the font you want to use from the second column, Family.**

   The first column, Collections, lets you group font families. OS X has already built several collections into the Fonts window. You see how to add new collections and how to add font families to collections later in this section. Font families can be in more than one collection. Collections are just an organizing mechanism for font families.

Figure 4-11:
Set fonts
with the
Fonts win-
dow.

4. Select the typeface from the Typeface column.

Typefaces are somewhat intuitive. Font families are developed by different vendors, and they may use different naming conventions. For
example, one vendor's italic may look like another vendor's oblique in
different font families.

Figure 4-11 illustrates an issue with font families that you should be
aware of. Not only do vendors use different typeface names (such as
oblique versus italic), but one vendor's typeface variation is another
vendor's font family. Notice that the Gill Sans font family in Figure 4-11
has a Bold typeface. Just below it is another font family called Gill Sans
Ultra Bold, which is exactly what its name suggests. But it isn't another
typeface for Gill Sans; it is its own font family.

5. Select the size you want to use.

You can type a font size in the size box at the upper right of the Fonts
window, you can click to select a font from the scrolling list of font sizes,
or you can use the slider at the far right of the Fonts window to quickly
move to the size you want.

You can close the Fonts window, if you want, by clicking its close button. If you do more formatting, however, just click in your iWork document window and keep working; the Fonts window remains open behind the document window.

Previewing fonts

If you select text in your document (rather than using the insertion point to set the font for new text that hasn't been typed), you can see the selected text change as you work with the Fonts window. But what do you do if you want to experiment directly in the Fonts window?

Use the small dot in the top center of the Fonts window, shown in Figure 4-11, to pull down an area that provides a live preview of your selection (see Figure 4-12).

Figure 4-12:
See your
font choices
in action.

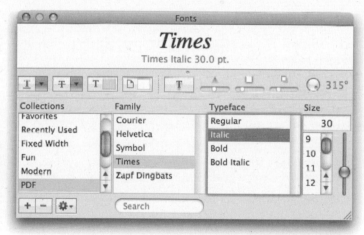

Setting basic effects

At the top of the Fonts window is a set of controls for font effects. You can show or hide this area using the Font panel actions, which you display using the gear icon in the lower left of the Fonts window.

If you're using the preview feature of the Fonts window, be aware that it reflects the choices for font family, typeface, and font size. The settings for font effects, such as underlining and color, are shown just below the preview pane in the Effects pane, but they aren't shown in the preview pane.

Actions are menus that pop up from a window. They're always shown with the gear icon. Figure 4-13 shows the Fonts window actions.

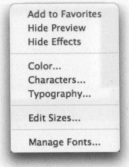

Figure 4-13:
Fonts
window
actions.

The first four buttons for font effects provide common controls:

- ✔ **Underlining:** The icon with an underlined *T* sets underlining. Use the pop-up menu to choose from None, Single, Double, and Color. The Color option is a single underline with the color you choose. You already know how to choose the color. Select this choice, and the Colors window opens.

- ✔ **Strikethrough:** The icon with a *T* and a strikethrough bar sets the options for strikethrough settings. The strikethrough options are the same as for underlining.

- ✔ **Text color:** The third icon opens the Colors window to let you set the text color.

- ✔ **Paragraph color:** The fourth icon opens the Colors window to let you set the paragraph's background color.

Applying text shadows

The five controls at the right of the Effects pane all control text shadows.

Shadowed text isn't as easy to read as unshadowed text. Use it for headlines and labels — short sections of big letters.

Here is how to set up text shadows:

1. **Select the text you want to shadow.**

2. **Open the Fonts window by clicking the Font button on the toolbar or by choosing Format⇨Font⇨Show Fonts.**

3. **Click the text shadow button (fifth from the left in the Fonts window).**

   This button toggles text shadowing on and off. The text shadow button should be highlighted. If it isn't, click it again.

   The slider to the right of the text shadow button changes the opacity of the shadow.

4. **Move the slider to the right to make the shadow more opaque.**

   You may want to experiment with the sliders in their most extreme positions to see their effects. Keep watching the selected text in the iWork document window to see what happens.

   Click elsewhere in the document to deselect the text: It's hard to distinguish between the highlighting of the selection and the text shadowing.

5. **Use the next slider to blur the far edge of the shadow more (to the right) or less (to the left).**

6. **Use the final slider to move the shadow farther away from the text it shadows (called the *offset*).**

   If you're experimenting, try moving this slider all the way to the right. That lets you see the shadow clearly. If you're having trouble, choose View➪Zoom➪Zoom In to zoom the window. You can also use the zoom control at the left of the bottom window frame of your iWork document.

7. **Drag the wheel to set the angle for the shadow.**

   A setting such as 320 degrees usually looks good. On a computer screen, most people are used to an assumed light source at the upper left of the screen, so shadows normally are drawn below and to the right of the object they shadow.

Customizing typography

You can gain even more control over your fonts by using typography options that are supported for some fonts. Here's how to gain access to the typography options:

1. **In your iWork document, select the text to which you want to apply the typography options.**

2. **In the Fonts window, select the font.**

3. **Choose Typography from the Fonts window actions (the gear icon at the bottom of the window).**

   The Typography dialog shown in Figure 4-14 opens.

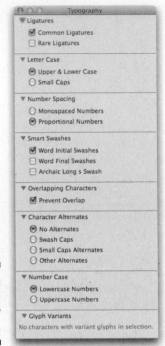

The typography options vary for each font. Some fonts support none of them; others, such as Helvetica Neue and Hoefler Text, support many of them.

Managing font collections

Font collections are sets of fonts that you want to be able to find quickly. You can add any fonts to your collections. By default, the following collections are provided for you: All Fonts, English, Favorites, and Recently Used.

If you want to add a new collection, click the add button (the + symbol) below the Collections column in the Fonts window. You can name your collection; it will be alphabetized automatically.

To remove a collection (but not the fonts within it), select it and then click the delete (– symbol) button below the Collections column.

To add a font family to a collection, just drag it in. To remove it, drag it out. This change affects only the collection: Nothing happens to the font itself.

The Fonts window Actions menu lets you add a selected font family to the Favorites collection.

Working with fonts and text on iOS

Double-tapping within a text box or within a Pages word-processing document lets you edit and select the text inside the box. When you've selected one or more words in a text box, you can open the Info popover so that you can set styles, lists, and layouts with the buttons at the top, as shown in Figure 4-15.

Yes, the interface shown in Figure 4-15 is the same as shown previously in Figure 4-9. However, in Figure 4-9, you manage text settings for the selected text box and the text within it; in this case, you manage text settings only for the selected text within the text box.

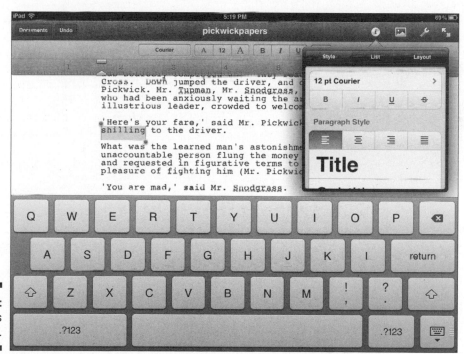

Figure 4-15: Set styles for text.

Here's how you can set styles, lists, and layouts:

✔ **Setting styles:** As you see in Figure 4-15, there are two sets of style settings. At the top, you can set the text attributes for the selected word(s). Paragraph styles affect the entire paragraph in which the words occur.

Tap the font name at the top of the popover to show the text options you see in Figure 4-16. You can set the font size and the font itself from there.

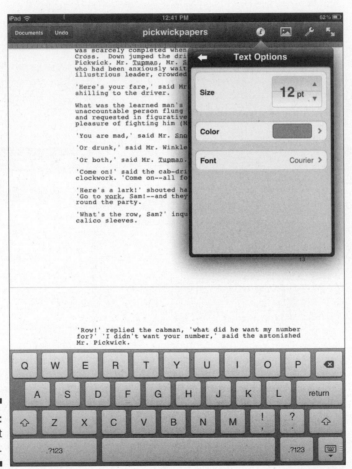

Figure 4-16: Set text options.

Tap the color, and you can change the color of the selected text (see Figure 4-17).

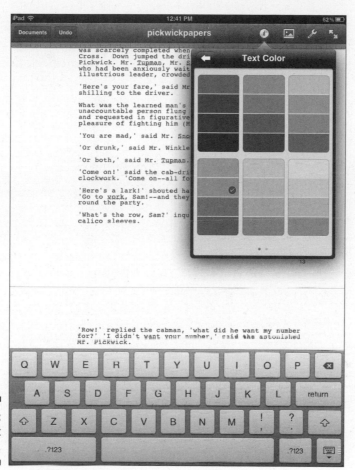

Figure 4-17:
Set the text
color.

✔ **Setting lists:** With the list settings shown in Figure 4-18, you can format a list. Each line of text that is terminated with a return has the appropriate list bullet at the beginning of the line. You can use the arrows at the top right and left of the popover to create sublists. Settings such as numbered and lettered lists are automatically updated with the next number or letter. These settings are for the selected text (not the paragraph).

✔ **Setting layouts:** The layout settings shown in Figure 4-19 let you set line spacing and the number of columns in a paragraph. These settings apply only to the current paragraph.

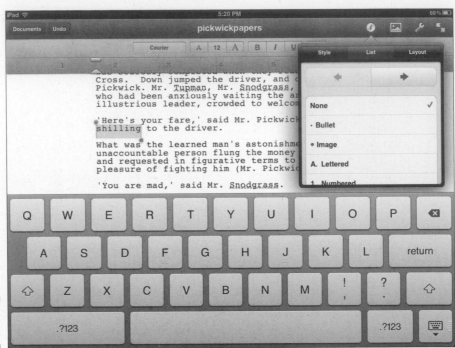

Figure 4-18:
Format lists.

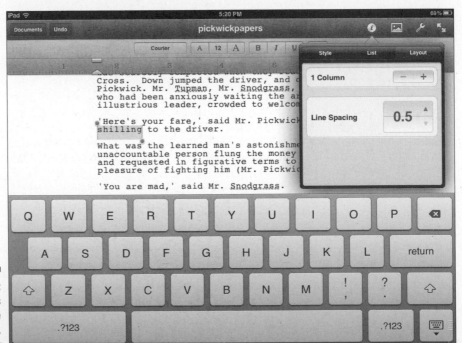

Figure 4-19:
Set columns
and line
spacing.

Integrating the text box with a document

Figure 4-20 shows how the text box appears if you create it in *The Pickwick Papers* word-processing document on OS X.

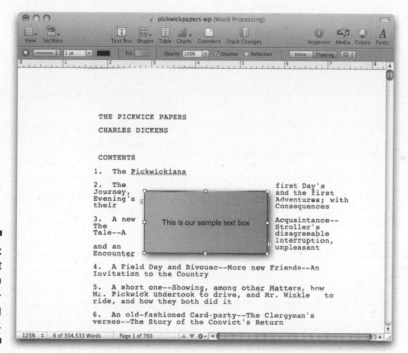

Figure 4-20:
Add a text
box to
a word-
processing
document.

As you can see in Figure 4-20, just putting a text box into a default position in a document can make the existing text look peculiar. You can make things look better in three basic ways. You'll probably use a little bit of each of them, as you experiment with the best size, shape, and position for the text box:

- **Resize the text box.** Click the text box to show its eight handles. Resize it as you want. (A single click selects the text box; a double click lets you edit the text.)

- **Move the text box.** Notice that as you move the box, the text wraps around it. Often, this wrapping of the text is what you want.

- **Use Wrap inspector to change how text wraps around the text box.** Wrap inspector is shown in Figure 4-21 and is described in the following section. Note that you can turn off text wrapping by deselecting the check box shown in Figure 4-21 on OS X; on iOS, it's controlled by the Arrange tab in Text settings.

Figure 4-21:
Use Wrap
inspector
to integrate
the text box
with the text
around it.

Wrapping around the text box

As shown in Figure 4-21, Wrap inspector on OS X has three sections. The Object Placement section of Wrap inspector is disabled for floating text boxes, which is the type of text box you create in this section. On iOS, Wrap settings are chosen from the Arrange settings. Change the Automatic settings (the default) by tapping on Wrap to configure wrapping, as shown in Figure 4-22.

The principles of wrapping text around a text box are the same as wrapping text around any shape.

What's the best way to wrap text?

There is no single answer to the question of the best way to wrap text. However, you can consider some general issues that apply to text boxes and any other objects around which text is wrapped.

You may choose to have embedded objects placed at the left of your document (using wrap right or wrap larger). This provides a consistent look and can make the text easier to read.

Another choice applies particularly to documents that will be bound like a book. On pages that will appear on the left side of the book (generally even-numbered pages), place the embedded objects at the left. For pages on the right side of the book (generally odd-numbered pages), place the embedded objects at the right. When the book or booklet is bound, it will be easier to see the embedded objects or text boxes if they're closer to the edge of the page than if they're closer to the binding, where you may have to stretch the book flat to see them.

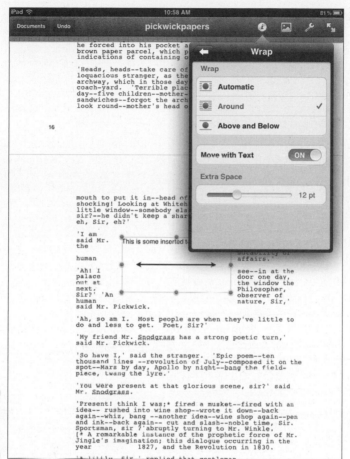

Figure 4-22:
Set wrap-
ping on iOS.

The issue of wrapping text around something in a word-processing document or a page layout document is tricky in any program. Usually when you set options and settings for text, a shape, or anything else, those options and settings govern the object's appearance and performance. In the case of wrapping, the options govern the appearance and performance of objects next to the text box.

Pages implements wrapping in a simple yet powerful way. Refer to Figure 4-8 to see what happens when you insert a text box into a section of text. The existing text moves to accommodate the text box. Wrap inspector lets you specify how and if that existing text will move and wrap. The settings are for the text box (or for any object inserted into the existing text), but those settings affect the existing text, not the text box. (There is actually a bit of interplay because the inserted text box and the existing text interact, but basically the existing text adjusts itself based on the text box's settings.)

Setting how the text box causes wrapping

Use the Object Causes Wrap check box to turn wrapping on and off. When the option is turned on, you then click whichever of the five wrapping techniques you want to use. From left to right, they are as follows:

- **Wrap left:** Text flows to the left of the object; there is no text to the right of the object. Usually if you use wrap left, you place the text box at the right side of the document.

- **Wrap both sides:** This is the default setting. Text flows on both sides, and the text box is centered. This option works well if the text box is relatively narrow and the page is relatively wide, but most of the time, it's the worst choice because you wind up with very short sections of text on the two sides.

- **Wrap right:** This is the reverse of wrap left. If you do this, generally place the object at the left.

- **Wrap larger:** This option wraps text on one side or the other depending on which side is wider.

  Use wrap larger instead of wrap right and wrap left. Move the text box to the right or left, and the text will automatically flow to the other side. The result is the same as carefully setting wrap right and wrap left. As an added benefit, if you edit the document, perhaps adding other text boxes, you just need to reposition the text boxes to one side or the other, and the document's text will flow the way you want it to: to the side opposite the text box.

- **No wrap:** Text doesn't wrap around either side of the text box but continues below the text box.

Setting how the text box causes text fitting

The last set of options on Wrap inspector handle text around irregularly shaped objects. You can also specify the distance between the text box and the text that is being wrapped around it.

With all these settings, experiment with the results in your document.

Creating an Inline Text Box for a Word-Processing Document

A floating text box is fixed to a place on the page. It floats in the sense that because it is fixed to a place on the page, the text that is next to it floats as you add or remove text in the document. When you do everything properly, the reader doesn't notice the difference between a floating text box and an inline text box. But a mistake is easy to spot. In this section, I show you an example of how you can get into trouble and how to prevent it.

In Figure 4-23, a floating text box has been placed in a word-processing document. The text in the document references the text box as being to the right of the paragraph.

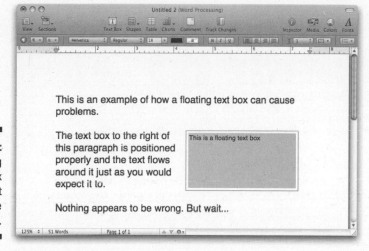

Figure 4-23: A floating text box doesn't move on the page.

In Figure 4-24, some text has been added at the beginning of the document. The text reflows to incorporate the added text, but the floating text box stays where it is on the page. The reference to the text box being at the right of the paragraph no longer makes sense because that sentence has flowed down the page and is now below the text box. (That's the floating part — the text has floated past the text box.)

Something worse can occur. Instead of text referring to a text box at the right of a paragraph, there may be no reference to the text box. That can puzzle the reader who now has to try to figure out why that text box is next to that paragraph.

Word-processing documents allow you to change floating text boxes to inline text boxes. Inline text boxes are tied to a specific place in text rather than to a specific place on the page. You can create inline text boxes in two ways:

✔ **Use Wrap inspector to change the Object Placement setting to Inline rather than the default Floating.**

✔ **Place the cursor where you want the text box to appear and choose Insert⇨Text Box.**

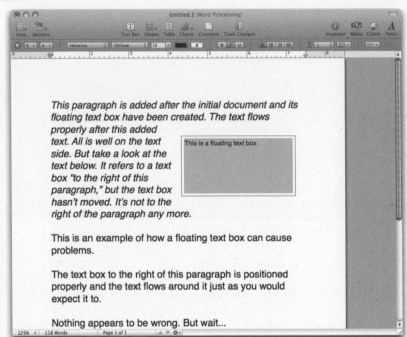

Figure 4-24:
References
to the text
box or other
embedded
shapes
no longer
match up.

Figure 4-25 shows an inline text box next to the paragraph that refers to it. When the text box is selected, an insertion point appears in the text. As you move the text box, the insertion point moves. The text box will stay at that point in the text, although its specific positioning is set by the Object Causes Wrap settings in Wrap inspector.

If text is added at the beginning of the document, as shown in Figure 4-26, the text reflows, and the inline text box moves with its accompanying text.

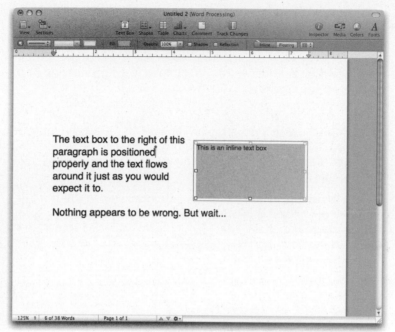

Figure 4-25:
An inline
text box is
fixed to text.

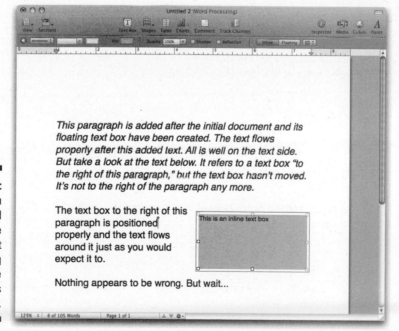

Figure 4-26:
You can
safely add
or delete
text without
disturbing
the inline
text box's
link.

Flowing Text between Text Boxes

Sometimes you want to put more text in a text box than will fit in it. If you're working with a floating text box in either a word-processing or page layout document, you can flow text between several text boxes. You do this for several reasons:

- **To flow text in a page layout document:** Although word-processing documents automatically flow text from page to page as you add it, in a page layout document, the only way to flow text is from one text box to another (and, perhaps, another and another . . .).

- **To handle page jumps:** When a story begins on the front page of a newspaper and is continued inside the paper, the inside continuation is referred to as the *jump*. (On websites, articles sometimes have a few lines of text followed by a link that says Click Here to Read More. That, too, is called a jump.)

Creating a text flow link

Here's how you flow text between text boxes:

1. **Create a text box.**

   If you're in a word-processing document, it must be a floating text box; in a page layout document, it will automatically be a floating text box.

2. **Type or paste the text into the box.**

   In Figure 4-27, the entire text of *The Pickwick Papers* has been pasted into the text box. (Yes, all 300,000 words. Pages and your Mac are very powerful!) The clipping indicator in the center of the bottom of the text box indicates that there is more text than is shown — it's the square with the plus sign in it. The triangle indicators at the near top-left and near bottom-right let you specify the flow of the text, as explained in the next steps. If there's no more text, there's no clipping indicator.

3. **Click the right arrow box at the lower right of the text box to begin the link.**

   You can link to a text box on any page of your document:

   - To link to an existing text box, click the existing text box.

   - To link to a text box that will be automatically created, click in the document at the approximate location for the new text box. Figure 4-28 shows the link to a text box on the next page of the document. Note that there is still more text to be flowed because the clipping indicator in the center of the new text box still contains a + symbol.

   When the link is created, the right arrow box becomes a solid blue box.

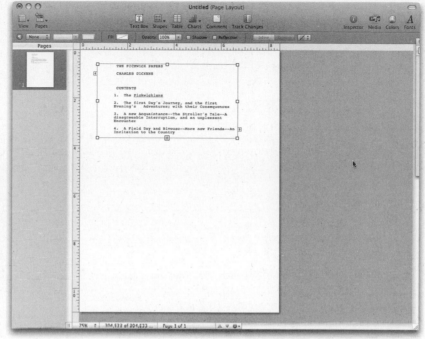

Figure 4-27:
Text in a floating text box that overflows shows a clipping indicator.

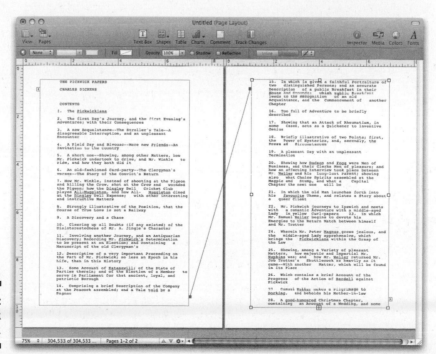

Figure 4-28:
You can link text boxes.

You can link any number of text boxes, and you can resize each one as you want. To remove a link, drag the solid blue box for the link you want to break off the text box. The link will disappear and the blue box will revert to being an arrow.

Joining two text boxes

You can use the procedure in the preceding section to join two text boxes, each of which has its own text. Link them, and the text becomes a single flow. As you resize the text boxes, you will see that the text flows from one to the other.

Adding Objects to Text Boxes

You can insert objects into text boxes, as shown in Figure 4-29. They behave as inline text boxes do: You position them relative to the text in the text box, and they stay in that relative place.

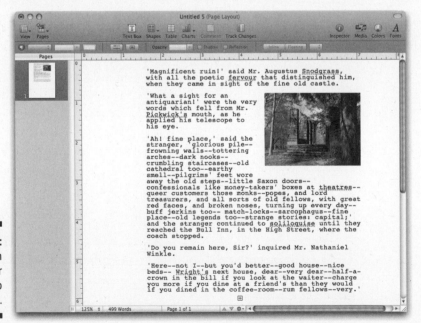

Figure 4-29:
You can add other objects to text boxes.

Here's how to add a graphic to a text box. The same technique works for other objects, such as tables and charts:

1. **Select the text box.**

2. **Click to set the insertion point approximately where you want the graphic to be.**

3. **Insert the object using the Insert menu.**

   - For a graphics file, choose Insert⇨Choose.

   - For a table, choose Insert⇨Table.

   - For a chart, choose Insert⇨Chart.

   - For a shape, choose Insert⇨Shape.

   You can't insert a text box into a text box.

Chapter 5

Working with Colors, Fonts, Shapes, and Images

*i*Work blurs the lines between page layout, spreadsheets, and presentations, so, in many ways, it doesn't matter where you start. As you continue, you can add colors, fonts, shapes, and media to any of those documents — and you do it all in the same way. This chapter collects those additional document objects and shows you how to work with them. Caution: You'll soon see that the folks at Apple have made it possible to work almost the same way with colors, fonts, shapes, and images. There's not much to learn once you know the basics.

Using Selection Buttons and Info on iWork for iOS

Although iOS has no menu bar, remember that with many apps (including the iWork apps for iOS), tapping an object on the screen can bring up *selection buttons* just above the object you have tapped. The selection buttons are context-sensitive, so they vary depending on the object you have tapped. Figure 5-1 shows selection buttons for a word that's selected on a Keynote slide.

As you see in Figures 5-1 and 5-2, arrows at either end of the selection buttons let you view more buttons.

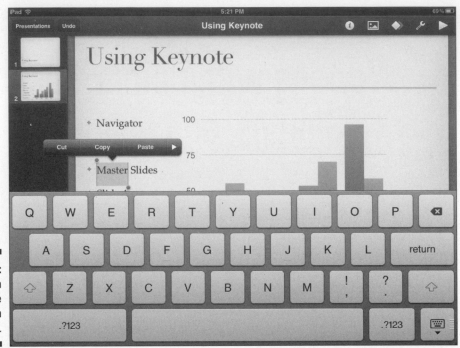

Figure 5-1:
Selection
buttons are
shown with
a single tap.

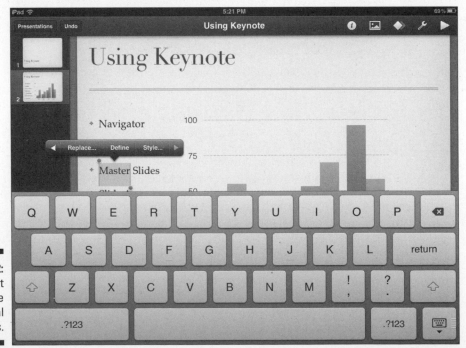

Figure 5-2:
Arrows let
you see
additional
buttons.

In addition to selection buttons, when you select an object by tapping it, you can open the Info popover from the right side of the toolbar. The Info popover, too, is context sensitive. For example, with Numbers for iOS, tapping a cell brings up a popover with buttons at the top to let you format the table, its header, and its cells as well as the format of the cell (number, currency, stepper, and so on). Tapping a text box brings up a popover with buttons for style and for text (including the font and style). Also, because a text box can float above or below other objects, an Arrange button lets you move the text box forward or back on the screen. (Cells in spreadsheets do not move forward or back: They all exist in the same layer of the document.)

Using Color in Your Documents on OS X

Color has become an essential part of today's documents both on paper and on the screen. The days of black-and-white printing for most documents is long gone. You can use color to create the most garish and distracting documents that confuse and annoy people, but you can also use color to enhance your communication and make your work more attractive.

One of the Mac's most useful features is a consistent and integrated approach to color management. While not all applications on the Mac use the common interface, all iWork applications use it. So do many applications from Apple and third parties. You set color for text, graphics, and graphics in iWork in one place: the Colors window. The following sections provide you with a fast way to set a color. Then, you find out how to use the advanced features of the Colors window.

The Colors window is a floating window that appears only when the application is active. That means if you switch to another application by clicking one of its windows (or by launching it), the Pages window will remain visible behind the other application's windows, but the Colors window and any other floating windows will disappear. When Pages once again becomes active (most commonly when you click one of its windows in the background of another application), its floating windows come forward and become active. In addition, the Colors window reappears, in its last location. Other floating windows discussed in this chapter, such as the Font panel and the Inspector window, have the same behavior.

The Colors window is part of Mac OS X and is used in many applications, not just iWork.

The process for applying a color depends on how you're using the color. You can

✔ Color a selected object.

✔ Color a nonselected object.

✔ Add a color to your palette in the Colors window.

✔ Copy a color from an object in the window.

Rather than using the centralized Colors window on Mac OS X, with iOS, you generally color each type of object in its own settings.

Coloring a selected object using the Colors window

To color a selected object, such as text or a graphic element, follow these steps:

1. **Select the object you want to color.**

2. **Click the Colors button on the toolbar or choose View⇨Show Colors to open the Colors window, shown in Figure 5-3.**

   If the color wheel isn't shown as you see it in Figure 5-3, click the color wheel button at the top left of the Colors window. If you don't see the set of five buttons across the top of the Colors window, click the oblong button at the top right of the window and then click the color wheel button at the left.

   To brighten or darken the colors in the color wheel, use the slider at the right.

Figure 5-3:
Use the Colors window.

3. Click a color from the color wheel.

The center of the wheel is white. It shades into other colors:

- Yellows in the upper right

- Reds in the lower right

- Blues in the lower left

- Greens in the upper left

The selected color is applied to the selected object automatically.

Saving a color in your color palette

The Colors window lets you save swatches of color in a *palette* at the bottom of the window. This palette shows up in all Colors windows. It consists of ten rows of swatches; its width is determined by the width of the Colors window. Figure 5-4 shows the palette with all ten rows shown in a widened window.

Using the steps in the preceding section, select the color you want. But instead of dragging the color to the object to color (in Step 4), drag it to a swatch in the color palette.

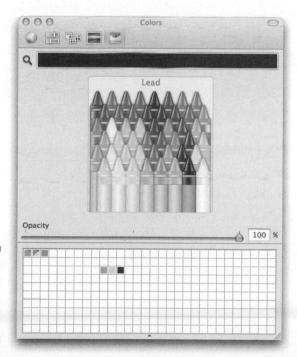

Figure 5-4:
Use the Colors window palette.

Organize the colors in your palette so that you know what you'll use them for. You can leave spaces, as shown in Figure 5-4 so that colors for your website are separated from colors for your brochures, for example. If you put the green for your website next to the green for your Keynote presentation backgrounds, you may have trouble telling them apart. Millions of colors are available on modern computers such as the Mac; using a selected subset makes your work elegant and consistent. It also makes it much easier to set colors in your iWork documents.

Coloring a selected object using the palette

After you've set up colors in the palette, the process of coloring a selected object is much simpler.

1. **Select the object.**
2. **Click the Colors button on the toolbar or choose View⇨Show Colors to open the Colors window.**
3. **Double-click the color from the palette.**

Coloring a nonselected object using the palette

Likewise, the process for coloring nonselected objects is simpler with the palette:

1. **Click the Colors button on the toolbar or choose View⇨Show Colors to open the Colors window.**
2. **Single-click the color you want.**

   The color appears in the color well.
3. **Drag the color from the color well to any object you want to color.**

Copying a color from the screen

You can copy any color you see onscreen to the color well. This color can be a from a website, photo, or interface element of an application.

Colors themselves aren't copyrighted, but combinations of them may be copyrighted logos and images.

To copy a color from the screen:

1. **Click the Colors button on the toolbar or choose View➪Show Colors to open the Colors window.**

2. **Click the magnifying glass to the left of the color well.**

3. **Move it over the color on the screen you want to copy.**

   The pixels under the magnifying glass are enlarged, and you can position the center of the magnifying glass directly over the color you want.

4. **Click.**

   The color is placed in the color well.

5. **Apply the color to objects in your document or place it in your palette.**

Graphics often have a row of pixels along their edges to make them appear better on the screen. You may think that you have a red circle on a background of a blue square, but when you look at the individual pixels, you may find one or two rows of pixels in intermediate colors that make the image more attractive and remove fuzziness. For that reason, make certain that you center the magnifying glass on the color you want and not on the special pixels at its edge.

Setting opacity

Opacity refers to the degree of transparency of the color — the extent to which objects behind it can be seen. After you select a color, you may want to set its opacity with the slider at the bottom of the window. Lower numbers (dragging the slider to the left) make the color more transparent so that objects behind it are visible.

Advanced color management

The Colors window gives you as much control as you want over color. If you want red, you can just click a red crayon. If you want exactly the shade of red that you remember from your first grown-up prom gown, you can have that. But before you go too far, you should know that color is one of the most subjective perceptions we have. Artists and philosophers as diverse as Wolfgang Goethe in the 18th century and Josef Albers in the 20th century wrote and thought perceptively about color (and they didn't agree).

Colors look different in different lighting conditions; even more important, *reflected color* (that is, color that is reflected from a wall, painting, or physical object) looks different from color that is transmitted (such as on a computer screen or a projection screen). You can use whatever color model you want.

If you're trying to match colors on other documents, they may be specified in one of the slider models and values, so it is easiest to use them.

You can use different color models for different objects in the same document. The only way to accurately match colors is to use the actual method that will be used to display them. Don't even try to match a color in a newspaper with a color on a flat-panel TV screen.

The Colors window (shown in Figure 5-5) gives you as much or as little complexity as you want. At the top of the Colors window, five buttons let you choose between five *color pickers* — ways of comparing and identifying colors:

Figure 5-5:
Use RGB
sliders to
set a color.

✔ **Color wheel:** Maybe you learned about the color wheel in school. The center point of the color wheel is always white. Individual colors move out from there, with greens in the upper left, blues in the lower left, reds in the lower right, and yellows in the upper right. The colors merge into one another. When you click a color in the color wheel, it fills the box just above the color wheel. You can set the brightness for the entire color wheel with the slider at the right.

✔ **Color sliders:** The second button lets you select from among color sliders, which allow you to specify a color using numbers. These color sliders may seem to have more precision than the color wheel, but they actually have less because the numbers are integers: one value for gray scale, three for RGB and HSB, and four for CMYK. If you want a color that is just between grayscale 65 and 66, for example, you can't compromise on 65.6. In the color wheel, are least theoretically, every gradation is possible. (The hardware limits the actual gradations.) Four separate models are supported for sliders:

- **Gray scale slider:** This slider shows shades of gray. You can move it until the color in the box at the top of the Colors window is the shade of gray you want. You also can type a percent from 0 percent (black) to 100 percent (white).

- **RGB sliders:** This color model uses three numbers to define the colors red, green, and blue (hence RGB). Each can have a value from 0 to 255 as shown in Figure 5-5. As you move the slider or type a number, the color at the top changes. If you want a basic red, set red to 255 and set the blue and green values to 0. RGB colors are often used to set colors for the web and other screen-display devices.

- **CMYK sliders:** These sliders behave just like RGB sliders, but they use a different model based on four values: cyan (C), magenta (M), yellow (Y), and black (K). CMYK is often used to specify colors that will be used in printing.

- **HSB sliders:** This is yet another color model based on three values: hue, saturation, and brightness. This model is often used in television.

✓ **Palettes:** Here, you find palettes of color. You can also create your own. Perhaps the most commonly used palette is Web Safe colors, shown in Figure 5-6. These are the colors that are safe to use on the web for all displays on all operating systems and all browsers. If you're designing documents to be published on the web, you should use these colors. To select a color, use the Palette pop-up menu at the top of the Palettes tab of the Colors window to select Web Safe and then click whatever color you want. The color will appear in the color well at the top of the Colors window.

Create and name a palette if it will be used for a specific project. The palette at the bottom of the Colors window applies to all of your iWork projects and documents.

Figure 5-6:
Use Web
Safe colors
for docu-
ments to be
published
on the web.

✔ **Spectrum:** The fourth button from the left is another attempt to represent all colors, but in a different layout from the color wheel. Give it a try and click the color you want to use.

✔ **Crayons:** If you don't have to precisely match colors, maybe you're longing for a simple box of crayons. That's exactly what the last icon, shown in Figure 5-7, provides.

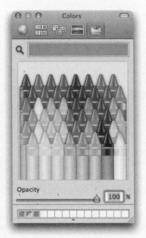

Figure 5-7: Get out the crayons!

Creating Shapes

Shapes work the same way in all iWork applications. Usually, the toolbar is the easiest way to create shapes. iWork has two kinds of shapes:

✔ **Predrawn shapes:** iWork can create predrawn shapes, such as circles and arrows. You can modify predrawn shapes.

✔ **Custom shapes:** Draw any shape that you want. You can constrain the shape to horizontal or vertical as well as to a regular shape (that is, a circle instead of an oval, or a square instead of a rectangle).

Creating shapes with iWork for Mac

Inspectors are the interface elements that let you change settings, such as colors, line widths, arrowheads, and the distance created around a shape as you move it through other objects. You can also use an inspector to place an image in an object. This chapter shows you how to use inspectors.

Inserting a predrawn shape from the toolbar

Follow these steps to insert a predrawn shape from the toolbar in any iWork document:

1. **Click Shapes on the toolbar.**

   Hold down the mouse button to bring up the menu of shapes shown in Figure 5-8.

   The bottom shape is the *custom* shape. You use custom shape later in the chapter.

2. **Select the shape you want.**

   The shape is inserted in the center of the document.

Figure 5-8:
Select a
shape to
insert.

Inserting a predrawn shape with the mouse

You can use the mouse to add a predrawn shape in the size and location that you want. Here's how:

1. **Create or open your iWork document.**

2. **Hold down the Option key while you click the Shape button on the toolbar.**

3. **Using the mouse, draw the shape.**

As you move the mouse, the size of the shape grows or shrinks. Also, instead of automatically being placed in the center of the document as is the case when you use the Insert command in the menu bar, the shape is placed where you started drawing it.

Inserting a shape from the menu bar

You can also use the Insert menu command to insert a shape rather than using the toolbar:

1. **Open or create your iWork document.**

2. **Choose Insert⇨Shape⇨<the kind of shape you want>.**

The shape is created. If you want to edit it, continue with the next section.

Creating shapes with iWork for iOS

Use the Insert button at the right of the toolbar to insert any object into your iWork document. The Shapes button lets you insert predrawn shapes, as you can see in Figure 5-9. (Note that the T inserts a text box; you can use any of the other shapes and then type into them.)

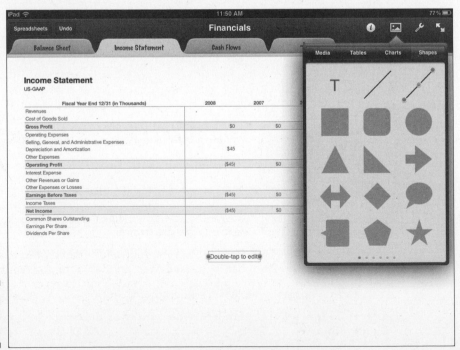

Figure 5-9:
Add a shape.

Editing a shape on Mac OS X

After you create a shape, you can change it. Click the shape to select it, and you see a *bounding box* and eight *handles,* small boxes along the bounding box, as shown in Figure 5-10.

Four handles are in the corners of the shape; the other four are located at the midpoints of the bounding box edges. The bounding box is the smallest rectangle that can contain the shape. Even if the shape isn't rectangular, it will fit inside a rectangle. Shapes such as triangles have a different number of sides, but the functionality is the same.

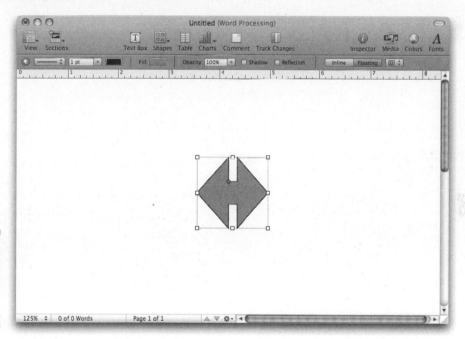

Figure 5-10:
Select a shape to show its handles.

Here are the types of edits you can perform on a shape:

- ✔ **Resize the shape:** Drag one of the four corner handles to enlarge or reduce a shape's size.

- ✔ **Reshape the shape:** Drag one of the four midpoint handles to change the shape's proportions. The midpoint handle in the top line moves the top line up and down; the midpoint handle in the bottom line moves that line up and down. Similarly, the midpoint handles on the left and right lines move them in and out.

✔ **Move the shape:** Drag inside the bounding box to move the entire shape. Don't use one of the handles because that will resize or reshape the shape.

✔ **Change special sizes:** Some shapes have additional handles:

- **Arrow depth:** A small handle lets you vary the length of the arrow shaft.

- **Double-arrow width:** The double-headed arrow has a tiny handle in the center of the shape that you can drag back and forth to change the distance between the two arrowheads.

- **Star and polygon points:** When you select a star or polygon, a slider below the shape lets you change the number of points, as shown in Figure 5-11. Note the small round handle between two of the points. Drag it in or out to make the valley deeper or shallower.

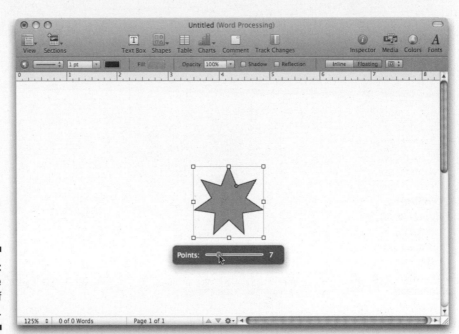

Figure 5-11: Change the number of points.

Editing a shape's geometry

The changes to a shape described in the preceding section don't change the basic geometry of a shape. The formula that describes a circle, a rectangle, or another shape is the same regardless of its values. For example, a circle is always round; a rectangle is always rectangular, with four sides. A special case of a rectangle is a square with four sides of identical length.

There are many reasons for changing a shape's geometry, such as realizing that it would look better as another shape. Editing the shape preserves its color and other attributes.

To change a shape's geometry:

1. **Select the shape you want to edit.**

2. **Choose Format⇨Shape⇨Make Editable.**

   In addition to the handles, red circular controls appear in the middle of each arc of the shape, as shown in Figure 5-12.

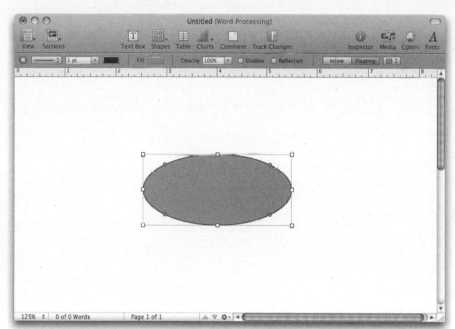

Figure 5-12:
Make a
shape
editable.

3. **If you want to change an arc, drag the circular control to the new position, as shown in Figure 5-13.**

   The clicked control has a control handle.

4. **Pull either end of the handle to change the arc.**

   Compare Figure 5-13 with Figure 5-14 to see how these control handles modify the shape.

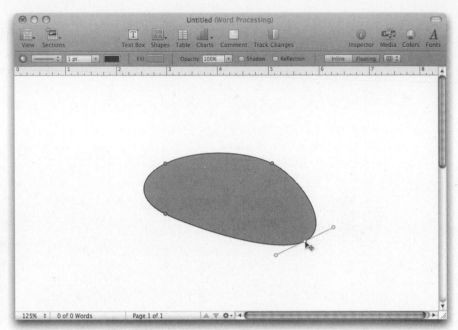

Figure 5-13:
Change a
rounded
shape.

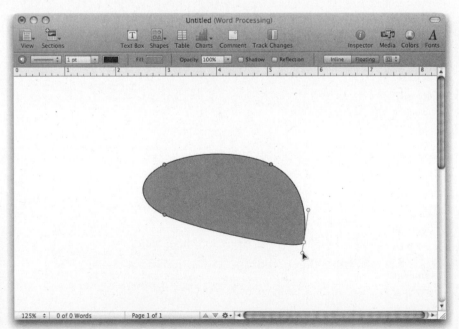

Figure 5-14:
Change an
arc.

Adjusting shape settings on iOS

Whether you've created a shape with iWork for iOS or iWork for Mac, you can select a shape and adjust its settings. Tap the shape to select it and then tap Info at the right of the toolbar. As you see in Figure 5-15, you have three tabs at the top of the popover: Style, Text, and Arrange.

Style Options at the bottom lets you set the fill, border, and effects. For fill, you have a number of preset colors to choose from. As you see in Figure 5-16, you can change the border color, width, and pattern.

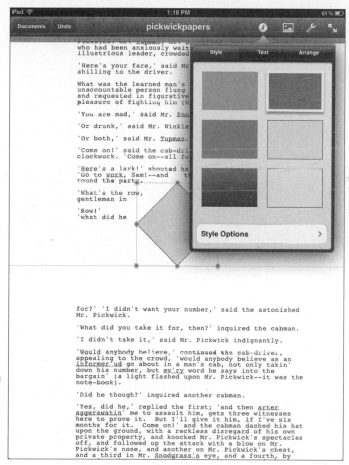

Figure 5-15:
Adjust
shape
settings.

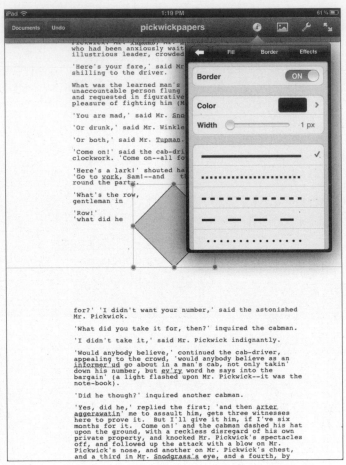

Figure 5-16:
Set border
options.

Effects, shown in Figure 5-17, let you adjust the shadow (if any) and the *opacity* of the shape (that is, the degree to which you can see through it to objects behind it).

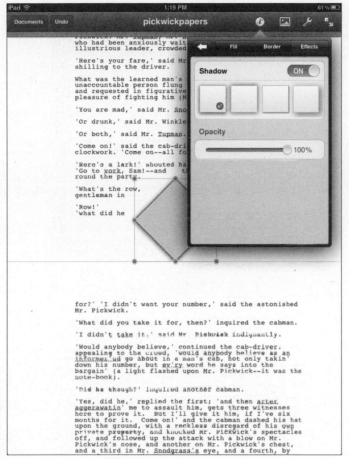

Figure 5-17:
Adjust
effects.

Arrange, shown in Figure 5-18, lets you set the back-to-front positioning, wrapping around the shape, and vertical alignment.

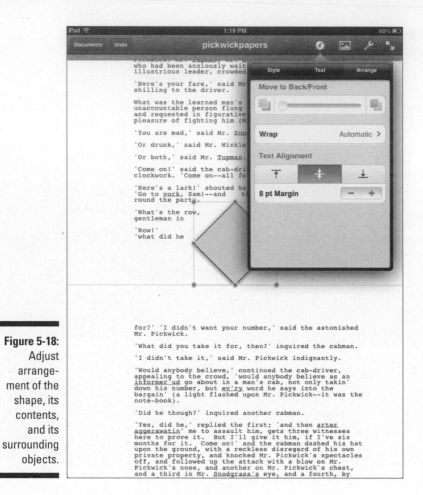

Figure 5-18:
Adjust
arrange-
ment of the
shape, its
contents,
and its
surrounding
objects.

You can choose from several wrapping methods as shown in Figure 5-19.

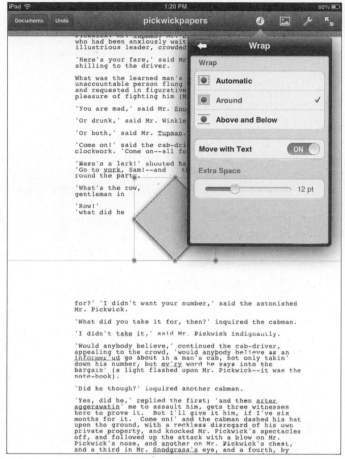

Figure 5-19:
Choose the
wrapping of
text around
the shape.

Formatting Graphics with Graphic Inspector on Mac OS X

As you can see in Figure 5-20, Graphic inspector has five main sections. Not all of them are available for selected graphic objects. For example, a graphic object that doesn't contain an image cannot be shown with an apparent mirror reflection of the image. The five sections of Graphic inspector let you adjust the following attributes of objects:

✔ **Fill:** You can fill selected objects with solid colors, images, gradients, or combinations of images and colors.

✔ **Stroke:** You can set the attributes for a line object or the line that borders an object. The attributes you can set are color, the line width, its endpoints (arrows), and its appearance (solid, dashed, and so on).

✔ **Shadow:** Set a shadow for the selected object. The settings are the same as for text shadowing, described in Chapter 3, except instead of using the outline of text characters for the shadow, you select a color from the Colors window to shadow the exact shape of the selected object.

✔ **Reflection:** If an object contains an image, this setting automatically produces a reflection of the image outside the object with greater or lesser opacity. It is generally best to use either a shadow or a reflection; using both produces peculiar results.

✔ **Opacity:** This setting lets you choose whether the object hides anything behind it (100%), is totally transparent (0%), or is somewhere in between. Note that the setting is for the entire graphic object; you can separately set opacity for its border (using Stroke settings) or its center (using Fill).

Figure 5-20:
Use Graphic
inspector.

Beyond the general settings described here, you can do some simple tasks with Graphic inspector, such as

✔ Fill an object with color

✔ Create a gradient fill

✔ Place an image inside a graphic

✔ Use a tinted image fill

✔ Choose stroke settings

I describe each of these processes in the following sections.

Filling an object with color

The settings for shadows, opacity, and reflection are similar to settings for text in Chapter 3. Here's how to fill an object with a color:

1. **Select the object you want to fill with a color.**

2. **Display an inspector.**

3. **Click the Graphic button to display Graphic inspector.**

4. **Select Color Fill from the Fill pop-up menu.**

    A color well appears.

5. **Use the color well to select the color you want.**

6. **If you want to adjust the opacity, use the Opacity setting.**

Creating a gradient fill

In iWork, a *gradient* is a pattern that changes from one color at one side to another color at the opposite side. Gradients can provide elegant effects in your documents, but they also can lead you astray. If your document will be printed, test the gradient effect on a printer as early in the process as you can. Different types of printers handle colors in different ways. What appears as a smooth gradient transition on your screen may have ugly bars and be not at all smooth or elegant on some printers — particularly those designed for black-and-white printing.

To create a gradient fill, follow these steps:

1. **Select the object you want to fill with a gradient.**

2. **Open or create an Inspector window.**

    Choose View➪Show Inspector, View➪New Inspector or click Inspector on the toolbar.

3. **Click the Graphic button to display Graphic inspector.**

4. **Select Gradient Fill from the Fill pop-up menu at the top of Graphic inspector, as shown in Figure 5-21.**

5. **Use the color wells to select the colors to start and end the gradient.**

    The top color well is the starting color.

    If you select a color with an opacity of less than 100 percent, it appears with a diagonal bar through it in Graphic inspector. On the screen or when printed, the opacity effect is generated and the bar is not shown.

6. **In the Fill area, select the angle of the gradient.**

   You have three ways to select the angle. The right-pointing arrow automatically selects 0 degrees; the downward-pointing arrow selects 270 degrees. Use the wheel to select any other angle or use the text box to enter the angle.

Figure 5-21:
Fill the object with a gradient fill.

Placing an image inside a graphic

One of the most common tasks is to fill a graphic object with an image. There are many reasons for placing an image inside an object rather than just inserting the image (or pasting it) into the document itself. First, inside an object, the image can be framed or highlighted by the object itself. Second, if your images are of different sizes, you can place them inside objects of the same size, shape, and orientation to make your document look cleaner.

Here's how to place an image inside a graphic:

1. **Select the object you want to fill with an image.**

2. **Display an inspector.**

3. **Click the Graphic button to display Graphic inspector.**

4. **Select Image Fill from the Fill pop-up menu, as shown in Figure 5-22.**

Figure 5-22:
Use Image
Fill.

5. **Click the Choose button and select an image file to insert into the graphic object.**

   A small version of the graphic appears in the Inspector window.

   You've seen a color well; the similar looking object in Figure 5-22 that contains the image is called an *image well*. When Graphic inspector is open, you can drag a file from Finder into the image well rather than clicking the Choose button.

6. **Scale the image.**

   A small pop-up menu (set to Tile in Figure 5-23) is now available. These are the possible settings, as shown in Figure 5-23.

Figure 5-23:
Scale the
image.

- **Scale to Fit:** If the image and the object have the same dimensions, the image simply is placed in the object. If the dimensions are different, the image is resized as best as possible. In some cases, part of the object may not be shown. Scale to Fit is a quick way to scale an image in which the center is the most important part, and it doesn't matter if you can't see some of the edges.

- **Scale to Fill:** In this case, the image is kept as large as possible, but all of it is shown. In some cases, this may leave fairly large sections at the top or sides. This is a good choice if you want to make certain that the entire image is shown.

- **Stretch:** The image fills the object. If they're different shapes, the image is distorted as necessary. This sometimes works well with images when you don't care a great deal about the detail. If you stretch an image of a pine forest, the pine trees may turn out taller or wider than they are in the original image, but as long as the image and object are roughly the same shape, the trees in the image will still be recognizable as pine trees.

- **Original Size:** The image isn't resized. It may not all be visible in the object.

- **Tile:** This is like the Original Size setting, but if the image is smaller than the object, the image is repeated (at its original size) as many times as necessary to fill the object.

Using a tinted image fill

The last choice for filling an object is Tinted Image Fill, which combines an image and a color. Here's how to do that:

1. **Select the object you want to fill with an image.**

2. **Display an inspector.**

3. **Click the Graphic button to display Graphic inspector.**

4. **Select Tinted Image Fill from the Fill pop-up menu, as shown in Figure 5-24.**

Figure 5-24:
Use Tinted
Image Fill.

5. **Click the Choose button and select an image file to insert into the graphic object.**

   A small version of the graphic appears in the image well, below the Fill menu.

6. **Scale the image.**

   For details, see Step 6 in the preceding section.

7. **Use the image well to select the color to use.**

   The Choose button selects an image file for the image well; clicking the image well brings up the Colors window so you can choose a color. The diagonal line in the image well indicates that the color isn't opaque. (If the color is opaque, you won't see the image, and the entire process is pointless: Just use the Color Fill option.)

The settings for shadows, opacity, and reflection are similar to settings for text, discussed in Chapter 3.

Choosing stroke settings

The only other item in the Graphic inspector to examine is the Stroke settings. When you select a graphic object, you can set the stroke of its border — the color, width, and type of line (solid, dotted, or dashed). In addition, certain types of graphic objects are basically lines with a beginning and an end. For those, you can set the type of endpoint, as shown in Figure 5-25, if you have chosen Line from the pop-up menu in the Stroke area.

Figure 5-25:
Set stroke
options.

Using Images in Your Documents

A picture is worth a thousand words as the saying goes. Images are at the heart of the Apple experience — everything from the design of the devices themselves, to the look and feel of the software, and on to the tools that let you create and manipulate images.

Adding images to your documents on OS X

You can add images to any iWork document. Use Insert⇨Choose to select the file you want to insert. Once the file is inserted in your iWork document, you can move and adjust it. You make some of these adjustments with Metrics inspector or Graphic inspector; others you do by directly manipulating the images.

Masking images with shapes

When you have a graphic in an iWork document, you can mask it with shapes so that only part of the image is shown. This replaces the cropping you may have performed in other applications. What appears is the part of the image that shows through the shape.

Follow these steps to mask an image:

1. **Select an image in an iWork document.**

2. **Choose Format⇨Mask to place a mask on top of the image.**

   You can also choose Format⇨Mask with Shape to use a predrawn shape, such as a triangle or circle.

3. **Drag the handles at the corners of the mask until it is the size and shape you want.**

4. **Drag the image until the part you want to show is over the mask.**

5. **Use the Edit Mask slider below the mask to enlarge or shrink the image itself.**

   Figure 5-26 shows the process in action.

6. **Repeat Steps 3 to 5 until you're satisfied and then click out of the image.**

   What is shown is only the part within the mask, as shown in Figure 5-27.

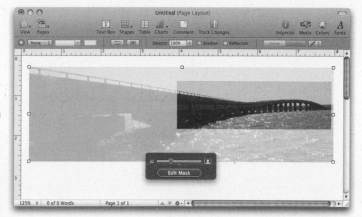

Figure 5-26:
Experiment
with the
mask and
the image.

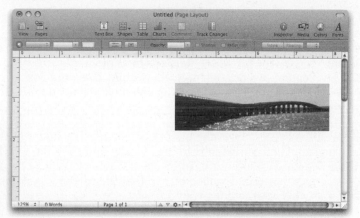

Figure 5-27:
The image is
masked.

Checking and setting positions with Metrics inspector

Metrics inspector, shown in Figure 5-28, lets you control the size and location of objects. For many people, the easiest way to arrange objects (including inserted graphic files) is by moving them around to the approximate position you want and then using the mouse to resize or reshape them. For finer control, however, you can specify exact coordinates for each object. iWork uses X/Y coordinates for the units you've chosen in Preferences. The origin (0,0) is the upper-left corner of the document.

You can flip objects. You can also constrain an object's proportions so that as you're resizing it with the mouse, you don't distort the image that it contains.

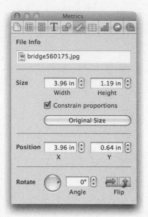

Figure 5-28:
Use Metrics inspector to position objects.

Adjusting images

Images can be used throughout iWork. You can use images as title graphics identifying chapters or other sections of a document, but they frequently are used as the content of a document itself. Nothing prevents you from creating a spreadsheet in Numbers that contains columns of information about items: prices, names, and images.

For example, a chapter about the history of Quebec City might have an image of the 400-year-old city walls next to the chapter and the title. Within a chapter on 16th-century architecture, an image of Quebec City may be placed beside an image or another walled city so that the reader can compare two or more styles of city wall construction.

Whether an image is used on its own or inserted into a graphic object, you can adjust the image inside iWork. The adjustments that you make apply only to the inserted image: The original image isn't changed.

The adjustments that you can make are common to image manipulation; you can make the same adjustments in iPhoto, Aperture, and Photoshop.

Follow these steps to adjust an image in iWork:

1. **Select the image in the iWork document.**

2. **Choose View➪Show Adjust Image to open the Adjust Image window, shown in Figure 5-29.**

3. **Make changes to the image.**

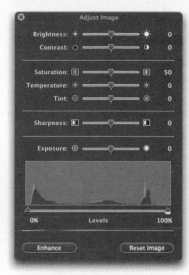

Figure 5-29:
Change image settings in iWork documents.

Adding images to your documents on iOS

One important feature that distinguishes Apple software from many other products is how easily you can use graphics and video in the documents you create. It's probably not surprising for you to see Pages templates with photo placeholders in them, and it certainly makes sense that Keynote templates often include photos. In today's world, you expect images in word-processing documents and presentations. But spreadsheets? Take a look at the Numbers templates to see how the people at Apple are suggesting you rethink your understanding of spreadsheets.

You can add photos, images, and video — easily and productively — to any iWork for iPad document. You have two ways to do this:

- ✔ Use the Insert button at the right end of the toolbar.
- ✔ Use a template that includes a placeholder image.

Using a template with a placeholder image requires one more step than using the Insert button. Here's how this process works:

1. **Create a document based on a template that includes a placeholder image.**

   Some templates contain several placeholder images. Figure 5-30 shows Photo Portfolio template in Keynote, for example.

   Notice in the lower-right corner of the image a button that matches the Insert button at the right end of the toolbar at the top of the Keynote window. This indicates that the image is a placeholder.

Indicates a placeholder figure

Figure 5-30:
Create a
document
with
placeholder
images.

2. **Tap the placeholder button to open a list of your photo albums, as shown in Figure 5-31.**

   You can browse photos on your iPad as well as albums you have created in iPhoto or other programs, such as Photoshop Elements, and synchronized to your iPad. Select the image you want to use instead of the placeholder.

Figure 5-31:
Choose a
photo.

3. **Double-tap the image to show the masking control (see Figure 5-32), which lets you adjust the size of the image.**

4. **Adjust the slider to change the image mask.**

The slider adjusts the size of the image. It starts with the image the same size as the frame, but if you move the slider all the way to the right, as you see in Figure 5-33, the image is shown dimly filling the entire screen. You can drag the image around so that the part you want is inside the frame. You can also use the eight handles on the frame to change its size and shape. This is a hands-on way to handle tasks such as cropping images. Rest assured that the original image file is unchanged by these steps: You're only changing the image's appearance within the document.

Masking control

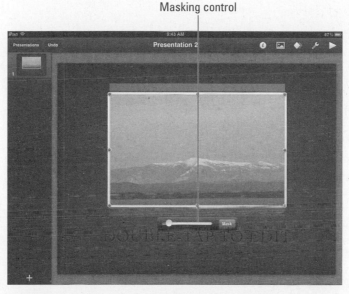

Figure 5-32: Double-tap to mask the image.

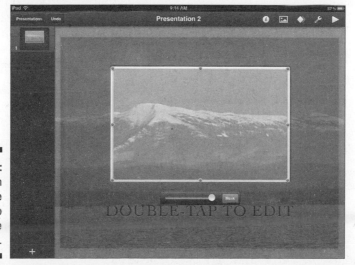

Figure 5-33: You can adjust the slider to change the image mask.

Using Media Browser

The basic media manipulation programs (iPhoto, iTunes, and iMovie) let you assemble images, audio, and movies into groups and categories. iWork Media Browser lets you browse these files in the categories you've created in the iLife applications. From Media Browser, you can drag media files into your iWork documents without worrying about where they're stored on disk.

To display Media Browser, choose View➪Show Media Browser. The window shown in Figure 5-34 appears.

Once you've placed media files in your iWork documents, you can use QuickTime and other inspectors to adjust the appearance and behavior of the media files. In the case of images, you can place them inside objects as described previously in this chapter.

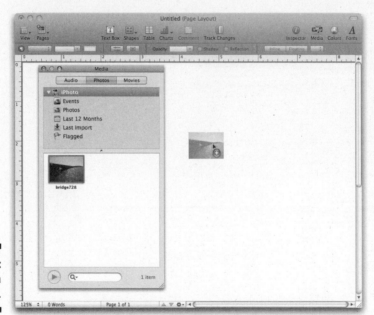

Figure 5-34: Use Media Browser.

Chapter 6

Working with Tables and Charts

In This Chapter

▶ Adding tables and charts to your documents

▶ Changing settings in tables and charts

Tables and charts provide a structured and efficient way of presenting data. iWork provides you with standard ready-to-go layouts (particularly in iWork for iOS), as well as highly customizable options.

This chapter shows you how to create tables and charts using iWork for Mac as well as iWork for iOS. If you're using Numbers, you can use additional features (see Part III, "Counting on Numbers").

Creating Tables and Charts

Charts and tables present data in a highly structured way, which can help make your documents clearer. Numbers has its own very sophisticated tables, but Keynote and Pages also provide powerful tables.

Tables provide the data that drives charts in iWork. Tables can also be a convenient way of formatting data that may consist of text, numbers, or even images.

Pages' charts are among the most sophisticated and simple features of the Pages program.

Creating a table with iWork for Mac

In any iWork app, click Table on the toolbar to create a table (see Figure 6-1). Just as with shapes, if you hold down the Option key while you click Table, you can then draw the table where you want it.

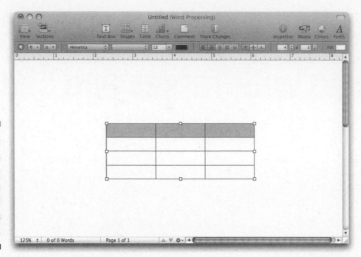

Figure 6-1:
You can create tables in Keynote and Pages documents.

As you can see, tables, like shapes, have handles in their corners and on the midpoints of each side. You can drag the handles and resize just as you drag and resize shapes. The default table for Pages documents has three columns, a header, and three rows beneath the header. In Keynote, the default table is a simple three by three table. (Numbers offers much more specific tables; see Chapter 13.)

Creating tables with iWork for iOS

To create a table with iWork for iOS, tap Insert in the toolbar to insert objects into your iWork document. At the top of the popover, tap Tables to see the preformatted tables, shown in Figure 6-2. Note that tables and other insertable objects have several variations (usually having to do with color schemes). Swipe left or right to see the various choices. The dots at the bottom of the popover show you where you are in the sequence.

Creating charts with iWork for Mac

To create charts with iWork for Mac, click Charts on the toolbar to open the chart menu shown in Figure 6-3.

Two-dimensional charts are shown in the first column; three-dimensional charts are shown in the second. To create a chart of a specific type, simply click it, just like you click a shape or a table. If you hold down the Option key while you click a chart type, you can draw the chart in the location and size you want.

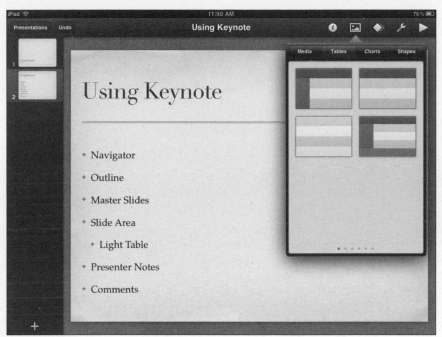

Figure 6-2:
Select a
table to
insert.

Figure 6-3:
Choose a
chart type.

If you choose to create a two-dimensional chart, such as the combined bar/
line chart, the chart itself behaves just like a shape or a table, with eight

handles, as you can see in Figure 6-4. A legend is also created (in Figure 6-4, it's above the chart) and is in its own draggable and resizable shape.

But there's more. A floating window containing data for the chart is also opened. (The window is below the chart in Figure 6-4.) And still more! Chart inspector also opens. (You can see how to use Chart inspector in the next chapter.)

You can edit the chart data in Chart Data Editor. You add rows or columns and switch how the chart is drawn. Pages takes care of everything for you. For example, suppose that you want to change the value in Region 1 for 2007 from 17 (the default value created by Pages) to 170. You type the new value in the Region 1/2007 field and leave the field by clicking out of it or by pressing the tab key. (Until you leave the field to finish editing the data, Pages will not redraw the chart.)

As shown in Figure 6-5, Pages not only moves the point but also rescales the chart so that the value of 170, which is significantly larger than any value in Figure 6-4, is shown properly.

If you've chosen a three-dimensional chart, you get one more item: a controller for the chart's position in three-dimensional space. The controller is shown in the upper left of Figure 6-6. As you drag the arrows up and down or right and left, the chart rotates (but the controller stays still). Notice that as you move the chart in space, its shadow adjusts appropriately.

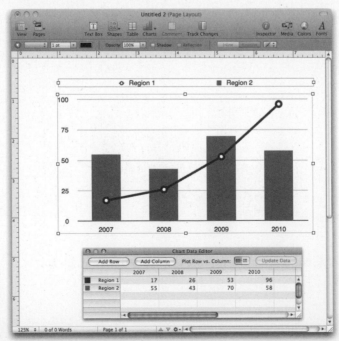

Figure 6-4:
Create the chart.

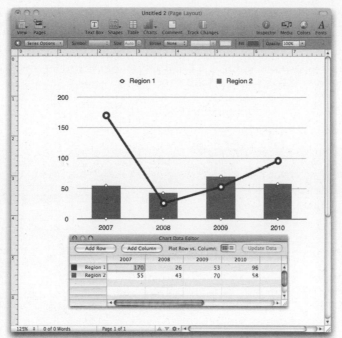

Figure 6-5:
Edit the
chart data.

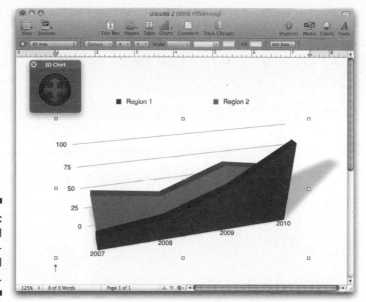

Figure 6-6:
Control
three-
dimensional
charts.

Creating charts with iWork for iOS

In the same way that you create tables, you can create charts. The difference is that you tap Charts instead of Tables at the top of the popover. You have several different types of charts to choose from, as you can see in Figure 6-7. In addition, just as with tables, you can swipe right and left to see different color schemes for each of the chart types.

Figure 6-7: Create a chart with iWork for iOS.

Adjusting Table Settings with iWork for Mac

When you create a table, Table inspector (see Figure 6-8) opens automatically. If you have to do something with an inspector to finish your current task, iWork opens it automatically, as is the case when you create a table. At any time, you can go back, open an inspector, and modify your settings.

Note the two tabs at the top of the window. You use the Table tab to control the general formatting of the table and the Format tab to control specific settings for each cell.

Figure 6-8:
Use Table inspector to modify table settings.

Setting cell and table properties

Table inspector handles general table formatting. Seven sets of settings are available:

- ✔ **Body Rows and Body Columns:** Use the steppers (arrows) or type numbers to set the number of rows and columns in the table.

- ✔ **Headers & Footer:** Three buttons let you set left, top, and bottom headers and footers. Each is a pop-up menu; you can select 0 to 5 rows or columns for each type of header and footer. The default value is 0.

- ✔ **Edit Rows & Columns:** To edit a row or column, first select a cell in the relevant row or column. Then click the action menu and make your choice (see Figure 6-9). To merge cells, you need to first select the cells to merge.

- ✔ **Column Width and Row Height:** Here's where you adjust the settings for the column and row specified by the currently selected cell. If you select the entire table with a single click anywhere in the table, these settings apply to all rows and columns. You can click column or row borders (see Figure 6-10) to select them so that you can change their settings (such as color or line width in Table inspector) or to drag them to resize the columns or rows. (Note the double lines and the double-headed arrows when the cursor is over a row or column.)

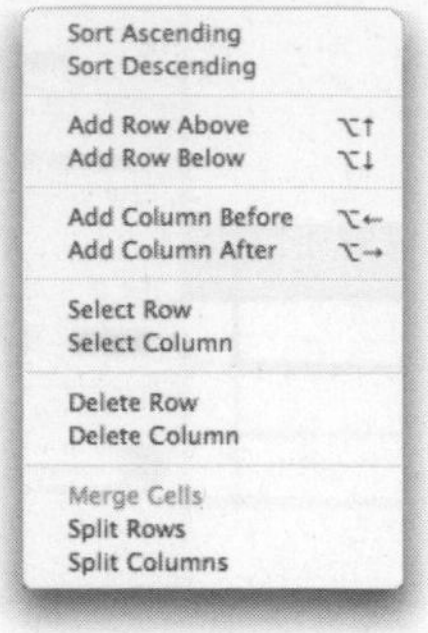

Figure 6-9:
Edit rows
and col-
umns with
the action
menu.

> Sort Ascending
> Sort Descending
>
> Add Row Above ⌥↑
> Add Row Below ⌥↓
>
> Add Column Before ⌥←
> Add Column After ⌥→
>
> Select Row
> Select Column
>
> Delete Row
> Delete Column
>
> Merge Cells
> Split Rows
> Split Columns

In addition to setting column width and row heights, you can use the Automatically Resize to Fit Content check box in Table inspector for any selected cell, row, or column. iWork will adjust the table appropriately. This adjustment can leave you with different-sized cells, rows, or columns, but each one will be the right size for its data.

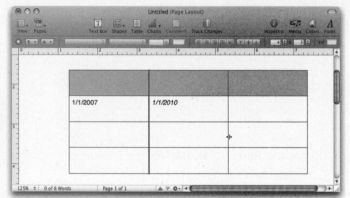

Figure 6-10:
Drag row
or column
borders to
select them.

✔ **Cell Borders:** Select a cell or group of cells and adjust their borders here. You can also select a row or column border, as shown in Figure 6-10, to format it using these controls. You can control the position of the borders (left, right, top, bottom, and so on), the shape of the line (solid, dotted, or whatever), and its color by using the color well at the right of the Cell Borders section.

✔ **Cell Background:** You can set the background for a cell with the same options available for fills in Graphic inspector: none (the default), color fill, gradient fill, image fill, and tinted image fill.

✔ **Table Options:** You can let the Return key move to the next cell. If this option is turned off, the Return key functions simply to insert a Return within the cell so that you can create multiple lines or paragraphs within the cell.

Setting formats and formulas for cells

You use the Format tab in Table inspector to format selected cells. Basic cell formats for numbers, currency, date and time, and other data types are provided. When you choose a format, Table inspector changes to show the specific settings for it. Figure 6-11 shows the Currency settings.

Figure 6-11: Format cells for currency, numbers, and other formats.

Setting a conditional format

In addition to setting a format for a cell, you can provide a conditional format that varies based on a condition you specify. Figure 6-12 shows an example of conditional formatting that you can construct for yourself to test. Conditional formatting has been applied to each cell in the Last Order column. The condition is simple: If sales have increased (that is, the last order is greater than the first order), make the Last Order cell background gray and display the text in bold and italic.

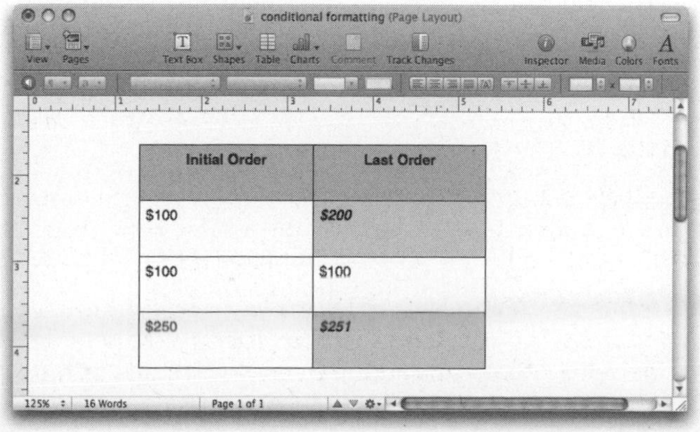

Figure 6-12: Conditional formatting changes a cell's format based on data conditions.

Here's how to construct conditional formatting:

1. **Select a field in the Last Order column.**

2. **In the Format tab of Table inspector, click Show Rules.**

   The Conditional Format dialog, shown in Figure 6-13, appears.

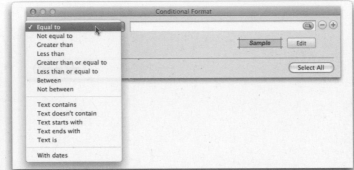

Figure 6-13:
The conditional formatting rules dialog.

3. **From the pop-up menu, choose Greater Than, as shown in Figure 6-14.**

Figure 6-14:
Select a cell to use in the comparison.

4. **Select the cell or value to be used in the comparison.**

   If this cell or value is greater than the value in the Last Order field, the conditional formatting is applied. To use a specific value, type it in the value field to the right of the pop-up menu. To use the value in a cell for the comparison, click the blue oval to the right of the value field to open the cell reference field. Click the cell that contains the value you want to use.

5. **Click the Edit button to specify how the cell should be formatted if the condition is true.**

   As shown in Figure 6-15, you can set the text color; bold, italic, underline, or strikethrough formatting; and the fill color for the cell background.

Figure 6-15:
Specify the
formatting
to use if the
condition
is true.

The comparison value or cell is part of the rule. If you copy and paste cells, that comparison value will not be adjusted automatically.

Setting a formula

Although tables are not full-fledged spreadsheets, they have many spreadsheet features. For example, you can add a third column to the table shown in Figure 6-12 to display the order goal. A formula computes a 50 percent increase by multiplying the value in the Initial Order cell by 1.5. Here's how to do it:

1. **Create a new column.**

   You can click a cell in the Last Order column and choose Add Column After from the action menu in the Edit Rows & Columns section of the Table tab.

2. **Type** Goal **in the header of the new column.**

3. **Click in the first data cell of the Goal column.**

4. **From the Format pane of Table inspector, use the pop-up menu in the Function section at the bottom (see Figure 6-16) and choose Formula Editor.**

   If you want, you can choose any of the other formulas that are built into iWork.

Figure 6-16:
Select a
formula or
use Formula
Editor.

5. **In the formula reference field that opens above the selected cell, type your formula.**

You can use a combination of text and mouse clicks in the fields you want to use. In this case, click in the Initial Order field and type *** 1.5**, as shown in Figure 6-17.

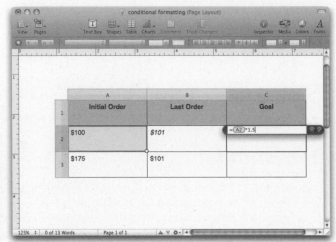

Figure 6-17:
Create the
formula.

6. **If the formula is correct, click the green check mark at the right to accept it.**

   If you want to close the formula reference field without accepting the format, click the red X at the right.

7. **Choose Format⇨Table⇨Fill⇨Fill Down to fill the formula down the other cells in the column.**

Adjusting Table Settings with iWork for iOS

On iOS, adjusting table settings are a bit more straightforward because almost all adjustments go through the Info button at the right of the toolbar. The drill is the same for almost all iOS apps: Tap an object to select it and then tap the Info button.

If you've selected a table, Figure 6-18 shows your choices for the tabs at the top of the popover: table settings (and table options at the bottom of that screen), headers, and forward-to-back arrangements.

Figure 6-18:
Adjust your
table.

Adjusting Chart Settings with iWork for Mac

When you create a chart, Chart inspector opens automatically. You can also open it by clicking the inspector's Chart button, as shown in Figure 6-19. Chart inspector provides you with detailed settings for your chart.

Figure 6-19:
Use Chart
inspector.

You'll probably use the following settings most often:

- ✔ **Edit Data:** Click this button to open Chart Data Editor, which is shown in Figure 6-20.
- ✔ **Show Title:** This is the name of the chart.
- ✔ **Show Legend:** This lets you identify which chart elements refer to which data sets.

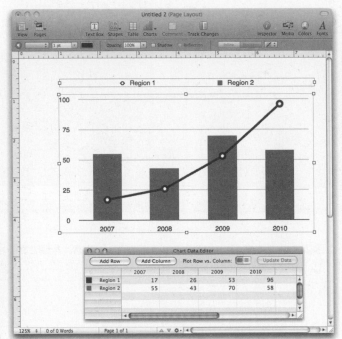

Figure 6-20:
Use Chart
Data Editor
to edit the
chart's data.

Adjusting Chart Data and Settings with iWork for iOS

You have an extra step for working with charts using iWork for iOS. With iWork for Mac, you can show the underlying table for the chart on the screen along with the chart. With iWork for iOS, the underlying table is behind the chart. Here's how you get to the underlying table:

1. **With the chart visible, tap once to show the command bar, shown in Figure 6-21.**

2. **Tap Edit Data.**

   The chart flips over to show you the underlying data table, shown in Figure 6-22.

Figure 6-21:
Show the
command
bar.

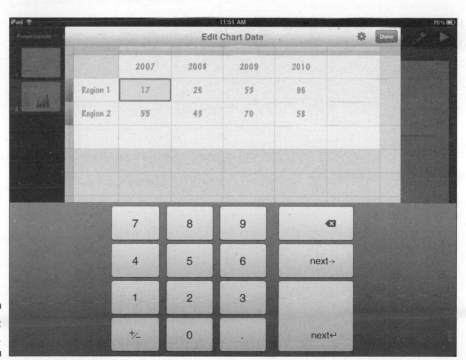

Figure 6-22:
Edit data.

3. Tap Done at the right of the command bar to finish.

Adjusting chart settings with iWork for iOS is the same process as it is with tables: Select the chart by tapping it and then use the Info button, shown in Figure 6-23. The interface is different from iWork for Mac, but the settings (and appearance) are the same.

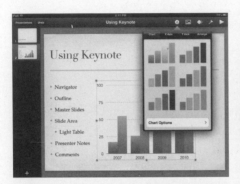

Figure 6-23:
Adjust chart
settings.

Part II
Turning the Page with Pages

The 5th Wave   By Rich Tennant

"I love the way this program justifies the text in my resume. Now if I can just get it to justify my asking salary."

In this part . . .

On OS X, Pages is two apps in one: It lets you create word-processing documents in much the way that you do with Microsoft Word, but you can also use it to create page layout documents much as you would do in Adobe InDesign or Quark Xpress. Pages for iOS provides you with a single interface to the page layout world, but you can still edit your iWork for Mac word-processing documents on your iPhone or iPad.

Pages provides you with advanced tools, such as automatic creation of tables of contents as well as controls over page numbers in various sections of your documents. As with all the iWork applications, you can add graphics, QuickTime movies, charts and tables, and hyperlinks to your documents.

You see how in this part.

Chapter 7

Getting to Know Pages

· ·

· ·

For each of the three iWork apps, the basic tools described in Part I come into play. For example, although tables and charts in Numbers spreadsheets can be more complex than tables and charts in Pages and Keynote, the basics are the same.

Pages is the word-processing app (and, in fact, it's two word-processing applications on Mac). This chapter and the others in Part II provide an introduction to the features, tools, and technologies you find in Pages.

The basics of Mac OS X as well as of iWork apply to each iWork app, including Pages. For example, there's nothing special about printing with Pages: It's the way you print in any Mac OS X or iOS application.

Two Faces of Pages Documents

Pages lets you work with two different types of documents: word-processing documents and page layout documents. This distinction can make it easier for you to think about how you lay out your documents, but in fact, the documents are fundamentally the same underneath. On iOS, you'll find that the distinction is not made.

Perhaps the biggest difference is that word-processing documents can generate a table of contents automatically based on the styles you apply to parts of the documents. (Usually, these styles are applied to headings and subheadings.)

Although you can't create a word-processing document with Pages for iOS, if you've created one with Pages for Mac, you don't have to worry if you start to edit it with Pages for iOS. (Perhaps you've used iCloud or iWork.com to move it back and forth.) Pages for iOS skips over the table of contents, but it doesn't destroy it — and it also doesn't automatically update it. When you're back on the Mac, Pages for Mac can pick up and regenerate the table of contents with changes you may have made with Pages for iOS.

Word-processing documents

A word-processing document in Pages (as in any word-processing program) lets you type what you want without worrying about page breaks and line breaks. If you type a sentence that is longer than the page is wide, Pages automatically breaks the sentence where necessary and continues on the next line as you type. This is known as *wrapping* the line. Likewise, when you come to the bottom of the page, Pages creates a new page and continues your text on that page. This process continues for all your text as well as for any tables, pictures, or graphics that you add to it. Everything flows along from line to line and from page to page and even from column to column within multicolumn documents. Figure 7-1 shows a word-processing document in Pages for Mac.

Figure 7-1:
A Pages word-processing document.

Looking at Mac OS X 10.7 (Lion) Windows

Lion integrates some of the popular iOS user interface features with Mac OS, but never fear: It's still the Mac, and it still works the same as it always did . . . just better in some ways. One of the features of Lion is full-screen mode. Although not every Mac app supports full-screen mode, many of them do, including all iWork apps. In the upper-right corner of the window is a small double-arrow button that lets you expand the window to take over the screen, as shown in the figure. When you move the pointer up to the top of the screen, the menu bar appears along with a button at the right to switch out of full-screen mode.

There are a few other interface differences that you'll notice in Lion. For example, you can resize a window from any edge. Also, Lion supports multitouch gestures just as on iOS. This means that you can scroll up or down with two fingers in the content area; scroll bars are shown when you are actually scrolling — just as on iOS. Use the General pane in System Preferences to switch scrolling preferences between the various behavior styles.

You can manually control how Pages wraps text. You can use the Return or Enter key to start a new line. On Mac, you can insert a *page break* wherever you want to force Pages to begin a new page.

Other formatting techniques you can use for word-processing documents are discussed in Chapters 8 and 9.

Page layout documents

A page layout document lets you design a page using objects that don't move. The objects can be the same tables, pictures, and graphics that you can add to a word-processing document, but they don't flow. They stay where you place them. Figure 7-2 shows a page layout document. (Note that in this document, left and right pages use different formats and show up properly in the thumbnails at the left of the window.)

As you can see in Figures 7-1 and 7-2, graphics can appear in both types of documents. In fact, you can't tell by looking at a document which type of document it is. But when you open the document in Pages, you can tell immediately which type it is. If you were to type a new paragraph at the top of Figure 7-1, the graphics in the middle of the page would move down as that paragraph was inserted. If you were to type more text into the page layout document in Figure 7-2, the graphics wouldn't move.

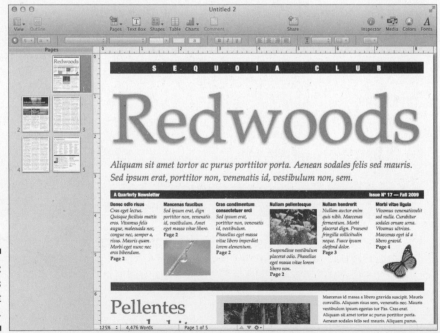

Figure 7-2:
A Pages page layout document.

Text boxes

Everything on the page in a page layout document (such as the page shown in Figure 7-2) is a self-contained object that contains text or graphics and remains where you put it. A special kind of object is a *text box*. You can type text in a text box, and the text will flow and wrap just as it does in a word-processing document. Although the text flows and wraps, it never extends beyond the text box, so the text box itself stays where you place it.

On Mac OS, you can link text boxes so that text will flow automatically from one to the other. They're particularly useful in newsletters and brochures where you might want to have several text boxes on the first page, each one linked to other text boxes later in the document that provide the continuation of the text.

On iOS, you can't link text boxes, and if you have linked text boxes in a document, they are unlinked when you open it on iOS. This is different from the behavior of tables of contents. If you have a table of contents in a word-processing document built with Pages for Mac, opening it with Pages for iOS doesn't harm the table of contents; when you're back on the Mac, you can continue. With linked text boxes, however, once you've opened the document with Pages for iOS, the links are gone (but you're warned).

You can use text boxes in both word-processing and page layout documents. If you place a text box within the flow of text in a word-processing document, the text box provides a second set of flowed text within the main text flow. As you can see in Chapter 8, you can set options so that the text box itself stays put or flows as a single entity with the text in which it is embedded. Furthermore, you can place objects inside text boxes so that the text box can contain flowing and wrapped text and graphics that will never extend beyond the boundaries of the text box. And if you want, you can place a text box inside a text box, but that is likely to produce a very strange-looking document.

Document types

Choosing the right document type isn't difficult. Each document type can contain the same objects (text, tables, shapes, and images); the main difference is whether the objects move as you type.

If you're creating a letter, report, or novel, you probably want a word-processing document. You don't want to worry about page breaks except when you manually insert them at the end of a chapter or section. If you add graphics, you probably want them to flow with the text.

On the other hand, if you're creating a flyer or brochure, you generally want things to stay where you place them. A one-page flyer must stay on one page. You can achieve this effect with a word-processing document by watching how much text and other information you add to the document, but it is generally easier to use a page layout document.

In the cases of brochures and newsletters, you may want a distinct difference in the layout of the first and second pages. By using linked text boxes, you can type the text on the first page and let it flow automatically to a text box with a different format on a later page. After you've set up the text boxes, Pages will take care of everything as you add or delete text: You don't have to worry about the format.

You won't find a Pages Police to tell you what type of document to use. Apple has given you the tools to achieve your goals in many ways. If you're more comfortable working in word-processing documents, you can make them look like page layout documents, although it will probably entail more work. If you're more comfortable working in page layout documents and graphics programs, you can make them look like word-processing documents. (You can even use Numbers to type letters and memos if you're happier working in spreadsheets.)

Choosing Basic Templates

Throughout iWork, Apple provides you with templates for documents, spreadsheets, and presentations. These provide starting points for your own work. You can always start with a blank page and do everything yourself, but many people like to use a template either as-is or customize it. This section provides an introduction to the Pages templates.

Word-processing templates

As you can see in Figure 7-3, Pages provides templates for a variety of types of word-processing documents. The list of template types gives you an indication of the kind of documents that are usually created as word-processing documents rather than page layout documents. The first category consists of blank documents that you can work with as you see fit. One is vertically oriented (portrait), and the other is horizontally oriented (landscape).

When you select a category, Pages shows you the first page of the various templates available so that you can get an idea of the design. When you move the pointer over the first page, you see an interior page. If you want to explore a template in more depth, simply select it and click the Choose button, or double-click it. Either way, Pages will create a document based on the template.

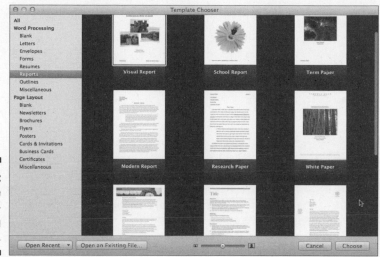

Figure 7-3:
Browse the word-processing templates.

In Figure 7-3, you can see Lion in action with multitouch gestures. The content is being scrolled with two fingers on the trackpad. When it is scrolled, the scroll bar appears, as does the pointer. You don't need to use the scroller (the movable control within the scroll bar), but it appears to give you an idea of where you are within the scrolling document. Compare Figure 7-3 with Figure 7-4, which is the comparable window running in Mac OS X 10.6 (Snow Leopard).

Figure 7-4:
Browse the page layout templates.

Page layout templates

The page layout templates, shown in Figure 7-4, also begin with blank documents. Then you can see the types of documents that lend themselves to page layouts. As with word-processing templates, you can get a preview of the documents and their design.

Creating a Document

As you can see, the multitude of templates in Pages lets you quickly get started creating effective and attractive documents. After you choose a template, you're ready to create your document.

Chapter 2 shows you the various ways to create documents with Pages for Mac and Pages for iOS using templates, iCloud, and iWork.com. This section covers the Pages for Mac-specific issues.

From a template with Pages for Mac

Creating a document from a template takes four simple steps:

1. **Choose File⇨New Document from Template Chooser or use the keyboard equivalent, ↑-⌘-N.**

   The Template Chooser dialog (refer to Figures 7-3 and 7-4) appears.

2. **Select the template category you want to use for either a word-processing or page layout document.**

   For example, in Figure 7-4, the Newsletters template category is selected.

3. **Select the specific template you want within the category.**

4. **Click the Choose button in the lower-right corner.**

   The Template Chooser closes, and your document is created.

From a default template with Pages for Mac

By default, the New command in the File menu functions exactly like File⇨New Document from Template Chooser (see preceding section). However, you can set a preference to bypass Template Chooser and automatically create a new document based on the same document template each time you choose File⇨New. You do this with the Preferences window, shown in Figure 7-5.

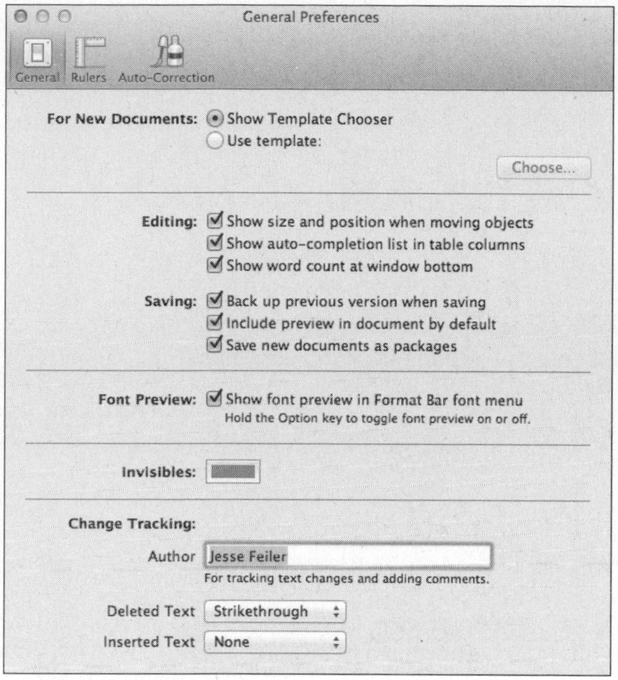

Figure 7-5:
You can
set prefer-
ences for
the behavior
of all Pages
documents.

Pages, like all iWork applications, lets you set preferences. These preferences apply to all documents you create and edit with the application. Here's how to set preferences for Pages:

1. **Open the Preferences window by choosing Pages⇨Preferences or pressing ⌘-, (comma).**

2. **Click the General button at the top of the window to show the General settings.**

3. **Click the Use Template radio button.**

   The Template Chooser opens.

4. **Select the default template you want to use for the New command.**

   From now on, the New command will use that template. To change the default template, simply repeat these steps.

From scratch with Pages for Mac

To create a document from scratch, use Template Chooser to create a blank word-processing or page layout document as described in the "From a template with Pages for Mac" section.

Alternatively, set the default template to a blank word-processing document or a blank page layout document and choose File➪New, as described in the "From a default template with Pages for Mac" section.

Setting Pages Preferences for All Documents with Pages for Mac

As you can see in Figure 7-5, you can set a number of other preferences that apply to all documents you open with Pages. If you change preferences and then open a document that you worked on previously with other settings, the new settings will apply. In general, *preferences* are for the application, and *settings* are for individual documents.

If you share your computer with other people, you don't have to worry about interfering with their preferences. Pages (like all applications on Mac OS X) stores preferences separately for each account on the computer.

With Pages for iOS, you don't have preferences that apply to all documents. As with many iOS apps, app-wide settings are set not in a Preferences menu command but within the Settings app. With Pages for iOS, these settings currently allow you to use or not use iCloud and to use or not use the restore option.

When you open Preferences by choosing Pages➪Preferences or pressing ⌘-, (comma), you can select any of the three sets of preferences by clicking the appropriate button at the top. The default is General preferences. If you've opened and then closed Preferences while Pages is open, it reopens to the preference you last viewed during that session.

General preferences

The General Preferences pane has six sets of preferences:

- ✔ **For New Documents:** The first preference lets you choose the behavior of the File➪New command, as described in the preceding section.

- ✔ **Editing:** These preferences help you as you're editing the document. They're particularly useful in making Pages behave like other word-processing applications you may be accustomed to (or making Pages not behave like other word-processing applications whose features you detest).

    • You can control whether the size and position of movable objects are shown as you move them.

- You can display an auto-completion list in table columns for partially typed words.

- You can choose whether to have the document's word count shown at the window bottom.

✓ **Saving:** These preferences control options when you save a document.

- You can automatically back up the previous version of a document as it was at the last save command; the file has BACKUP added to the name. Note that only one backup copy is saved. You can drag those old copies to a new location on your hard drive so that you can keep several older backups if you want.

- You can automatically add a preview of the document to the file so that the preview is visible in Finder windows. You can override this preference with an option in the Save dialog for an individual file, as shown in Figure 7-6.

- You can save new documents as a Mac OS X package that includes supporting files. (A *package* looks like a regular file, but if you Control-click it, you can open it to see the individual files within it.) You probably don't want to use this advanced feature, but it can't do any harm unless you need to share your documents with someone else. In that case, the supporting documents are copied into the package and you can share it with other people.

Figure 7-6:
Choose
whether to
save a
preview
image with
the Pages
document.

✔ **Font Preview:** The format bar can list font names in a standard font or using the particular font for each font name. This preview gives you an idea of what the font will look like.

✔ **Invisibles:** Invisible characters, such as tabs and returns, normally aren't displayed in a document, but their effects are visible. You can use the View➪Show Invisibles command in any Pages document to display those characters. View➪Show Invisibles is a per-document setting, not a global preference for all documents. However, the color you use to display invisibles is a global setting, and you set it in General Preferences. Click the color well to open the Colors window, as described in Chapter 3.

✔ **Change Tracking:** The last settings control how change tracking is stored and displayed. This feature keeps track of every change to the document with before-and-after versions, dates, times, and who made the changes. You can enter the name to be associated with the changes and control how deleted and inserted text is formatted.

Rulers preferences

The second set of preferences control the rulers you can display around your document. Click the Rulers button to display the following settings, shown in Figure 7-7:

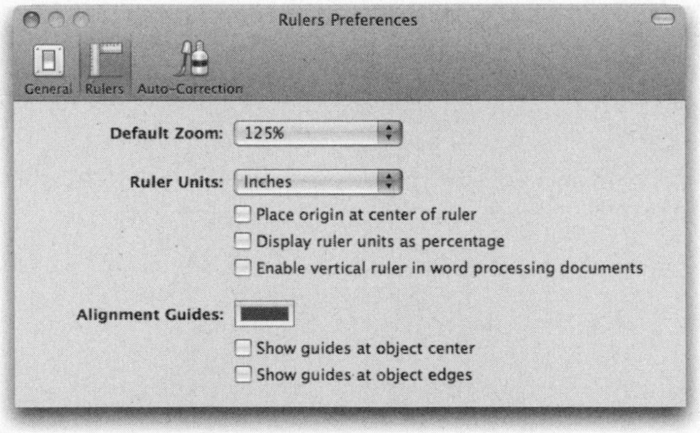

Figure 7-7:
You can
set several
preferences
for the ruler.

✔ **Default Zoom:** You can always adjust the window's zoom factor using the pop-up menu in the lower left of the window. By default, the window zooms to 125 percent. This reflects the fact that when a document is printed, smaller font sizes are generally used than when the document is displayed on a monitor.

✔ **Ruler Units:** You can choose inches, centimeters, points, or picas. You can also set the origin of the rulers. The origin is the 0,0 point — that is, the point that is 0 on both the horizontal and vertical rulers. You can place it at the upper left of the document, with numbers increasing to the right on the horizontal access and down on the vertical access. Or you can place it in the center of the document with larger numbers going to the right and smaller (even negative) numbers going down to the left margin. Instead of units, you can display a percentage. Finally, you can choose whether a vertical ruler is shown in word-processing documents. (It appears in page layout documents at all times when rulers are shown.)

✔ **Alignment Guides:** The alignment guides help you position objects accurately. You choose the color of the guides from the color well. You can also choose whether to display them at the edges or centers of objects (or both).

Auto-Correction preferences

The Auto-Correction preferences let you configure Pages so that certain keystrokes are automatically transformed into specific characters and symbols. As with the General preferences, the Auto-Correction preferences apply to all documents — unless you change them. If you change them, the changes take effect from then on; nothing is changed in documents you have opened previously.

To change the auto-correction preferences, follow these steps:

1. **Open the Preferences dialog by choosing Pages⟿Preferences or pressing ⌘-, (comma).**

2. **Click the Auto-Correction button at the top of the Preferences dialog to show the Auto-Correction Preferences pane, as shown in Figure 7-8.**

3. **Use the check boxes to adjust the various corrections as you want.**

   You can also add new ones with the + in the lower left.

Basic Auto-Correction preferences

There are two sets of Auto-Correction preferences. The first six are check box choices that are common to many word-processing applications:

✔ **Smart Quotes:** Smart quotes are sometimes called curly quotes. They look like " and " or, in the case of single quotes, ' and '. Your keyboard has straight quotes, " and " and ' and '. When smart quotes is turned on, Pages automatically converts straight quotes that you type to the appropriate smart quotes.

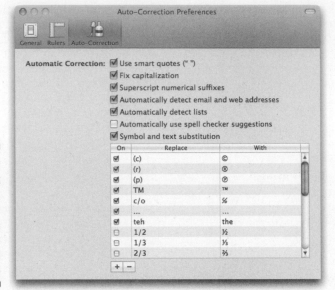

Figure 7-8:
Set preferences for abbreviations, shortcuts, and corrections.

To know whether to use opening or closing quotes (" or "), Pages relies on spaces. If you type a space and then "Hello, how are you" and then another space, Pages recognizes the space before the first quote and turns it into an opening quote. Then Pages recognizes the space after the closing quote and turns it into a closing quote symbol. If you're using quotes in phrases where the spaces aren't in the standard positions, check that the substitution is what you want.

✔ **Fix capitalization:** This preference helps correct capitalization mistakes that occur if you're typing quickly and accidentally capitalize the first two letters of a word, such as *THis*. With this preference set, as soon as you finish typing the word and press the space key, Pages automatically corrects the word to *This*. This preference doesn't correct any other capitalization errors, and it doesn't refer to a dictionary or other source to determine whether a word should be capitalized. If you really meant to capitalize the first two letters, just retype the second letter as a capital, and Pages will defer to your typing.

✔ **Superscript Numerical Suffixes:** This preference converts plain text to a superscript numerical suffix. If you type 1st when this preference is set, Pages will convert it to 1st.

✔ **Automatically Detect Email and Web Addresses:** Just as its name says, this preference converts text that appears to be an e-mail address or a web address to a hyperlink. You can then click the link and open your e-mail program to begin typing a message or open your browser to go to the web address. (See the next section for how to turn off this preference on a case-by-case basis.)

✔ **Automatically Detect Lists:** This basic preference comes into play when Pages thinks you're typing a list. If this preference is set, Pages begins to format the list according to the styles you've set. You can change the list settings (and turn the list back into plain text).

✔ **Automatically Use Spell Checker Suggestions:** Instead of just flagging a potential spelling error, Pages can make suggestions for a correction. In many cases, you can just click a suggestion and go on with your work.

Modifying auto-detected e-mail and web addresses

It's great to have hyperlinks in your Pages documents. You and the people with whom you share your documents can just click the link to go to a web address or to open and address a new mail message. Having the ability to auto-detect e-mail and web addressees makes it even easier to add them to your Pages documents as hyperlinks.

There's only one problem: How do you edit the link and its text? If you click it, you're off to your browser or e-mail program. Here's how to modify an e-mail or web address that's active in a Pages document:

1. **Scroll the page so that the link is in view, but don't click it yet.**

2. **If the inspector isn't shown, choose View➪Show Inspector or click the Inspector button at the right of the toolbar.**

   Chapter 4 discusses inspectors.

3. **Click the Hyperlink tab, shown in Figure 7-9.**

Figure 7-9:
The
Hyperlink
tab of the
inspector.

4. **At the bottom of the pane, select the Make All Hyperlinks Inactive check box.**

   Now you can edit any link in the document by clicking it.

5. **When you're finished, select the Make All Hyperlinks Active check box to clear the check mark.**

Setting symbol and text substitution

The second group of auto-correction settings controls symbol and text substitution. The bottom part of the Auto-Correction Preferences window consists of a table of substitution rules. A number of rules are installed automatically in Pages, and you can add your own. In addition, a check box at the left of each substitution rule determines whether that rule is turned on.

The default rules in Figure 7-8 handle different types of substitutions:

✔ You can create special characters, such as ½, by simply typing 1/2, without using modifier keys such as opt or .

✔ Common typos such as *teh* for *the* can be corrected automatically.

You can add your own rules easily:

1. **With the Auto-Correction Preferences window visible, click the + button, which is in the lower left, as shown in Figure 7-10.**

   A new line is added to the bottom of the scrolling list. The check box in the On column is set automatically, and the pointer is positioned in the next column (Replace).

2. **In the Replace column, type the text that you want to replace.**

3. **Using the mouse or the tab key, move to the next column (With) and enter the new text.**

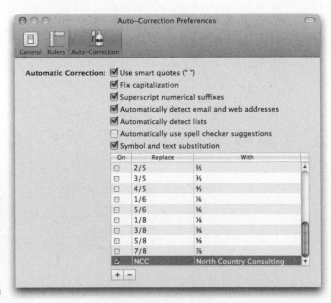

Figure 7-10: Add a new auto-correction rule.

You can use a similar process to remove a substitution rule. Scroll to the rule you want to remove, select it by clicking in the row, and then click the – button to remove it.

Rather than removing a rule, consider just turning it off. That way, if you change your mind, the rule is still there.

Saving Your Work with Pages for Mac

As with any Mac OS X application, you save your work using File⇨Save, as shown in Figure 7-11.

You can expand the Save dialog by clicking the downward-pointing arrow next to the filename, as shown in Figure 7-12.

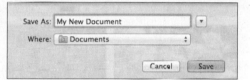

Figure 7-11:
Save your
work.

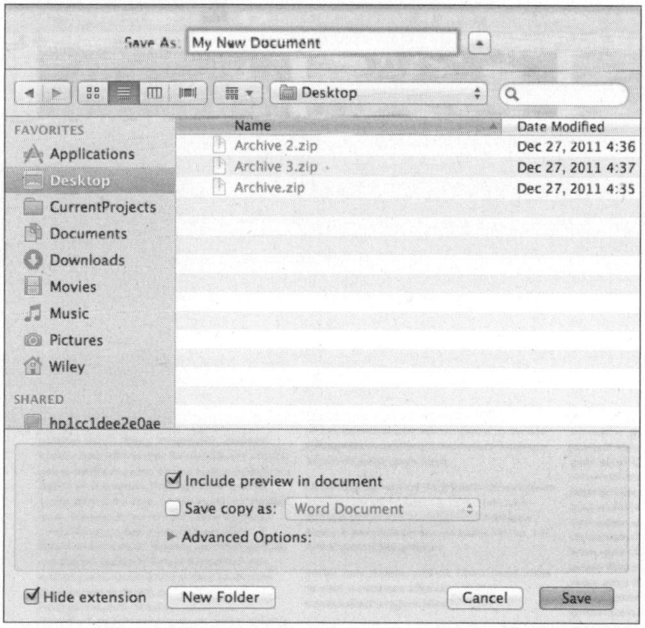

Figure 7-12:
You can
specify
additional
options for
the Save
command.

The Pages-specific options in this dialog give you greater control over what is saved. Note, however, that each of these options can increase the size of the file:

✔ **Include Preview in Document:** This is a preview of the document's contents for display in Finder.

✔ **Save Copy As:** Pages formats have changed with new releases. You have an option to save a copy in the prior format. This is useful if you're exchanging documents with someone who doesn't have the latest version of Pages. If you're sharing files with people who are using Microsoft Word, you can also choose to save a copy in Word format.

✔ **Copy Audio and Movies into Document:** These files can be very large. If you're saving the document to send to someone who will print it, there's no reason to include these files.

✔ **Copy Template Images into Document:** The Pages document that you see on the screen can include images from its template as well as images you've inserted in the document. In some cases, the template images should be saved in the document so that it's complete. In other cases, the template images are just placeholders, so there's no reason to save them with the document.

Lion does an automatic save about every five minutes, so your recent keystrokes are preserved. Your versions are your points at which you want to be able to return.

If you want to go back to a previous version, choose File➪Revert Document. That command opens a Time Machine–like display, shown in Figure 7-13. You can then select the version that you want to go back to.

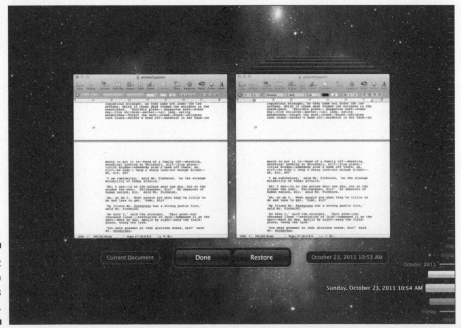

Figure 7-13:
Revert to a previous version.

Working with versions on Mac OS X 10.7 (Lion)

With iOS, you don't worry about saving your documents: The apps do it for you. (Although you don't worry about saving the document, certain steps do let you indicate that you're done or want to cancel the process, and you often have an Undo button in the toolbar.)

These features are so useful that the developers at Apple brought them back to the Mac in Lion. When you're running Pages for Mac, the File menu (see figure) looks a bit different. When you're tempted to save a document, instead you save a *version* of the document.

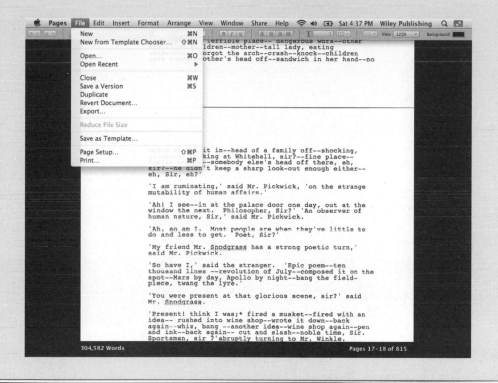

What this new interface does is remove the need for you to create multiple versions saved under various names (Version of Friday before restructuring, Version of Wednesday after meeting, and so on). You just save a version whenever you want to draw a line in the sand that you may want to come back to. Fortunately, the keyboard equivalent is ⌘-S, just like the old Save command, so you can use it just as you always did, but you don't have to rename each version.

In the document's title bar, you'll notice a small downward-pointing arrow when you're using versions. As you see in Figure 7-14, this arrow lets you revert to a previous version, and it also lets you lock a document. This can be very handy in keeping your documents under control. If you haven't touched a document in a while, it will automatically be locked. When you try to edit it, you're asked if you want to continue: A click of the mouse lets you move on.

Figure 7-14:
Choose
what you'd
like to do.

Creating a Template from a Document with Pages for Mac

To create a template from a document, you use the same dialog and the same options as the Save dialog discussed in the preceding session. When you're ready to save your document as a template, choose File⇨Save As Template.

The only difference between the Save dialog and the Save As Template dialog is that by default the template is saved to a folder called My Templates inside your home directory. The path is `<home>/Library/Application Support/iWork/Pages/Templates/My Templates`. The newly created template now appears in Template Chooser.

To remove a template, remove it from the folder in your home directory.

Chapter 8

Editing Word-Processing Documents on Mac

*1*n Chapter 6, you can see how to create Pages documents — both word-processing and page layout types of documents. When you find yourself looking at a blank word-processing document or a document based on a template, this chapter tells you what to do next.

Word-processing documents exist only in Pages for Mac. On iOS, the functionality is provided by text boxes in page layout documents. However, if you move a word-processing document to an iOS device using iCloud, e-mail, or iWork.com, you'll see that the document works just fine. Some of the text document features aren't supported on iOS, but your text and styles are just fine. For these reasons, this chapter focuses on Mac OS.

This chapter deals with the major entities in your word-processing document, such as paragraphs, headers, and footers. In Chapter 9, you can see how to fine-tune both page layout and word-processing documents. You can use the format bar, which is discussed in Chapter 9, for fine-tuning or for quick shortcuts.

Managing Paragraphs

One of the nice things about a word-processing document is that you can just start typing. The text flows as you type; new pages are created as needed, and formatting is basically taken care of for you.

Is iWork WYSIWYG?

WYSIWYG (What You See Is What You Get) isn't really the case on the computer screen. Myriad settings influence what you see. The display resolution changes the size of everything on the display, and system-wide settings such as Font Smoothing in System Preferences modify text on the screen in subtle ways. Inside applications, you can zoom in or out of a document. Look in the lower left of a Pages document, and you see that the default zoom factor is 125 percent: Text is larger on the screen (all other settings and options being equal) than it is on a printed page (although you can change the zoom factor for a printed page, too). You can change the default zoom by choosing Pages➪Preferences and clicking the General tab.

The default zoom is 125 percent for a good reason. As a general rule, font sizes that are comfortable to read on a printed page are hard to read on a screen. You may have noticed this difference when you created text documents and then printed them. Depending on the font, a font size of 10 or 12 is comfortable for reading on the screen but looks more like a headline than body text when printed. Pages has built-in styles that look good for printed documents. To make these styles more legible on the screen, the zoom factor is set to 125 percent rather than 100 percent.

Whenever you're creating an iWork document that will be presented on some device other than the computer you're working on, proofread the document on the device that will be used. That means doing the final proofreading of a document that will be printed by printing it and looking at the printed copy. If it will be printed on a specific printer, have a test run with the actual printer and paper that will be used. If you're preparing Pages documents or Keynote slides for a presentation, proofread the slides on the screen you will be using, if possible. If the image is to be projected, check to see that it is sized properly and that the potted palm at the side of the platform doesn't obscure critical parts of your slides.

If your document is lengthy, however, page after page of type can become difficult to read. You can communicate your message more effectively if you use some of the tools described in this chapter. Even a short document can often benefit from organization, and the most basic form of organization is paragraphs.

Your word-processing document consists of paragraphs. (Technically, it could have no paragraphs but be made up of tables, images, and media files, but normally at least one paragraph exists.) In a word-processing document, paragraphs flow one after the other by default. Pages inserts page breaks as needed. You can modify this default behavior in a variety of ways, such as by manually inserting page breaks (even within a paragraph) or by forcing Pages to handle pagination in special ways for given paragraphs. This section shows you the principal paragraph management settings.

Paragraph settings apply to the entire paragraph — for example, you might make a paragraph single-spaced or double-spaced. You can select the paragraph you want to apply settings to in two ways:

✔ Position the pointer in the paragraph and triple-click.

✔ Click anywhere in the paragraph.

It doesn't matter where in the paragraph you click because the paragraph settings are the same for every location in the paragraph.

Setting vertical spacing

Three vertical spacing settings for paragraphs are available: the space between lines, the space before the paragraph, and the space after the paragraph. (The before and after spaces aren't additive — they're used to compute the actual space between any two paragraphs.)

Here's how to set vertical spacing for a paragraph:

1. **Click in the paragraph for which you want to adjust vertical spacing.**

2. **Open an inspector.**

3. **Click the T button at the top to display the Text settings.**

4. **Click the Text tab.**

   The inspector looks like Figure 8-1.

5. **Set the line spacing using the slider, the stepper arrows, or the box.**

   You can also use the small pop-up menu below the text box (which is currently set to Multiple). The default line spacing is one line. The height of the line is determined by the tallest font in the line; as a result, it can appear that a single paragraph has several different line spacing values, but it is the font variations that cause them.

Figure 8-1: Set vertical spacing in a paragraph.

6. **Set the space before and after the paragraph with the sliders, steppers, or text box.**

   Pages automatically handles potential conflicts between interparagraph spacing settings as follows:

   - **First paragraph:** There is no space before a first paragraph regardless of the setting.

   - **Last paragraph:** Likewise, there is no space after a final paragraph.

   - **Conflicting settings:** If the space after a paragraph and before the next paragraph is the same, that's the space that's used. If they differ, the larger space is used.

Setting indents with an inspector

The preceding section shows you how to set vertical spacing. This section and the one that follows deal with horizontal settings.

To set paragraph indents with an inspector:

1. **Click in the paragraph for which you want to adjust horizontal spacing.**

2. **Open an inspector.**

3. **Click the T button at the top to display the Text settings.**

4. **Click the Tabs tab.**

   Controls appear at the bottom of the inspector, as shown in Figure 8-2.

5. **Click the stepper arrows or type in the boxes to set the first line indent, left indent, and right indent.**

Figure 8-2:
Set
paragraph
indents.

Indenting the first line of a paragraph is a common style. Other times, the first line of the first paragraph of a section is indented.

Make sure that your paragraph boundaries are visible. If the space between paragraphs is the same as the space between lines in a paragraph, and the paragraph has no first line indent, the break between paragraphs is difficult to see.

If you need to group several paragraphs, use headings or subheadings, as I do in this book.

Setting indents with the ruler

You don't have to use Text inspector to set the indents for a paragraph. You can use the ruler instead:

1. **If the ruler isn't visible, choose View➪Show Rulers or click the View button on the toolbar.**

   The ruler is shown in Figure 8-3.

2. **Drag the downward-pointing triangle on the left to set the left margin.**

   The first line indent marker is the rectangle right above the triangle. By default, the first line indent moves with the left margin. To adjust the first line indent, drag it separately, as shown in Figure 8-4.

Figure 8-3:
Set paragraph indents from the ruler.

Using decorative caps

In addition to indents for the first line of a paragraph or for the first line of the first paragraph in a section, you can use a decorative cap for the first character of a paragraph. Typically, this technique is used at the beginning of a chapter or section. The first character uses a distinctive font and a much larger size than the text of the rest of the paragraph. The first character of a paragraph is a good place to use very elaborate letters. Explore the Fonts window to see what you can work with.

Figure 8-4:
Set the first
line indent
with the
ruler.

3. Drag the downward-pointing triangle on the right to set the right margin.

The ruler and Text inspector work together. If both are visible, changes made in one are automatically reflected in the other.

Setting tabs

You can set tabs for a paragraph using Text inspector:

1. Select the paragraph.

2. Open Text inspector and click the Tabs tab (refer to Figure 8-2).

If you need a new inspector, choose View➪New Inspector or View➪Show Inspector; you can also click Inspector on the toolbar if no inspector is visible.

3. Click the + button beneath the list of tab stops in the lower left.

A new tab appears. It will be located to the right of the previous tab at a distance set in the Default Tabs box.

4. **If you want to change the new tab, double-click the new value in the Tab Stops list and then change it.**

   For example, in Figure 8-2, the Default Tabs value is set at .5 inch, so all new tabs are in increments of .5 inch. I started with tabs at 0.5, 1, and 1.5. In the figure, the 1.5 tab is being edited to move it to 1.75.

5. **Select the type of tab from the Alignment list, at the right.**

   The most common tab is a left-aligned tab. A left-aligned tab produces a column with an aligned left side. Right- and center-alignment function similarly. Decimal tabs align the column based on a character that you specify in the Decimal Tab Character box. Most often, the Decimal option is used to align numbers on their decimal point.

6. **If you want, choose a tab leader.**

   Tab leaders (characters that link the text and the next tab) can improve readability when there is a fairly long distance between the text and the next tab. For example, in this book's table of contents, dots are used as leaders between the chapter titles and the page numbers.

Setting pagination

Finally, you can set options for the interaction of pagination and paragraphs. These settings are available in Text inspector in the More tab, as shown in Figure 8-5.

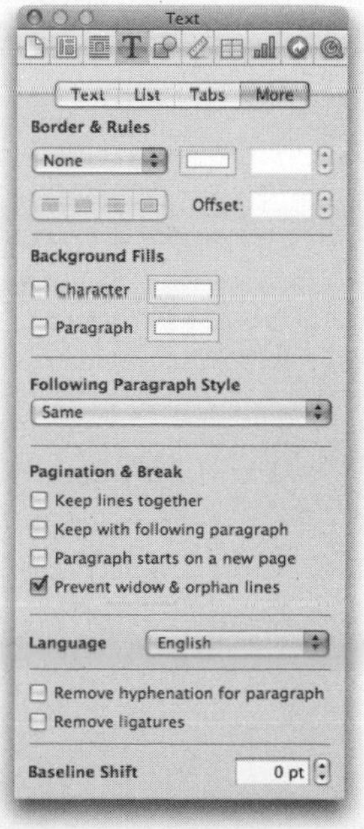

Figure 8-5: Set pagination preferences.

The pagination settings are in the Pagination & Break section of the inspector. Turn any setting on or off to get the effect that you want.

In the case of a preference such as Keep Lines Together, Pages will do its best, but if the paragraph has five pages of text in it, there is no way Pages will be able to fit it onto a single page.

The only setting that is guaranteed to take effect is Paragraph Starts On a New Page. Pages can easily do that.

The last setting, Prevent Widow & Orphan Lines, generally is turned on because it makes the document look better. Widow and orphan lines are single lines at the top or bottom of a page, respectively. If the line is short (perhaps a single word), a widow or orphan can look peculiar. Forcing the previous line down so that you have at least two lines at the top or bottom of the page generally looks better.

Using Headers and Footers

You can improve the appearance of your documents by using headers and footers, which are special sections of text at a page's top and bottom, respectively, for information such as page numbers, dates, titles, and author names. When Pages inserts a page break, it places the appropriate footer at the bottom of the page and places the appropriate header at the top of the next page.

Headers and footers can contain constant text, such as the document name, or certain variable information, such as a date.

Most documents that are more than one page long benefit from headers and footers.

Constructing a header

Most of the Pages templates have headers and footers, but many of them aren't filled in. Choose View➪Show Layout to show all the layout elements on a page. Figure 8-6 is the Modern Report template with the layout shown. The page header is at the top.

Even without displaying the layout, you can click where you know the header is to activate it.

Figure 8-6:
Show the
layout.

To construct a header, type it as you would normally type any paragraph, but keep your text to a single line (two or three lines at the most). The longer the header and footer, the less room on the page for your text.

In the past, teachers assigned reports by page count. The advent of word processors and headers and footers allowed innovative students to fulfill the page count with a remarkably small amount of text and a remarkably large amount of header and footer information. Today, most teachers assign reports by word count, not page count, so the header/footer trick no longer works.

You can also insert special markers, located in the Insert menu, that will be used during pagination:

✔ Date & Time
✔ Page Number
✔ Page Count

Figure 8-7 shows a typical footer that combines text with some special symbols. At the left, the actual footer is

Page <page number> of <page count>

By default, footers and headers contain a right-aligned tab, so if you press the Tab key after inserting something at the left, whatever you type will be placed at the right. You can set additional tabs, if needed.

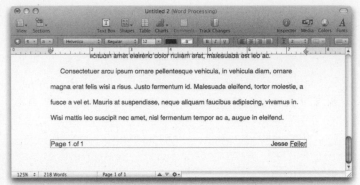

Figure 8-7:
Create a
footer.

Moving headers and footers

You can turn headers on and off and move them:

1. **Click in the section of the document you want to modify.**

2. **Open an inspector and click the Document button at the left.**

3. **Click the Document tab, as shown in Figure 8-8.**

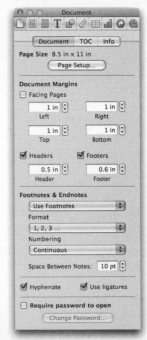

Figure 8-8:
Place head-
ers and
footers.

4. **Use the check boxes in the Document Margins section to turn the headers and footers on or off.**

   If you turn a header or footer off, its content is removed. If you subsequently restore it with the check box, it will be blank.

5. **To place the header or footer below the document's top margin or above its bottom margin, use the stepper arrows or text box.**

   The header or footer moves down or up, leaving more blank space at the top or bottom of the page.

Using section headers and footers

Pages word-processing documents are composed of sections. You can set separate header and footer options for any section:

1. **Click in the section you want to modify.**

2. **Open an inspector and click the Layout button at the top.**

   It's the button that's second from the left.

3. **Click the Section tab, as shown in Figure 8-9.**

Figure 8-9: Specify a special first page.

4. **Select the First Page Is Different check box.**

   The header and footer on the first page are removed. You can create new ones there. If you already created a header or footer, it continues to appear on pages after the first page.

Using the Sections Menu to Add and Reuse Sections

A document *section* is a part of a document. It can contain one or more pages, one or more paragraphs, or even nothing except the beginning and end markers for the section. You can adjust headers and footers for each section; you can also control whether page numbers restart at the beginning of a section (refer to Figure 8-9). An "empty" section is created with beginning and end markers so as to be able to manipulate the page number, header, and footer for a blank page.

For now, it's important to know just these basics and that most of the Pages word-processing templates come with several sections defined for the document even if they aren't shown. You can find out more about sections and how to create them in Chapter 12.

To select a section to insert into a document, click the Sections button on the toolbar or choose Insert⇨Sections. Figure 8-10 shows the sections for the White Paper template. The sections are well named and include a variety of pages. Experiment by adding various sections to your document to see what they look like. One of the advantages of using sections is that you can create a common look for different types of pages in your document.

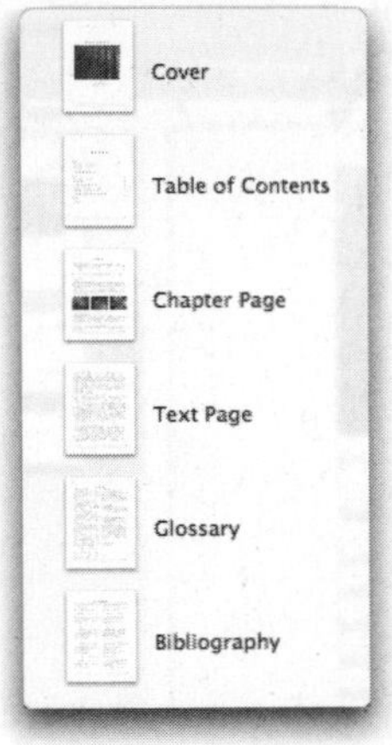

Cover	
Table of Contents	
Chapter Page	
Text Page	
Glossary	
Bibliography	

Figure 8-10:
Use
template
sections.

Navigating through a Document

When you have a document with many pages, a fast way to navigate through the document is to use thumbnails of the pages:

1. **Show page thumbnails by clicking the View button on the toolbar or by choosing View⇨Show Page Thumbnails.**

   A page thumbnail for each page in the document appears in the Pages pane on the left of the screen, as shown in Figure 8-11.

2. **To rearrange the sequence of pages, drag the thumbnails up or down.**

3. **To delete a page, select it its thumbnail and press the Delete key.**

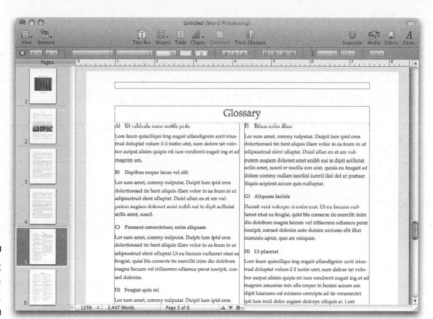

Figure 8-11:
Show the
thumbnails.

Chapter 9

Editing Page Layout Documents with Pages for Mac

All the iWork for iOS apps let you create and manage text boxes (see Chapters 4 and 5). Text boxes give you tremendous power and flexibility. Pages for Mac adds features to text boxes in page layout documents. In general, you can edit these features with Pages for Mac. Often, those edits remain intact even after you've moved a document to an iOS device for editing with Pages for iOS, although there are some exceptions. As this chapter describes, text boxes created with iWork for Mac have even more features.

Word-processing documents tend to be fairly simple: They consist of words that are built into sentences and paragraphs. You can add graphics and other elements, but most of the time, you're typing one word after another.

Page layout documents generally have a variety of objects, such as text boxes, graphics, and even movies and hyperlinks. You need to identify the components, know how to create and edit them, and put them all together.

As always with iWork, the easiest and fastest way to get started is to begin with one of the built-in templates. In this chapter, you create a document from a template. Then you explore what you've created, seeing how you create and customize each component. You can apply these steps to any page layout document, whether you construct it from a template or from a blank document.

Analyzing the Templates

The Page Layout templates are divided into nine categories:

- ✔ **Blank**
- ✔ **Newsletters**
- ✔ **Brochures**
- ✔ **Flyers**
- ✔ **Posters**
- ✔ **Cards & Invitations**
- ✔ **Business Cards**
- ✔ **Certificates**
- ✔ **Miscellaneous**

Each template comes with built-in styles, and many of them have placeholder text and pictures, which you replace with your own text and pictures. As with word-processing documents, as well as Numbers and Keynote documents, the templates not only provide a jumping-off point but also can give you ideas for the documents you want to create. These ideas can be specific, such as the types of information you should consider putting into a brochure, or general.

Open Template Chooser by choosing File⇨New From Template Chooser. As you click the various categories in Template Chooser and look at the thumbnails of the various templates, you get an excellent basic lesson in graphic design (something the people at Apple know from top to bottom). Figure 9-1 shows some newsletter templates.

To see a particular template full-sized, simply create a document from the template.

It's easy to spot the title in each template, even when the templates are thumbnail-sized. If you want to become an iWork pro, start training yourself to analyze what you're seeing. What makes the titles stand out from the rest of the elements on the template? Here are some of the ways in which the designers at Apple have done this:

✔ **Titles are large.** Here's where you can go to town with a distinctive font and a large font size.

✔ **Titles are brief.** If a designer has to work with a long title, such as *Sailing Newsletter,* one solution is to make *Sailing* much larger than *Newsletter.*

✔ **Backgrounds can help a title stand out.**

• Large type for the title with plenty of white space around it can help the title stand out.

• A color or an image behind the title can also help it stand out. If you use this technique, the color or the main color in the background image should not be used extensively elsewhere on the page.

Starting with a Simple Template

The built-in flyer templates are some of the simplest page layout documents. Generally, they are a single page, although a few of them have alternate page layouts (such as one version with tear-off slips for phone numbers and another one with no such tear-off slips). Because the flyer templates are usually a single page, they're a good place to start exploring exactly what goes into a page layout.

To create a template-based document — in this case, a flyer — follow these steps:

1. **Choose File⇨New Document from Template to open Template Chooser.**

   You can also use ⌘-N if you've set General Preferences to open Template Chooser.

2. **In the Page Layout group at the left of the window, click the Flyers category to show the templates for flyers.**

   Figure 9-2 shows you the range of choices for flyers in iWork.

3. **Double-click the For Sale template (the one with a large photo of a bike) to create a document based on it.**

   You can also select this template with a single click and then click the Choose button in the lower right. Your new document opens in its own window, as shown in Figure 9-3.

Figure 9-1:
iWork has
a variety of
newsletter
templates.

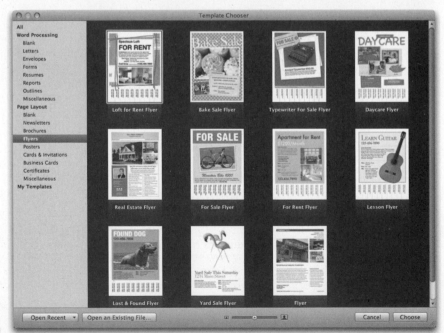

Figure 9-2:
Select a
template for
your
document.

Figure 9-3:
View your
new
document.

The first step in exploring a document is to know what you have in the document. Everything on a page in a page layout document is some kind of object, such as an image, a text box, a shape, a table, or a chart. Information (including colors and images) is always located within an object. Objects sometimes are grouped either with the Pages Arrange⇨Group command or conceptually in your mind and the minds of your users.

Here's what you should be able to identify in your new document:

- ✔ **Title:** The title is *For Sale* on a solid red background.

- ✔ **Image:** The image in this case is the bike. This is a placeholder image that you replace with whatever you are selling.

- ✔ **Description:** The description of what's for sale includes the name of what's for sale and its price in large text. It is followed by placeholder text. If you look closely, you may see your own phone number at the end of the text! You see in the section "Automatically Inserting Your Phone Number in the Flyer," later in this chapter, how Pages can pick up information on request from your Address Book and your Me card.

- ✔ **Tear-off tabs:** Ten identical tear-off tabs at the bottom have the name of the item for sale and the phone number for people to call.

Modifying the Title

Depending on what you're going to use the flyer for, you may or may not have to modify the title. Perhaps it will read *Free* or *Best Offer* rather than *For Sale*. Even if you're going to leave the text unchanged, you may want to alter other aspects of the title, such as its font or size. In this section, I show you how the title is constructed in the template and how you can modify it. (You can also use this information to create your own title on a blank document or another template.)

The title consists of bold text on a red background. Here's an important iWork design note: The text on the red background is created with two objects. See Figure 9-4, in which both objects are selected. Look for the two outlines: one around the red box, and the other around the text box inside the red box.

Figure 9-4:
The title
consists of
two objects.

Here's how to make changes to the title:

✓ **Change the text:** Double-click the text to select it all. You can then type replacement text. Alternatively, you can click where you want to make a change; then type the new text or delete the text you don't want.

✓ **Change the text formatting:** Double-click the text to select it all. Then do one of the following:

- • Use Text inspector to change the font, color, and other attributes. (For more information on these tasks, see Chapter 4.)

- • Use the Font window to change the font, color, and other attributes. (For more on the Fonts window, see Chapter 3.)

✓ **Change the background shape or color:** Click to select the background shape and then drag the handles of the background shape to change its size and shape. Change its color using the Fill section in Graphic inspector (see Chapter 4) or the Colors window (Chapter 5).

Changing the Image

You'll want to use your own image unless you happen to be selling a gray-and-yellow bike. In this section, I look at how the image has been placed on the flyer. Then you can simply replace it with your own image or change the image's settings, such as its angle on the page. If you just replace the image, your own image will appear tilted slightly to the right just as the placeholder image is.

Here's another design tip incorporated into this template. The photo of the bike is tilted a bit, just enough to draw your attention. Note, too, the light gray shadow behind the image. The shadow is subtle, but it helps to draw your attention to the image. Both techniques are used extensively throughout the iWork templates and in other examples of good design.

You can change the formatting of any image. If you insert a new image in a document, it will be inserted in its original orientation, but you can change it. If you're working from an image that has already been inserted and manipulated (such as this one), you can make further adjustments to it. Here's how to make the adjustments to an image such as the one in the For Sale flyer:

1. **Click the image to select it.**

   You can zoom in or out using the Edit Mask slider that appears below the image, as shown in Figure 9-5.

2. **If an inspector is not visible, click Inspector on the toolbar to show the inspector.**

   You can also choose View➪Show Inspector.

3. **Click the Graphic button at the top of the inspector.**

   Graphic inspector appears, as shown in Figure 9-6.

4. **Adjust the Stroke settings to change the border around the image.**

   You can change the width of the border, its shape, or its color. The template has the Stroke settings set to an unbroken, white, 10-point line. Figure 9-7 shows the image if you change the Line setting to None (no border).

Figure 9-5:
Use the Edit Mask slider below the image to change the zoom factor.

Figure 9-6:
Use Graphic
inspector to
adjust the
image.

Figure 9-7:
Use Graphic
inspector to
change the
border.

5. **Adjust the Shadow settings.**

You can turn the shadow on or off with the check box. The Shadow settings are increased in Figure 9-8 to make the shadow bigger and more prominent. Compare this image to Figure 9-3, which shows the results of the default settings (shown in Figure 9-6). For Figure 9-8, the settings were changed to Offset (24), Blur (30), and Opacity (100). Experiment to see what looks best to you, but remember not to go to extremes.

TIP

A subtle shadow with a suggested light source at the upper left is usually best, providing a slight 3-D effect and drawing attention to the image.

ForSale (Page Layout)
Tracking Bubbles
Tracking: On
Paused
Accept
Reject
View Markup
Pages
FOR SALE
Edit Mask
75%
Page 1 of 1

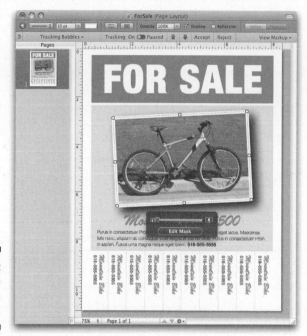

Figure 9-8: You can change the shadow.

Setting the Main Text

You adjust the text and its characteristics just as you adjust text in a word-processing document. Because it's placeholder text, you can't edit it. If you begin to type, you will simply replace it. That doesn't matter because the placeholder text is meaningless and you must replace it. To edit the text, just click in the text box, as shown in Figure 9-9, and type away.

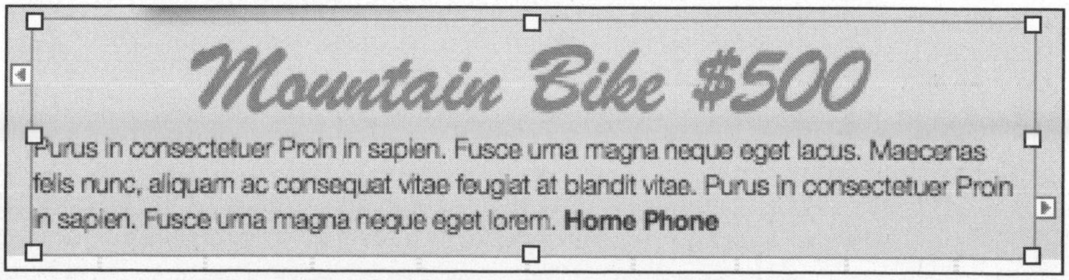
Mountain Bike $500
Purus in consectetuer Proin in sapien. Fusce urna magna neque eget lacus. Maecenas felis nunc, aliquam ac consequat vitae feugiat at blandit vitae. Purus in consectetuer Proin in sapien. Fusce urna magna neque eget lorem. Home Phone

Figure 9-9: Edit the text in the text box.

Automatically Inserting Your Phone Number in the Flyer

iWork provides the ability to merge data from Address Book with your documents. Several templates use the feature to automatically insert your phone number. For this insertion to work properly, you must have your own card in Address Book. Then you insert a Sender field in your document. Although the Flyers template has already completed the second step, this section walks you through both.

Creating a Me card in Address Book

Here's how you create a Me card:

1. **Launch Address Book.**

2. **Choose Card⇨Go To My Card to go to your card.**

   Congratulations! You have a Me card, and you don't have to create a new one unless the Me card is not yours. This can happen if you're using someone else's computer. Get their permission before proceeding with the next step.

3. **Type your name in the search field at the upper right of the window.**

   You don't have to click a button: Address Book finds any cards with the name you type.

4. **If you don't see a card with your name, create one by choosing File⇨ New Card and filling in your data.**

5. **With your card visible, as shown in Figure 9-10, choose Card⇨Make This My Card.**

   A small *me* appears in the lower left of your card image.

Using the Merge or Sender field

You can add two types of fields that interact with your Address Book data: Merge and Sender fields. You can see them both at work in templates for letters. The Merge fields in a letter contain information about the person you're writing to; the Sender fields in a letter contain your information.

These fields are already placed in many of the templates. The Sender fields pick up data from your Me card. The Merge fields pick up data from the appropriate Address Book record. Simply drag an address card from Address Book into your document, and the data for that person automatically appears in the Merge fields.

The Flyers template has a Merge field that picks up data from a selected Address Book card. This section shows you how to delete it and create a new Sender field that picks up your own work phone number from your Me card:

1. **Delete the existing Merge field by selecting it and pressing Delete.**

   In the For Sale flyer, the Merge field is the phone number at the end of the placeholder description text. Leave the placeholder text.

2. **Place the cursor at least one space after the placeholder text.**

3. **Choose Insert➪Sender Field➪Phone➪Work Phone, as shown in Figure 9-11.**

   In the document, the Sender field you've inserted appears, as shown in Figure 9-12, with the data from your Me card. If it doesn't appear, check the following:

   • Do you have a Me card?

   • Do you have a work phone on the Me card?

   • Have you finished editing the Me card? If you've just created it or just typed your work phone, try going to another card so that your update is captured.

The Me card is used by default for a Sender field, but sometimes you don't want that. Perhaps you're preparing this flyer for a friend, and you want to use her card instead of your Me card. Simply drag her card from the Address Book to the Sender field, and the Sender field automatically picks up the information from that card and retains it until you change it again.

Figure 9-10: Make certain your Me card is visible.

Changing the Info on the Tear-Off Tabs

At the bottom of the Flyers template are tear-off tabs that people can take with them to contact you. Each one is its own text box, which you can see if you click one. As always happens when you click a text box that has been rotated, it immediately returns to a horizontal state, as shown in Figure 9-13.

As you hover your cursor over the text box, you can see that the phone number is a Sender field. If you have changed the Sender field in the main text to your work number, you should change it here as well.

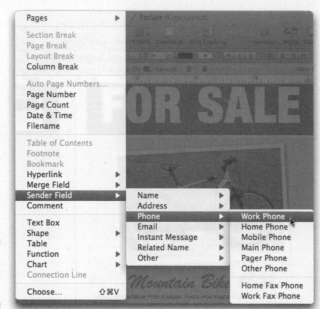

Figure 9-11:
Insert a
Sender field.

Figure 9-12:
The Sender
field is
inserted.

Mountain Bike $500

Purus in consectetuer Proin in sapien. Fusce urna magna neque eget lacus. Maecenas felis nunc, aliquam ac consequat vitae feugiat at blandit vitae. Purus in consectetuer Proin in sapien. Fusce urna magna neque eget lorem. 123-456-7890

Figure 9-13:
Each tear-
off tab is
its own
text box.

Chapter 10

Fine-Tuning Your Pages for Mac Documents

In This Chapter

▶ Formatting text from the format bar

▶ Managing styles

▶ Looking for text

▶ Moving around with thumbnails

*T*his chapter explores some of the Pages tools that improve your productivity and make your documents look better. You might consider some of these tools as advanced features in the sense that you can manage to produce fine Pages documents without using them. But if you think *advanced* means *complicated,* you're wrong. These tools can save you time — sometimes a lot of it — and make your documents easier to read and much, much easier to reuse.

Most of the features discussed in this chapter — the format bar, styles drawer, and thumbnails —appear only in Pages for Mac. (They use parts of the window that do not exist on iOS.) Searching for text is available on iOS, but it uses a different interface that is described in this chapter.

Using the Format Bar

One feature of iWork that makes it so easy to use is that you can usually accomplish something in many ways. If you want to change a font, for example, you can use the Fonts window, a style (see the next section in this chapter), the format bar, or Text inspector. The format bar brings together formatting controls from many places in iWork; it resembles toolbars in other programs, such as Microsoft Word.

You decide whether or not you want to display the format bar. When shown, the format bar appears across the top of the window below the toolbar. Figure 10-1 shows the format bar with the toolbar hidden (so that you can concentrate on the format bar). As you can see, the format bar is only one row of controls, buttons, and icons. That is part of a compromise: Tools such as inspectors and the Fonts window have more space to allow you more control over formatting features, but the format bar brings many formatting features together in one place.

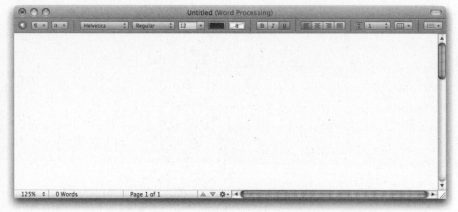

Figure 10-1:
The format bar is at the top of the Pages window.

The format bar has the following six sections (from left to right):

✔ **Styles:** The first section lets you manage styles for paragraphs and characters. For more control over styles, use the Styles drawer (described in the next section).

  • The round ¶ icon shows and hides the Styles drawer.

  • The ¶ pop-up menu lets you select a paragraph style for the current paragraph.

  • The *a* pop-up menu lets you select a character style for the currently selected text. If no text is selected, the character style will be applied to the next characters you type.

✔ **Font formatting:** These next five controls manage basic font formatting for the current selection.

  • Use the first pop-up menu to choose a font family.

  • Click the next menu to choose the typeface (such as regular, bold, or italic).

- • The third pop-up menu lets you choose the font size.

- • Click the color well to choose a color for the font.

- • Click the color well containing the letter *a* to choose the background color for the selected text.

For more control, use the Fonts window (described in Chapter 3).

✔ **Character styles:** Use the next three buttons — which represent bold, italics, and underline — to turn styling on or off for selected text. For more control, use Text inspector (described in Chapter 4).

✔ **Paragraph alignment:** The next four buttons let you choose the paragraph alignment as follows: flush left, centered, flush right, and justified. For more control, use Text inspector (described in Chapter 4).

✔ **Line spacing and columns:** The next two pop-up menus let you adjust vertical line spacing and columns. For more control, use Layout inspector (columns) and Text inspector (vertical line spacing).

✔ **Styles:** The last pop-up menu lets you choose a list style for a selected list (or to convert text into a list). For more control, see the List pane of Text inspector.

Formatting Text with Styles

Word-processing applications let you format text with underlining, italics, boldface, and many more features. With Pages, all you have to do is select the text in question and open the Fonts window (Format➪Font➪Show Fonts) or use Text inspector and select the desired character style. You're finished.

You can easily get carried away with text formatting. When used properly, formatting increases the readability of a sentence. When used in the wrong way, it <u>really</u> not only *doesn't* **help** but can ACTUALLY make a sentence much <u>*harder*</u> to read.

Styles let you set one or more formatting instructions and give them a name of your own choosing. You might use styles for two reasons:

✔ **Consistency:** Particularly when it comes to formatting such as underlining and italics, a style can help you be consistent. For example, you can construct several styles that serve specific purposes in your document. You could create a style called Emphasis that you use for anything that you want to emphasize. If you set the style to boldface and the font color to red, all emphasized words appear that way. Also, you wouldn't have to go back to figure out what you decided you would use for emphasis:

Just select the text and use the Emphasis style. If you were to print the document on a printer that doesn't support color, you could change the style to use, say, italics instead of boldface and red; the one change would affect all the uses of the style.

✔ **Simplicity:** Styles can be complex. It is typical for a style for a paragraph to include its margins, the spacing between lines, and sometimes even a border. You can construct a style and give it a name so that you can then apply all those settings at once to any given paragraph.

You can copy and paste styles. You can modify a style either for all its occurrences or on a case-by-case basis when you want to vary a single section of text or a paragraph. Creating a style in Pages is simple: You style some text or a paragraph, and then you specify that as a style that you name.

You can create styles for characters, paragraphs, and lists. Styles are easy to create, but the Apple developers of iWork are several steps ahead of you: Styles come with every iWork Pages template. You can modify them, delete them, or add more, but you always start with some styles.

Showing the Styles drawer

The *Styles drawer* helps you create, manage, and use styles. Even the simplest templates (the blank documents for both word processing and page layout) come with styles. To see your document's styles, you display the Styles drawer using one of the following methods:

✔ Choose View⇨Show Styles Drawer.

✔ Click the View icon on the toolbar and choose Show Styles Drawer, as shown in Figure 10-2.

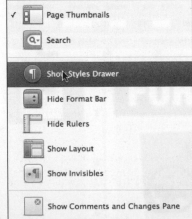

Figure 10-2:
Display the Styles drawer from the toolbar.

✔ In the format bar, click the ¶ icon all the way at the left, as shown in Figure 10-3.

Figure 10-4 shows the styles that come with the blank templates.

iWork has no such thing as a totally blank document. The closest you can come to a blank document is a document based on one of the blank templates.

Templates have styles that help implement their look and feel. For example, the For Sale flyer template is shown in Figure 10-5 with its styles. Notice how the styles are displayed using some of their characteristics. For example, look at the Heading style and match it to the text *Mountain Bike $500* in the flyer. The styles shown at the right of Figure 10-5 are displayed in a *drawer*.

Figure 10-3: Display the Styles drawer from the format bar.

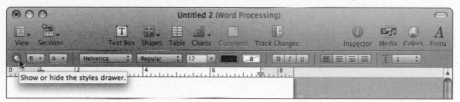

Figure 10-4: All templates come with styles.

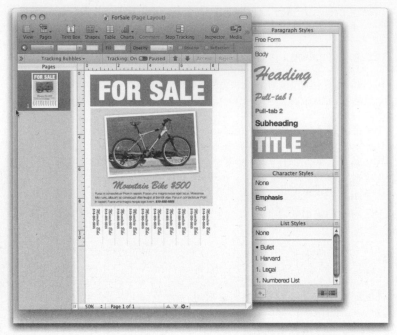

Figure 10-5:
The For Sale
flyer has its
own styles.

Drawers are a feature of Mac OS X. They slide out from the main window. As you resize the window vertically, the drawers automatically resize. You can drag the edge of the drawer to pull it farther in or out. Give it a bit of a shove with the mouse, and it will slide back into the window. (You can also use the Hide Styles Drawer command on the toolbar and in the menu bar; it replaces the Show Styles Drawer command when the drawer is open.)

A drawer normally opens on the right side of a window. If the window is close to the right edge of the display, it will open on the left side if there's room. If not, Mac OS X will nudge the window a bit farther toward the center of the display to make room for the drawer.

Using the Styles drawer controls

The Styles drawer has a lot of power. The Styles drawer has three sections: paragraph styles, character styles, and list styles. You can manipulate these sections as follows:

✔ **Resize sections:** You can resize the three sections by dragging the double-bar to the right of the heading for character and list styles. If you drag up the double-bar to the right of the character styles, for example, you enlarge the character styles section at the expense of the paragraph styles section.

✔ **Show and hide sections:** You can show or hide the character and list styles sections using the buttons in the lower right of the Styles drawer. The button with the letter *a* on it controls the character styles section; the one with the bulleted list on it controls the list section. The paragraph styles section is always shown.

To use an existing style, select the text you want to style. Then do the following:

✔ **Paragraph styles:** Click anywhere in the paragraph you want to style and click the style to use in the Styles drawer.

✔ **Character styles:** Select the character or characters to style and then click the style to use in the Styles drawer. If no characters are selected, the style will be applied to all the characters that you type starting with the next character.

One of the most common problems using styles in any application is not selecting characters to style. The new style will affect the next characters you type, but nothing changes on the screen until you type a new character. If you have accidentally not selected any characters, but are expecting a word to be changed to another color or font size, it can be frustrating.

✔ **List styles:** Select the entire list and then select a list style. Note that list styles are associated with paragraph styles, so selecting a list style will modify the associated paragraph style on a one-time basis.

Handling style changes

When you select a style in the style drawer, at the right of each style name is a downward-pointing triangle (a *disclosure triangle*) that you click to open a menu. This menu (see Figure 10-6) is where you control individual styles.

The downward-pointing triangle has another important function. It normally is gray, but if you override any of the styles' settings, it turns red.

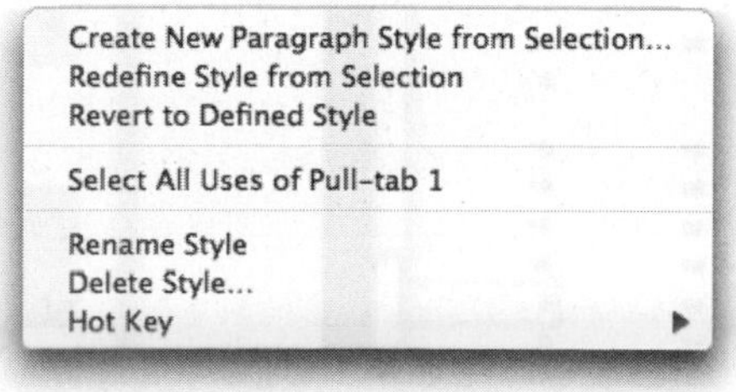

Figure 10-6:
Use the contextual menu in the Styles drawer to control styles.

Create New Paragraph Style from Selection...
Redefine Style from Selection
Revert to Defined Style

Select All Uses of Pull-tab 1

Rename Style
Delete Style...
Hot Key ▶

Changing style on a one-time basis

As you're editing your document, you can change font sizes and colors, margins, and all the other attributes of text. You always have some basic paragraph style even if it's the catchall Free Form style. As you make your formatting changes, the currently selected style will show a red triangle next to its name instead of the standard gray one. The first three items in the menu shown in Figure 10-6 let you decide what to do with the changed style:

✔ **Create a new style:** If you've deliberately made a change to the style, you can save it as a new style. For example, maybe you've decided that you would sometimes like the Heading style to be underlined. You can select a paragraph that uses the Heading style and underline it. The red triangle will appear, and you can choose to create a new style named, for example, *Underlined Heading.* The style will now appear in the Styles drawer.

• You're asked to provide a name for the new style, as shown in Figure 10-7. By default, the style has the name of the existing style with a number after it. It's a good idea to give it a more meaningful name right away. You also can choose whether to apply the style on creation. That means that as soon as it is created, it will be applied to the current selection. If you deselect this box, the style will be created and added to the list, but it won't be applied until you select some text and choose the style.

• If you're creating a character style, you can use the disclosure triangle to see which character attributes have been set, as shown in Figure 10-8. You can turn any of them on or off. If a character attribute isn't set in the character style, basic formatting (usually specified in the paragraph style) is used. The Select Overrides button in the lower right displays only the character style changes you've specified.

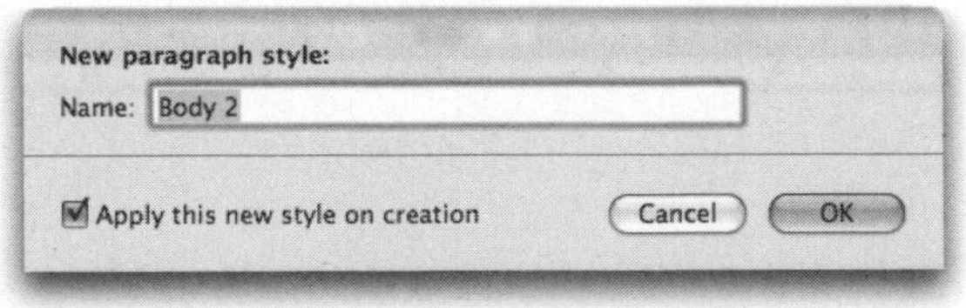

Figure 10-7:
Create a
new style
and name it.

New paragraph style:

Name: Body 2

☑ Apply this new style on creation   (Cancel)   (OK)

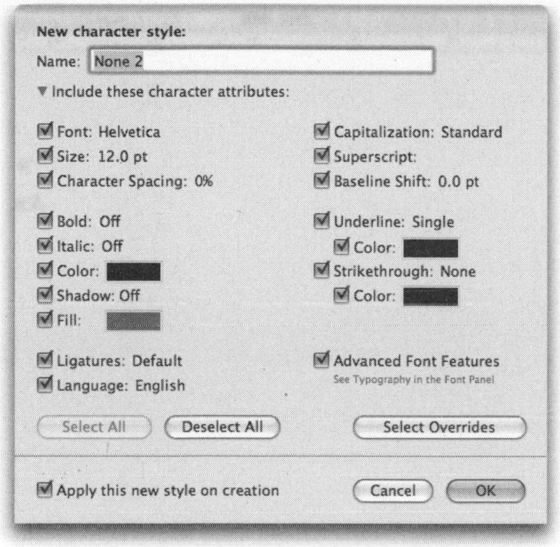

New character style:

Name: None 2

▼ Include these character attributes:

☑ Font: Helvetica
☑ Size: 12.0 pt
☑ Character Spacing: 0%

☑ Bold: Off
☑ Italic: Off
☑ Color:
☑ Shadow: Off
☑ Fill:

☑ Ligatures: Default
☑ Language: English

☑ Capitalization: Standard
☑ Superscript:
☑ Baseline Shift: 0.0 pt

☑ Underline: Single
  ☑ Color:
☑ Strikethrough: None
  ☑ Color:

☑ Advanced Font Features
  See Typography in the Font Panel

(Select All)   (Deselect All)   (Select Overrides)

☑ Apply this new style on creation   (Cancel) (OK)

Figure 10-8:
Specify character attributes for a character style.

✔ **Redefine the style:** If you decide that the Heading style would look better underlined, for example, select a paragraph that uses it and underline the paragraph. Then, in the contextual menu, choose Redefine Style from Selection. This changes the style. Now you have only one style, but it is the redefined one. All Heading paragraphs are now changed.

✔ **Revert to the defined style:** If you make a mistake or change your mind about the underlining or other formatting, choose Revert to Defined Style and your change is ignored. You are back to the original style without your modification.

✔ **Do nothing:** You don't have to do anything about that red triangle. If you made a formatting change and you meant to do it, so be it. Just move on. (There's no menu choice for doing nothing.)

Managing styles

Whenever you select a paragraph, a list, or some characters, the style name is highlighted. The name is also highlighted as you move the mouse over the style names in the styles list. You can use the downward-pointing triangle to open the menu shown previously in Figure 10-5 whether you've changed the style or not. Menu commands let you rename or delete the style. You can also associate a function key from F1 to F8 (at the top of the keyboard) with that style. That way, you can just select a paragraph, a list, or text and press the function key to apply the style. (On recent keyboards, press the FN key before pressing the function key you want: They have multiple purposes.)

Searching for Text

iWork has a powerful search feature on both iOS and Mac.

On Mac, you display the search tool shown in Figure 10-9 by choosing View⇨Search or by clicking the View icon at the left of the toolbar.

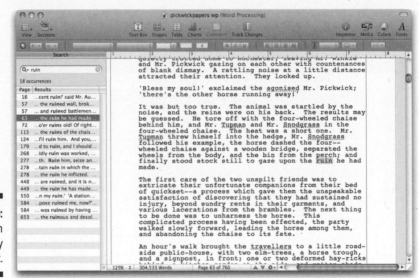

Figure 10-9:
Use search
to quickly
find text.

Type some text into the search box, and Pages will quickly find every occurrence in your document. In the search area, you see page numbers as well as the search string in context. Click an item in the list, and you immediately go to that occurrence in the document.

iWork indexes the text very quickly. And it indexes all the text. It will find your search string in a word-processing document, in a text box, and even inside an object if you've typed text there.

The search list is updated as you modify the document.

On iOS, you search for each item in turn:

1. **Use Tools (the wrench at the right of the toolbar) to choose Find, as shown in Figure 10-10.**

2. **Type the text you want to find.**

   As you can see in Figure 10-11, you have options to also replace text. You can navigate to the next or previous instance with the arrows.

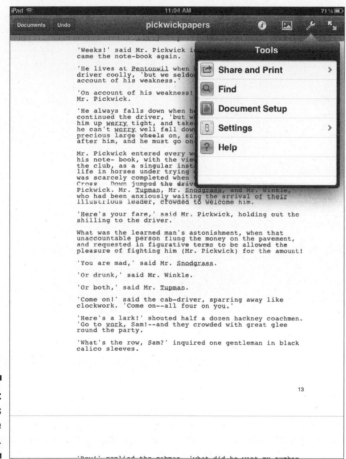

Figure 10-10:
Use Tools
to start the
find.

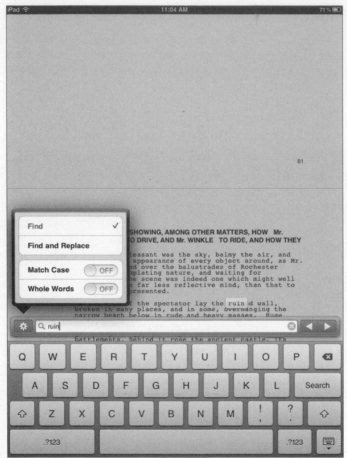

Figure 10-11:
Perform the
find.

Navigating with Thumbnails

iWork can provide thumbnails of your pages in sequence. Even though the thumbnails are small, you can often get a sense of what page you're looking at, particularly in a page layout document. You display thumbnails by choosing View⇔Page Thumbnails. Just click a thumbnail to go to that page.

Chapter 11

Improving Your Documents with Comments and Track Changes (Mac Only)

*T*he tools described in this chapter help you improve your documents by using features of iWork as well as comments and suggestions from other people. iWork has a variety of tools that make it easy for people to work together on documents. These tools are available in Numbers and Keynote as well as in Pages on Mac OS. They are not supported on iOS. They have the same overall functionality in all the applications, but they have slightly different interfaces.

iWork.com implements the commenting and track changes functionalities through the web so that multiple people can work on the same documents at the same time. See Chapter 1 for details.

Using Comments

Whether you're working by yourself or with others, you frequently need to make comments on your work. Sometimes comments are reminders; sometimes they're questions. For example, Figure 11-1 shows a typical comment questioning whether the date 1600 is the specific year or an approximation. You might leave this comment for yourself or add it to someone else's document. Either way, you need to deal with the comments.

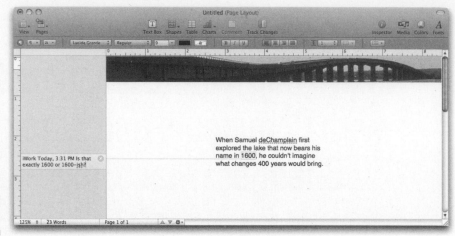

Figure 11-1:
The
Comments
pane
displays
comments
and links
them to
highlighted
text.

If you're reviewing a document (perhaps you're a teacher), your comments may not require action — you might write "Good!" or "You really understand why black ice is so dangerous."

Either way, the point is that you want to be able to comment on a document without your comment appearing in the document. If you insert a comment into the document itself, not only can it appear when you print the document, but its presence can change the flow of the document, perhaps adding several pages to the uncommented document.

Showing and hiding the Comments pane

Comments are shown in the Comments pane, which appears at the left of a Pages document (refer to Figure 11-1).

To show or hide the Comments pane:

- ✔ Choose View➪Show Comments or View➪Hide Comments on the toolbar.
- ✔ Click the pop-up View menu on the toolbar and make your selection.

There's another special way to display the Comments pane: Simply create a comment, and the Comments pane appears automatically.

Creating a comment

To create a comment, first select what it applies to. That can be a word, a paragraph, or even a page; it can be an object, a text box, or an image. If you can select it, you can comment on it.

Highlighting one or two characters is possible, but it can make the comment hard to find. If you have a question or comment about one or two characters in a word, highlight the entire word and make it clear that the comment applies only to those characters.

When you've highlighted the subject of the comment, the next step is to create the comment. You have two choices:

- ✓ Choose Insert⇨Comment.
- ✓ Click the Comment icon on the toolbar.

If necessary, the Comments pane appears. If appropriate (such as words within a stream of text), the subject of the comment is highlighted. In all cases, a line is drawn from the comment subject to the Comments pane, where a *comment bubble* appears. The comment bubble is placed at the end of that line with the current date and time. Click in the bubble to type your comment. If your comment is emphatic, feel free to italicize it. Use bold text if you want to drive your point home. Your Pages text-editing tools work in comments as well as in the body of your documents.

Your comment is now linked to the document. The comment moves around the document as you move objects in the document. You can always hide the Comments pane if you don't want to see the comments. If you want to remove a comment, click the X in the upper-right of the bubble, and it will be removed. Note that I said removed, not hidden.

Printing a comment

You can print comments along with your document. Printing comments is particularly useful if you're sharing a document with several people who may have to review it and act on the comments. Pages makes printing comments simple. If the Comments pane is displayed, comments are printed, as shown in Figure 11-2.

If the Comments pane isn't displayed, comments aren't printed, as shown in Figure 11-3. If you compare Figures 11-2 and 11-3, you see that the entire page image is made a bit smaller to allow for comments. This means that if you have a multipage document with comments only on some pages, all pages will be printed in the reduced size.

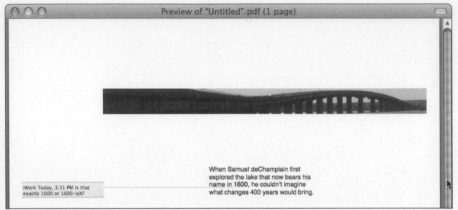

Figure 11-2:
You can print comments.

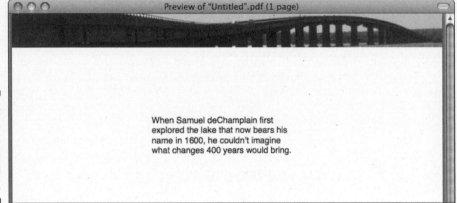

Figure 11-3:
You can hide comments in a printed document.

Tracking Changes

One of the best features of Microsoft Word is its ability to track changes. When Track Changes is turned on, Word keeps track of every change to the document, whether it's adding or deleting text, changing the format, or inserting page breaks. Microsoft Word has several ways of displaying the changes, each of which is identified with its date and time as well as who has made the change. If several people are working on a document, you can see all their changes together.

Pages has also implemented Track Changes functionality. It does almost everything that Microsoft Word does — and it handles Microsoft Word track changes documents. Figure 11-4 shows a Pages document with Track Changes turned on. In fact, the document was created in Microsoft Word. It started with one sentence: *This is a document without track changes turned on.* Track changes was then turned on, and I changed *without* to *with*. That counts as two changes: the deletion of *without* and the addition of *with*. The document was saved in Microsoft Word, and it was opened in Pages. When Track Changes is on, the tracking bar appears below the format bar, and the changes are shown at the left in *change bubbles*.

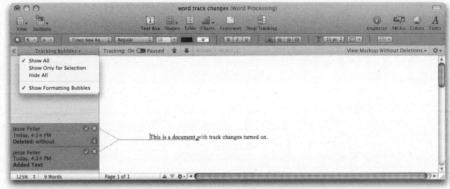

Figure 11-4:
Track Changes lets you trace your document's history.

Pages tracks changes to text and formatting, but it also tracks changes to objects in both word-processing and page layout documents, as shown in Figure 11-5.

Setting up Track Changes preferences

Preferences for Track Changes are set in General Preferences, shown in Figure 11-6. Just choose Pages⇨Preferences and click the General tab.

Untitled 2 (Page Layout)
View
Pages
Text Box
Shapes
Table
Charts
Comment
Stop Tracking
Inspector
Media
Colors
Fonts
Tracking Bubbles
Tracking: On
Paused
Accept
Reject
View Markup
iWork
Today, 4:40 PM
Formatted: Red
iWork
Today, 4:39 PM
Moved: Image
iWork
Today, 4:39 PM
Moved, Sheared: Image
iWork
Today, 4:39 PM
Added Text
Real Estate Watch
SUMMER 2009
MAECENAS PULVINAR SAGITTIS ENIM
ISSUE ONE
Lorem ipsum dolor sit amet, suspendisse nulla, rhoncus temp placerat fermentum
test
Donec arcu risus diam
125%
0 of 297 Words
Page 1 of 1

Figure 11-5: Changes in page layout documents are tracked.

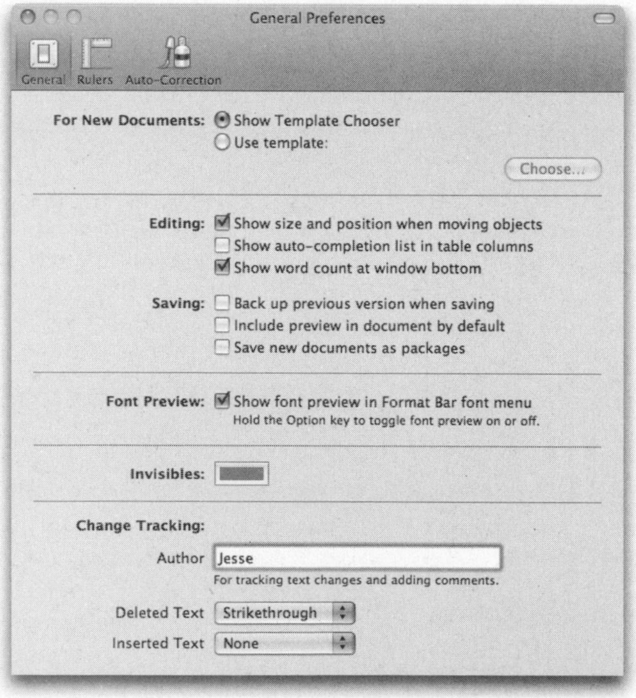
General Preferences
General
Rulers
Auto-Correction
For New Documents:
Show Template Chooser
Use template:
Choose...
Editing:
Show size and position when moving objects
Show auto-completion list in table columns
Show word count at window bottom
Saving:
Back up previous version when saving
Include preview in document by default
Save new documents as packages
Font Preview:
Show font preview in Format Bar font menu
Hold the Option key to toggle font preview on or off.
Invisibles:
Change Tracking:
Author
Jesse
For tracking text changes and adding comments.
Deleted Text
Strikethrough
Inserted Text
None

Figure 11-6: Set up Track Changes preferences.

At the bottom of the window is the Change Tracking section. The first item, Author, is the name that will be used for your changes. The name, like all the preferences here, applies to all your documents. Below your name, you can set preferences for how deleted and added text is displayed. This setting, too, applies to all your documents.

Inside your Pages documents, the changes are stored with all their details, including whether text has been added or deleted. Your preference determines how additions and deletions are shown on Pages documents on your computer. If you choose Strikethrough for deleted text, for example, that's how it will appear. If you give that document to someone else who has chosen Underline as the indicator for deleted text, that's how it will appear for them. Track Changes stores the action; your preferences (and your friends' preferences) determine how the changes are displayed.

Starting and stopping Track Changes

The tracking bar appears when Track Changes is turned on for a document. You turn on Track Changes (and show the tracking bar) by clicking Track Changes on the toolbar. The Track Changes icon immediately changes to a Stop Tracking icon.

After you have turned on Track Changes, changes from that point on are tracked as you make them — unless you pause tracking, as described later in this section. Each change is identified with your username and the date and time of the change. In addition, as shown in Figures 11-4 and 11-5, each change has a check mark and an X in the upper right of its bubble. The check mark lets you accept a change, and the X lets you reject it.

When you accept a change, the change bubble disappears, and the change is permanent (unless you change it again). When you reject a change, the change bubble disappears and the change is undone.

Track Changes stores its changes with the document each time you save it. If you have changes that haven't been accepted or rejected, you can't turn Track Changes off. If you try to stop tracking with unresolved changes, you see the dialog shown in Figure 11-7. At that point, you must either accept or reject all changes or click Cancel to accept or reject each individual change in turn.

Figure 11-7:
You must resolve all changes before stopping Track Changes.

All changes must be accepted or rejected to turn off Change Tracking.

Click Accept All Changes to keep the current version of the document. Click Reject All Changes to reject all tracked changes.

Cancel   Reject All Changes   Accept All Changes

Viewing (and not viewing) changes

Although you can't turn off Track Changes with unresolved changes, you don't have to see them. You can accomplish this in several ways:

✔ Show or hide the Comments and Changes pane by choosing View⇨ Show/Hide Comments and Changes Pane or by clicking the View menu on the toolbar. You can also click the double-arrow at the far left of the tracking bar. Changes will still be tracked, but you won't see them.

✔ Use the Tracking Bubbles menu at the left of the tracking bar to show or hide bubbles, as Figure 11-8 demonstrates. The bubbles disappear, but the Comments and Changes pane is still visible.

✔ If Page Thumbnails are shown, the changes are highlighted on the thumbnails, so you can quickly see which pages contain changes. You can click the thumbnail to go to that page immediately and deal with the change.

✔ Finally, if you hover your mouse over something that has been changed, you see a summary of the change, as shown in Figure 11-9. This summary can occur even if the change bubbles aren't visible, and it's particularly useful with text. Deleted and added text is highlighted in the document as it is changed, but the summary of the change adds the information of who did it and when.

Pausing Track Changes

Although you can't turn Track Changes off with unresolved changes, you can use the tracking slider next to the Tracking Bubbles pop-up menu in the tracking bar to pause Track Changes and to turn it back on. Pausing keeps Track Changes active (and keeps the tracking bar visible), but you can work for a while without your changes being tracked.

Figure 11-8: The Tracking Bubbles menu controls change bubbles.

✓ Show All
Show Only for Selection
Hide All

✓ Show Formatting Bubbles

Figure 11-9:
Hover your
mouse over
a change to
see details.

One reason for pausing Track Changes is if you are about to do a series of changes that will generate a number of change messages, each of which needs a response. Rearranging paragraphs in a lengthy document is an example of this: Each paragraph is marked as changed when it is deleted and then marked as changed when it is inserted in its new location.

Accepting and rejecting changes

You can accept and reject changes in several ways:

- ✔ For a given change, click the check mark (accept) or X (reject) button in the upper right of the change bubble. The change is accepted or rejected, and the bubble disappears.

- ✔ Highlight a particular change bubble and click Accept or Reject at the center of the tracking bar.

- ✔ Use the up and down arrows in the center of the tracking bar to move to the previous or next change, respectively. The arrows are deliberately placed next to the Accept and Reject buttons so that you can quickly navigate through the changes and deal with them.

- ✔ Accept or reject all changes with a single command from the Action menu at the far right of the tracking bar, as shown in Figure 11-10.

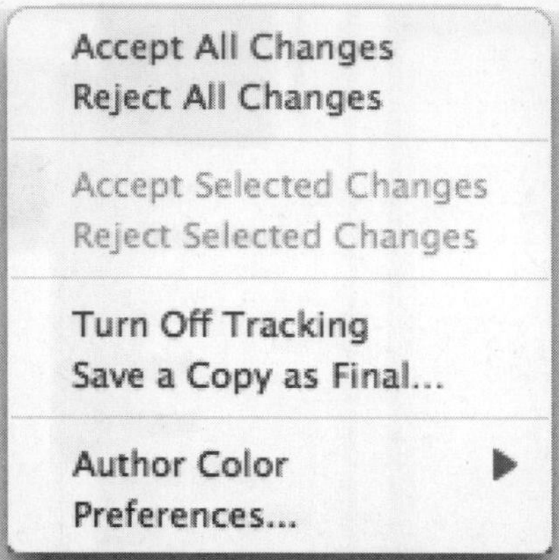

Accept All Changes
Reject All Changes

Accept Selected Changes
Reject Selected Changes

Turn Off Tracking
Save a Copy as Final...

Author Color ▶
Preferences...

Figure 11-10:
Use the
Action menu
for more
tracking
commands.

Printing a clean copy without changes

The Action menu contains another useful command: Save a Copy as Final. This command saves a copy of the document with all changes accepted. Your original document still has the changes for you to accept or reject, but you have a copy that you can print or send to someone.

Chapter 12

Working with Long Word-Processing Documents (Mac Only)

● ●

In This Chapter

▶ Using sections

▶ Formatting columns

▶ Paginating your document

▶ Creating a table of contents

▶ Creating ePub documents with Pages

● ●

*Y*our word-processing documents are already set up by Pages with a number of optional features: headers and footers, automatic page numbers, various margin controls, and the ability to create footnotes and to automatically update tables of contents (yes, *tables* — you can have several tables of contents in one document). These tools are valuable for all your documents, but they are particularly important for large documents.

Large documents — large Numbers spreadsheets and large Keynote presentations as well as large Pages documents — require special handling so that your readers don't get lost (and so that you don't get lost as you're writing the document!). The challenges of a large spreadsheet are different from those of a large presentation or a large word-processing document.

Don't let the title of this chapter mislead you. You can work with very large documents on Pages for iOS. However, when you have a long document, some features specifically help readers to navigate through and understand the document. These features include sections, tables of content, and pagination. It is those features (which, by the way, many people do not use) that are Mac-only.

Working with Sections for Improved Formatting of Long Documents

Word-processing documents consist of words, paragraphs, and pages. They also contain *sections*. Just as you can format words, paragraphs, and pages, you can also format sections. A section can be as small as part of a page or many pages long. In the case of a book, a section is usually a chapter.

Each section can contain its own formatting. Sections also may contain text that is either placeholder text you can replace or text that remains unchanged.

When you create a document from a template, all of the template's sections are available, but not all of them are inserted into the initial version of the document. For example, the Project Proposal template, which is in the Reports section of the template, has the sections shown in Figure 12-1 built into the template. You can add any of those to your document whenever you want. The initial version of the document created by the template has the Cover and Executive Summary already in place.

Figure 12-1: Templates come with at least one section already defined.

Adding a section to a document

Here's how to add a section to a document:

1. **Position the cursor where you want to insert the section.**

   Most sections in the templates automatically begin on a new page. You can change this setting for individual sections after you've inserted them.

2. **Insert the section:**

    • Choose Insert⇨Section to display a submenu of the document's sections (refer to Figure 12-1). Choose the one you want to insert.

    • Display the same menu by clicking the Sections icon on the toolbar and then choose the one you want to insert.

Rearranging sections

If you have page thumbnails displayed, you can use sections to improve your navigation. Figure 12-2 shows page thumbnails in a document that has two sections. The first section contains one page, and the second section has two pages. The second section is selected, as you can tell by the yellow border around its pages.

You can move a section by dragging it in the page thumbnails. As soon as you start to drag a page that is inside a section, the section collapses into a single page image with a number in the lower left showing you how many pages are in the section. Figure 12-3 shows what happens as you drag the two-page section in Figure 12-2.

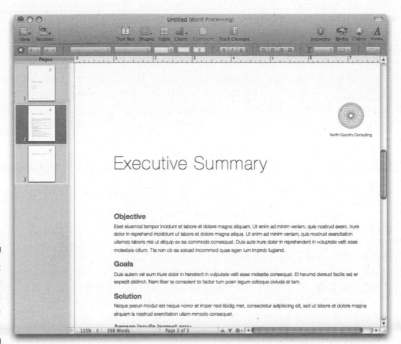

Figure 12-2:
Pages can
be grouped
into
sections.

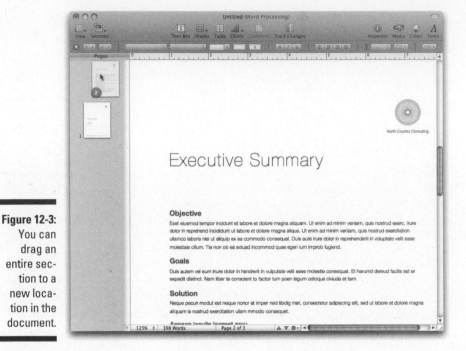

Figure 12-3:
You can drag an entire section to a new location in the document.

Formatting Your Document and Sections

Sections exist in every document. A page layout document in Pages has one section for each page. By default, a blank word-processing document has a single section. As you add pages, they're added to this section. You are never without a section in a Pages document, whether you know it or not.

The fact that you always have a section in a Pages document matters because many of the format settings you use actually apply to sections. In the basic case of a word-processing document with all the pages in one section, there is no practical difference between settings for the document and the section. But as soon as you have two or more sections in the document, those section settings become important.

When you're formatting text, you select whatever you want to format and use commands or the inspector to format the selected text. When you're formatting sections, you click anywhere in the section to format it using the inspector. If you're formatting a document, you do not need to click anywhere; as long as the document is open in your window, your inspector settings will apply to it. The only time you really have to worry about carefully selecting text to format is when you're working with part of a section. Otherwise, a click anywhere in the section will let you format the entire section, and a click anywhere in the document will let you format the entire document.

If the inspector is not visible, open it using one of these techniques:

> ✔ **Choose View➪Show Inspector to open the inspector.**
>
> ✔ **Click the Inspector icon, at the right of the toolbar.**

If you already have an inspector open, you can choose View➪New Inspector to open another inspector. If more than one inspector is open, clicking the Inspector icon on the toolbar closes all of them. You can also use the close box in individual inspectors to close them.

Most of the settings described here use Document inspector (the leftmost icon in the Inspector window) and Layout inspector (the next icon in the Inspector window).

Setting document information

Document inspector, shown in Figure 12-4, has three tabs:

> ✔ **Document:** This controls document settings such as margins.
>
> ✔ **TOC:** This controls the table of contents.
>
> ✔ **Info:** This displays the statistics for the document (the number of words, for example) and lets you enter a title and an author. This information is available as part of the file; it is not automatically displayed in the document itself.

Setting the document information is a good idea so that you can discover a year from now why you created the document. If you're working with a specific document length in mind (perhaps for a school assignment), Document inspector is where you check how close you are to your goal.

Setting document margins

Use the Document tab of Document inspector (see Figure 12-5) to set the document's basic margins.

If you're using a standard paper size, you can usually use the default settings. If you need to change the paper size, click the Page Setup button at the top of the inspector to open the standard OS X Page Setup dialog.

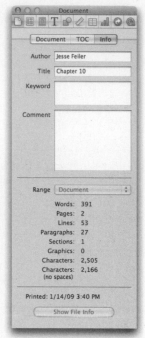

Figure 12-4:
The Info
tab of
Document
inspector
lets you
describe the
document.

Figure 12-5:
Set
document
margins
here.

The Facing Pages check box lets you create margins for a document that will be printed on both sides of the paper and prepared like a book. The left and right margins are changed to Inside and Outside, respectively. Visualize a book open to two facing pages. On the left page, the inside margin is the right margin (nearest the binding) and the outside margin is the left margin. On the right page, the opposite is true: The inside margin is the left margin and the outside margin is the right margin. Pages keeps track of which margin is which on different pages. That is, neither page is inside or outside. Each page has both an inside margin and an outside margin.

If you're planning to use facing pages, you have to help Pages by inserting blank pages where necessary. For facing pages to work, each part of the document must have an even number of pages. Fortunately, if you're working with sections, these blank pages are inserted for you automatically.

Setting multiple columns

One of the reasons for using sections is so that you can apply formatting to an entire section. In the cases of margins and columns, you may want to apply formatting to only part of a section; to do so, you create *layouts*. This section shows you how to set multiple columns for a layout.

Sometimes an entire section or even an entire document is presented in columns. Other times you have columns in only part of a document — perhaps only on part of a page.

You always have at least one layout in your document. If you want another layout, position the cursor where you want the new layout to begin and choose Insert➪Layout Break. Now you'll be able to change the formatting of either layout independently. If you want a section with columns, you would have your initial layout for the one-column text, then you'd insert a layout break to be able to format a two-column layout, and after that you'd insert a layout break to be able to format the remaining text as one column.

The most basic layout has a single column. You need to add new layouts only if you want to change to multiple columns (or back to one) or to change the margins just for that layout.

Use Layout inspector, shown in Figure 12-6, to set the column settings for each layout. Note that you can force a layout to begin on a new page; this command is available for every layout except the first one, which already starts on a new page.

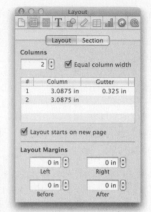

Figure 12-6:
Use Layout inspector to set columns.

Paginating your document

Use the Section tab of Layout inspector to control pagination of your document. You can number each section separately or number all the pages of the document together, as shown in Figure 12-7.

Here's a practical example of how you can use sections and automatic Pages tools to format a lengthy document such as *The Pickwick Papers* document, which you can download from the author's site as described in the Introduction.

Figure 12-7:
Control pagination from Layout inspector.

With the document still in one section, the section settings are shown in Figure 12-7. Insert a page number in the footer by choosing Insert⇨Automatic Page Numbers, which opens the dialog shown in Figure 12-8. Note that Pages provides you with the option to align numbers at the left, right, or center as well as at the inside and outside margins.

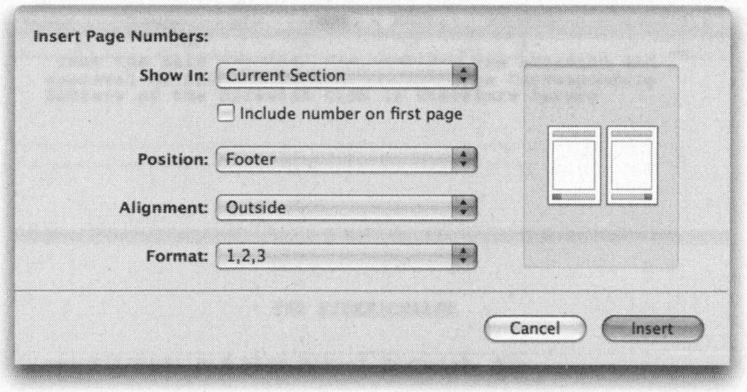

Insert Page Numbers:

Show In:	Current Section
	☐ Include number on first page
Position:	Footer
Alignment:	Outside
Format:	1,2,3

Cancel   Insert

Figure 12-8:
Insert automatic page numbers.

Now, break the document into chapter sections. You do this by positioning the cursor just before the start of each chapter and choosing Insert⇨Section Break. It's important to do this after you have formatted the unbroken section containing all the pages, because when you insert the breaks for each chapter, the settings from the previous section are carried forward. You can change each section, but in this case, you want each section to have the same type of formatting.

Sometimes making the first page different lets you add special formatting to it; other times, you want to add special formatting to the other pages. In this example, the first page is marked as being different, as shown in Figure 12-7. Type the name of the chapter into the header on the second page, and the chapter name will appear in the header of every page except the first one (which already contains the chapter title). Because the first page is marked as being different, if you type a header for this page, the header text will appear only on the first page.

If you indicate that each section should begin on a right-hand page, Pages will insert blank pages if necessary to force the first page of each section to be a right-hand page.

Creating and Updating Tables of Contents

Particularly when it comes to long documents, a table of contents is a great tool for your readers. Pages can automatically create a table of contents for you by relying on the styles you use in the document. You don't mark items to appear in the table of contents; instead you use a specific style for the table of contents items (there can be more than one), and that style is automatically picked up by Pages.

You don't have to use the styles that Pages provides: Any styles that you use in your document can be in a table of contents. However, you must use the styles consistently. For example, if you want each chapter title to be placed in the table of contents, the chapter title should always use a unique style. If you want headings placed in the table of contents, those, too, should use a unique style.

Here's how to create a table of contents:

1. **Create a table of contents page or section in your document.**

   • If you're using a Pages template, look for a section called Table of Contents. Position the cursor where you want to insert the table of contents and then either choose Insert➪Sections➪Table of Contents or click the Sections menu on the toolbar. This is the easiest method.

   • Position the cursor where you want the table of contents and choose Insert➪Table of Contents. This inserts the table of contents code into your document as part of an existing section rather than as a separate section.

2. **Specify the table of contents.**

   Open Document inspector to the TOC tab, as shown in Figure 12-9, to set up your table of contents. All the styles you've used in the document are shown. Select the check box to the left of each style that you want to appear in the table of contents.

   You can use the check box on the right to make the page numbers for entries into links that take you from the table of contents to the page in question. (Obviously, this works only with the digital version of documents.)

3. **Create the table of contents by clicking the Update Now button.**

   The table of contents will be automatically updated in the future whenever you save the document, but you can always regenerate it using the Update Now button. If the Update Now button isn't dimmed, you have changes that need to be indexed, and you should click it before saving or distributing the document.

   If the Update Now button is dimmed, chances are you forgot Step 1, creating the table of contents section in your document. Pages will have nowhere to place the table of contents so it can't generate it.

4. **Format your table of contents.**

   Go to the newly generated table of contents and open the Styles drawer, shown in Figure 12-10. (Choose View➪Show Styles Drawer or use the View menu on the toolbar.) The styles in the table of contents are named after the styles used for table of contents entries, but the style names are preceded by *TOC*.

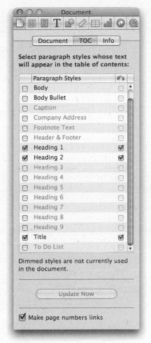

Figure 12-9:
Create a
table of
contents.

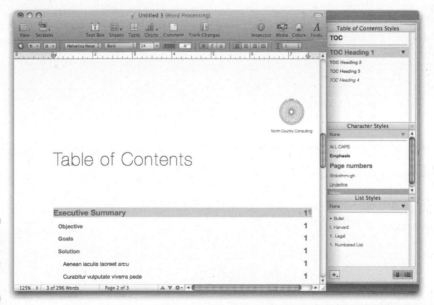

Figure 12-10:
Format your
table of
contents.

5. Select the table of contents and click the Tabs pane of Text inspector, shown in Figure 12-11.

One of the most common formatting changes for a table of contents is to add dots or dashes, called *leaders,* between the entry and the page number. As you see in Figure 12-11, a single tab stop is defined for each TOC style. Select that tab stop and choose the type of leader you want. The entry you selected changes immediately. If you don't like the look, try another leader character.

You can change other formatting as well. For example, you may want to indent subheadings in the table of contents beneath chapter or section titles. If you do so, you may want the subheading page numbers indented from the right.

6. Update the style.

Click the downward-pointing arrow next to the style name in the Styles drawer and choose Redefine Style from Selection, as shown in Figure 12-12. The formatting is applied to every entry that uses this style.

Your table of contents takes shape before your eyes. And Pages remembers your style changes, so the TOC styles appear the same whenever you update your table of contents.

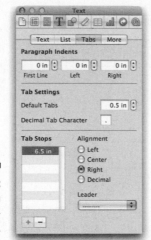

Figure 12-11:
Reformat a table of contents entry.

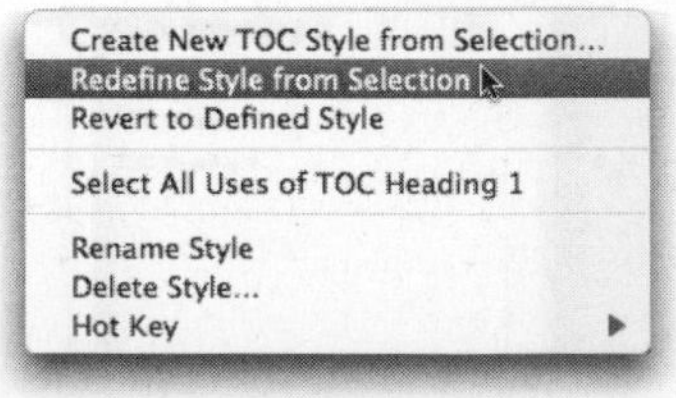

Figure 12-12:
Change the style.

Turning Your Pages Document into an ePub Book

You can share your lengthy Pages document with other people by exporting it as a PDF file, as a Pages document, or in a common format, such as Microsoft Word. All those options are available to you from Pages. There also is another choice: You can use the ePub format.

Books in Apple's iBooks store are published using the ePub format. On iOS, you can add ePub files that you create with Pages using iTunes as described in Chapter 1. Add them to the iBooks section in iTunes rather than to the Pages, Numbers, or Keynote section. After you add a document to iBooks, it can be synchronized across your various devices.

At this time, iBooks does not run on OS X. If you want to develop more sophisticated books, you can use Apple's free iBooks Author tool. You'll feel right at home as you explore it: It's very similar to the iWork apps.

Exploring ePub

PDF files are created by a program by using its printing code and then storing the image in a file rather than sending it to a printer, but ePub files use a different methodology. The ePub file that is created contains the content of the document as well as formatting instructions. It's not a page image. For that reason, ePub documents can adapt to different size screens. (This adaptation is particularly important on mobile devices with small and different-size screens.)

I use Pickwick Papers as an example of formatting in this book. It's used here as a demonstration of ePub. (You can download all the versions as described in the Introduction.) Figure 12-13 shows how a page from it appears in the ePub version when shown on an iPad.

Now, take a look at the same content when shown on an iPhone (see Figure 12-14). Although the text is small in both images (and both images have been resized in different amounts for readability), you can easily see that the chapter title has adjusted to the different size of the two screens. In addition, the lines of text have wrapped differently depending on the screen.

This is what a format such as ePub does: It takes the specified formatting and applies it to the device used for display rather than showing a static page image on whatever device you're using. This makes for easier reading and allows a number of other features to be implemented.

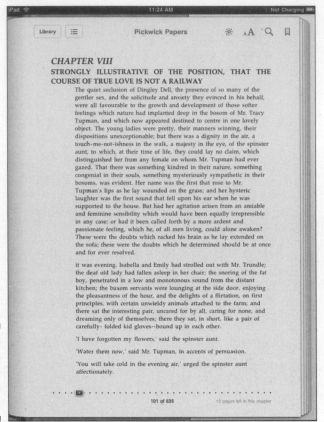

Figure 12-13:
View an
ePub file in
iBooks on
iPad.

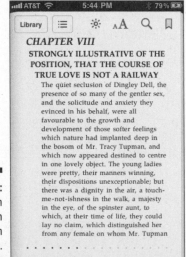

Figure 12-14:
View an
ePub file in
iBooks on
iPhone.

Managing digital rights

One issue that has bedeviled the e-book publishing business from its very beginning is the fact that once a digital version of a book exists, it can easily be transferred from one user to another. The work of the publisher and author can wind up being shared widely, which is a good thing in some cases, but in other cases, it would put publishers and authors out of business. The same issue applies to music, movies, and all other digitized data.

The ePub specification includes digital rights management (DRM), which is the software used to control authorized and prevent unauthorized copying of the content. ePub specifies how DRM fits into its structure, but it does not require DRM, and it does not specify a particular DRM system. That is why an ePub file designed for one device can be transferred to another ePub device but may not be readable on that device.

Books that are sold in the iBooks store have DRM encoded in them, and they are playable only on the iOS devices with valid authentication (that is, you've purchased them). However, because iBooks uses ePub, it can let you read non-DRM-encoded ePub files, and it's those files that Pages lets you create.

If you download and experiment with the ePub files, you'll see that on iPad, the image shown is page 101; on iPhone, it's page 278. Both pages show the beginning of Chapter VIII, but the actual page numbers are generated as the ePub file is displayed on the specific device. The reason it's possible to go to the same place on both books is that this page is the start of a chapter, and therefore it begins on a new page (although it's a different page). The table of contents is automatically generated, and these changing page numbers are displayed appropriately there.

Converting a Pages document to ePub

Whether you're creating your own Pages document from scratch for an ePub book or are modifying an existing one, the techniques are simple. They rely on two basic elements of Pages:

- ✔ Styles and tables of contents
- ✔ Wrap inspector

Styles, tables of contents, and the Wrap inspector are basic iWork features; you may want to slightly modify some of the settings as described in this chapter, but no new concepts are involved.

The fact that your ePub document will be displayed dynamically on whatever device is in use means that you cannot do the same kind of checking that you do with a PDF file. In that case, you can produce the PDF file and display it on any device or print it on any printer: It should appear the same in all cases because that's the goal. (There are some obvious exceptions: Printing a PDF file that uses color on a black-and-white printer will look different from viewing the file on a screen or printing the file on a color printer.)

Because you can't proofread and check the final result, it's important to check the issues that may affect the final result. There's really only one way of doing this if your destination is a mobile device with a small screen, such as an iPhone or iPod touch, and even a mobile device with a larger screen, such as an iPad. What you should do is prepare the first draft of your Pages document (maybe just the first few pages), export an ePub file, and then deploy it to the type of device you'll be using.

At that point, you can add it to your iBooks in iTunes, and it can automatically be synchronized with your iPad, iPod touch, or iPhone. You can also e-mail the ePub document to friends or post it on a website for downloading.

Depending on the document, you may want to add some steps to the process.

You generally can export a text-only document to ePub and successfully view it on any ePub reader, including the iOS devices. You can apply special formatting and embed objects (shapes, charts, tables, images, and text boxes), and they will be exported appropriately. However, you should consider some points that can affect the final result:

- You can't use multiple columns.
- Headers and footers are not supported, but page numbers are generated automatically. Remember, headers and footers have little meaning for ePub documents, because the pagination changes with each device the file is displayed on.
- If you have a number of embedded objects in your document, as the ePub document is reflowed for different devices, you may wind up with hard to read documents on iPhone.

Using styles

The styles used in the Pages version of this document are based on the Apple styles for their sample document. You don't have to use these or any other styles. What you do need to do is to set up the table of contents. Because the table of contents will be created automatically from your ePub file, this preparation is particularly important.

For many people, one of the major tasks here is to remove an existing table of contents that has been carefully typed. When the table of contents is created automatically, you don't have to worry about changing page numbers as you add and subtract pages, but you do have to set it up properly.

The key element here is the TOC tab of the Document inspector. Select the paragraph styles that you want to appear in the table of contents. You don't select page numbers as a style; rather, you use the check boxes under numbers at the right to indicate whether that particular style should also have a page number.

If you're planning to export the document to an iOS device (and in many other cases as well), use the option at the bottom of the window so that the page numbers are active links. That makes the table of contents particularly useful.

All of this won't do you any good if you don't use these styles or if you use them inappropriately. For some people, this is the hardest part to remember. You can use a basic style such as Body throughout your document, and you can format headings, chapter names, and so on so that they look right. However, although they have the right font, size, and style, they will still be Body style elements, and they won't appear in the table of contents unless you've added Body to the styles to be shown (and that creates a pretty useless table of contents because it contains everything).

This is an issue with all word-processing software: People don't use the styles because you can create a document that looks just fine without them. However, not using styles prevents you from using features, such as automatic table of contents creation, in most of these programs.

Exporting the ePub file

Export the ePub file as soon as you can — even before the Pages document is finished. You want to export it and try it on the target device as soon as possible so that you can go back and change settings if you have to. Pretty soon, you'll be able to look at the Pages document and pinpoint areas that may be problematic when you export the file and try it on an iOS device.

Here are the steps to export an ePub file.

1. **Save your Pages document.**

   The export command doesn't change the Pages file itself, but you should not leave the file unsaved.

2. **Choose File⇨Export and click the ePub button at the top right of the window.**

3. **Fill in the title and author; choose the genre as well, as shown in Figure 12-15.**

   This information appears in the user's library.

   4. Click the Next button.

   You see a standard Save dialog.

   5. Locate the folder for the new file and provide a name.

   If you'll be sharing the file with friends via e-mail or the web, it's probably safest to not hide the extension (.epub) with the check box at the bottom left.

   You may see a warning about the export, as shown in Figure 12-16. Just because warnings appear doesn't mean that the export failed. Read the warnings, and you'll be able to see things that don't convert to ePub.

   6. Distribute the file.

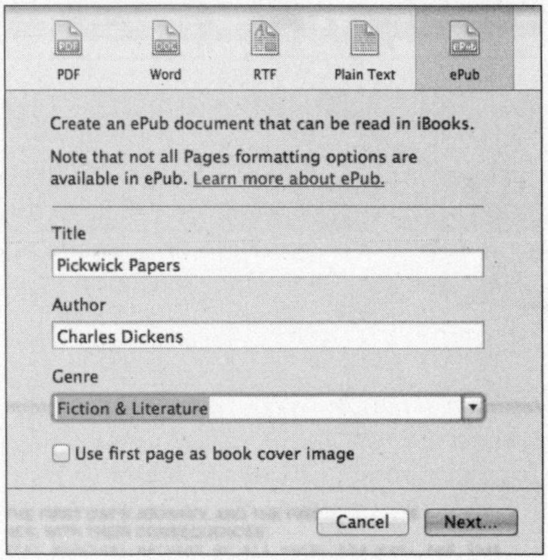

PDF	Word	RTF	Plain Text	ePub

Create an ePub document that can be read in iBooks.

Note that not all Pages formatting options are available in ePub. Learn more about ePub.

Title

Pickwick Papers

Author

Charles Dickens

Genre

Fiction & Literature ▼

☐ Use first page as book cover image

Cancel   Next...

Figure 12-15:
Identify your
ePub book.

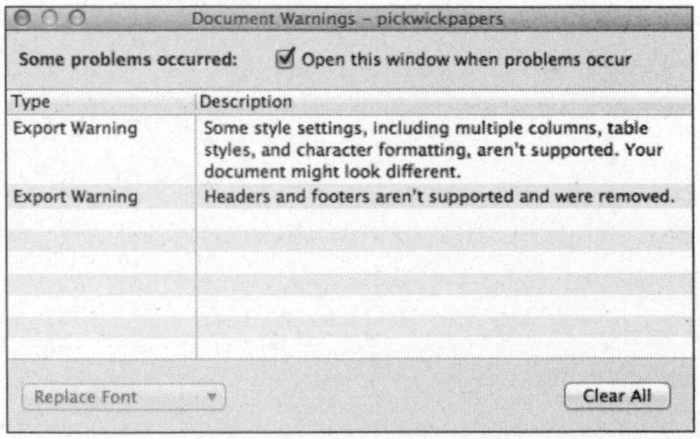

Figure 12-16:
Review any
warnings.

Document Warnings – pickwickpapers

Some problems occurred: ☑ Open this window when problems occur

Type	Description
Export Warning	Some style settings, including multiple columns, table styles, and character formatting, aren't supported. Your document might look different.
Export Warning	Headers and footers aren't supported and were removed.

Replace Font ▼   Clear All

Part III
Counting on Numbers

The 5th Wave
By Rich Tennant

"I started running 'what if' scenarios on my spreadsheet, like, 'What if I were sick of this dirtwad job and funneled some of the company's money into an off—shore account?"

In this part . . .

Numbers is the most recent addition to the iWork suite of applications. To call it a spreadsheet doesn't do it justice; it's like no other spreadsheet you've probably ever seen. Sure, you can create enormous sheets of rows and columns, but Numbers makes it easy to create useful and understandable spreadsheets. If you want to mystify people with your ability to throw hundreds (or thousands) of numbers on a page, you may want to look for another spreadsheet application. But if you want to use the iWork features to clarify your data and demystify all those numbers, Numbers is for you.

Chapter 13

Getting to Know Numbers

You've never seen a spreadsheet like a Numbers spreadsheet. Something about spreadsheets turns even the most imaginative and creative person into a zombie wandering through a maze with an infinite number of rows and columns. Well, in most cases, it's not infinite — in Microsoft Excel, somewhere around 1 million rows and 16,000 columns give you 17 billion cells you can use in your spreadsheet.

Numbers can be described in many ways, but one of the most direct ways is this: Numbers gives you every tool and technique the people of Apple could think of to help you manage your data without getting lost in 17 billion cells on a single spreadsheet. This chapter gives you an introduction to Numbers, starting with the basic design that tames spreadsheets and continuing with a guide to the features and functions in the Numbers window.

Of all the iWork apps, Numbers is the one with the fewest differences between Mac OS X and iOS.

Taming the Spreadsheet Jungle with Tables

In 1979, at the dawn of the personal computer era, the VisiCalc spreadsheet program, written for the Apple II, was one of the most popular programs. It was a fair representation of large accounting sheets with rows and columns that could accept any kind of data you entered. One spreadsheet was one file.

People quickly started bumping up against that limitation, and two changes came about over time:

✔ **Tables within spreadsheets:** Even though early spreadsheets were smaller than today's models, they still had almost unlimited rows and columns. People quickly learned that they could use a few rows and columns for a specific purpose, creating subspreadsheets or tables on that vast grid of cells. This made sense because within a single spreadsheet, it is possible to easily connect one set of cells to another. This means that these subspreadsheets and tables could automatically be updated if only one number was changed.

✔ **Linked spreadsheets:** There were issues with dumping multiple tables into a single spreadsheet. People clamored for the ability to have one spreadsheet automatically update and respond to updates in other spreadsheets in other files. Microsoft addressed this issue by creating documents called *workbooks;* each workbook can have a number of spreadsheets, all of which can communicate with one another. Today, when you create a Microsoft Excel document, you get a workbook with three sheets to start with.

The people at Apple took this decades-long history and designed Numbers in a radical, new way: It's designed not in the way software designers think people should use a spreadsheet, but in the way people have been using spreadsheets for three decades.

Adding tables to spreadsheets

When you create a Numbers document, you have three things to work with:

✔ **A Numbers document:** This is the container for everything. It's similar to a Microsoft Excel workbook.

✔ **One or more sheets:** You have one or more spreadsheets (*sheets* in the Numbers world of simplicity).

✔ **Zero or more tables:** The subspreadsheets or tables that people have been creating in Microsoft Excel and other spreadsheets exist in Numbers as formal structured tables. Numbers gives them a specific name: *tables.* (And, yes, you can have a Numbers document with no tables, but you have to have at least one sheet.)

The simple idea of making tables into an actual part of the Numbers application rather than letting people create them any which way leads to a major change in the way you can use Numbers when compared to an old-fashioned spreadsheet.

Working with tables

Now that tables are part of the software, Numbers can provide tools for managing them in ways that were not possible before (because tables as such never existed before for most people). You can see tables in action in documents created from the Numbers templates, such as the Travel Planner, which is used in this section.

Selecting tables

Because a table is a Numbers object, you can select it. Selecting a table isn't the same as selecting the cells in a subspreadsheet table. You don't have to worry about accidentally including or excluding cells that you don't want in the subspreadsheet table. A Numbers table has defined boundaries.

To select a table with Numbers for Mac, move the pointer over the border of the table until it changes to a black cross, as shown in Figure 13-1. You can also click the table in the Sheets pane at the left of the window. (You can find out more about the Sheets pane in the section "Exploring the Travel Planner document," later in this chapter.)

With Numbers for iPad and iPhone, just tap the table.

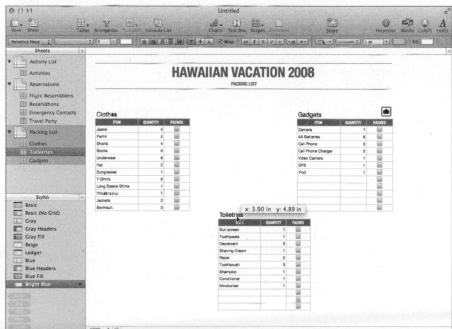

Figure 13-1:
You can
select
tables.

Numbers tables or iWork tables?

If tables are so important, and if Pages and Keynote both support them, why not just live your life with tables in Pages and Keynote? Until iWork '08 and the debut of Numbers, that's just what many people did. But many others found that although the tables in Keynote and Pages were powerful, they did not have all the features needed for spreadsheet development. Adding all that functionality to the basic iWork table structure would have added complexity to all iWork applications.

You now have the best of both worlds. If you want high-end spreadsheet tools, you can use Numbers, which has basic iWork shapes, text boxes, and media content features just like the other iWork applications. And if you want basic table functionality, you can use Keynote or Pages with the standard iWork tables. Just as the distinction between page layout and word-processing documents depends in many cases on an individual's preferences, the choice of tables in Pages or Keynote or tables in Numbers often is a matter of personal preference.

If you're accustomed to using spreadsheet applications, Numbers is probably a good choice for you. Although it goes dramatically beyond applications such as Microsoft Excel, Numbers still has a more "spreadsheety" feel. If spreadsheets give you a headache, try Numbers anyway, because it may cure that headache forever. If it doesn't, rest assured that you can do sophisticated table management in Keynote and Pages.

Moving and resizing tables

The sheet in Figure 13-1 has three tables. You can select a table and move it. As you drag it, you can see its current location. (This is a preference you turn on and off.)

Also, when a table is selected, the same eight handles you see on any selected shape in any iWork application are available so that you can resize the table.

Selecting table cells

You can select a cell in a table by clicking or tapping a cell. On Mac OS, when you select a cell in a table, *reference tabs* appear at the top and sides of the table, as shown in Figure 13-2. The reference tabs have row numbers and column letters — just like old-fashioned spreadsheets.

On iOS, selecting a cell in a table causes the column and row *frames* to appear, as shown in Figure 13-3.

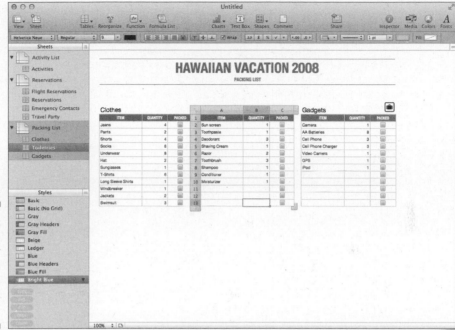

Figure 13-2:
Reference tabs appear in tables when cells are selected on Mac.

Figure 13-3:
Frames appear around tables when cells are selected on iOS.

Tap in a reference tab on Mac OS to select the entire row or column, as shown in Figure 13-4. You can also choose from commands that act on the entire row (or column).

On iOS, tap in a frame above or next to a column or row you want to select (see Figure 13-5). You can use the commands in the selection buttons, or you can use the Info popover to set the attributes of the cells in the row or column.

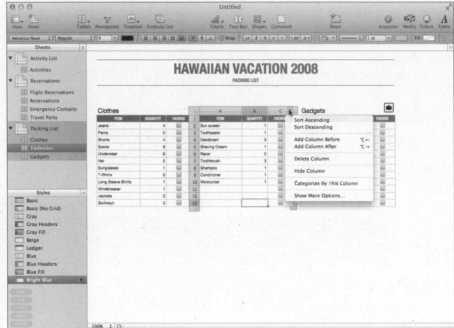

Figure 13-4:
Reference tab pop-up menus act on a row or column on Mac.

Creating a Numbers Document

The best way to get an overview of Numbers is to create a document and explore it. This section provides a high-level view. Later in this chapter and in the other chapters in Part III, you explore Numbers documents in more detail.

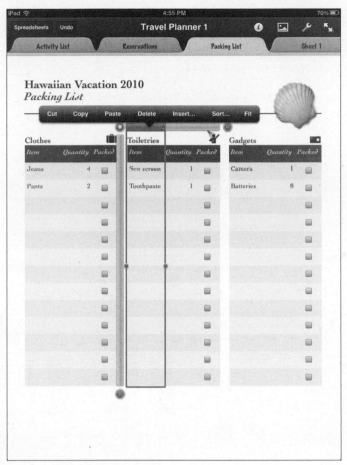

Figure 13-5:
Select an
entire row
or column
by tapping
in the row
or column
frame.

Creating the document

As with all iWork applications, you begin by creating a document from a template, as shown in Figure 13-6. Choose File⇒New Document from Template in Numbers to open this dialog.

On iOS, tap Spreadsheets at the left of the toolbar to open the popover to create a new document or open an existing one (see Figure 13-7). Tap + at the left of the toolbar to open the iOS templates.

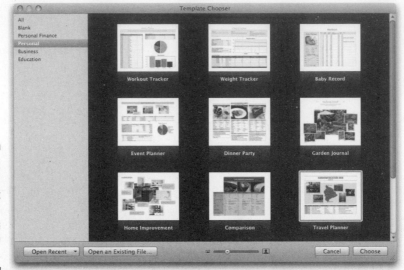

Figure 13-6:
Create a
document
from a
Numbers
template
on Mac.

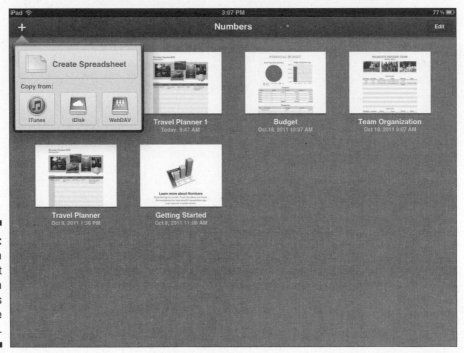

Figure 13-7:
Create a
document
from a
Numbers
template
on iOS.

As you browse through the templates, remember that on Mac, moving the pointer over a template's thumbnail image lets you see additional pages in the template. Explore the templates to get an idea of what you can do with Numbers. For most of this chapter, the Travel Planner template is used.

Create a document based on the Travel Planner template by double-clicking the Travel Planner template or by selecting it and clicking the Choose button in the lower right of the window. (On iOS, just tap the Travel Planner template.) Your screen will look like Figure 13-8.

Figure 13-8: Create a document from the Travel Planner template.

Exploring the Travel Planner document

The window shown in Figure 13-8 has six sections. The template has other sections, but this is the initial display. I go over each section in turn.

Sheet

The main part of the window displays a sheet from the document. The *sheet* can contain tables as well as other iWork objects such as shapes, text boxes, and media. You insert them from the toolbar or the Insert menu, as in any iWork application, which is a major difference between Numbers and other spreadsheet applications.

On Mac, choose Edit⇨Select All to select all the objects in the document. Figure 13-9 shows that the sheet has one table plus a text box for the title, a background shape for the title's background, a colored background for the center part of the sheet, five photos, a shape that is the map, and round shapes along with text boxes for the place names on the map. These objects are placed on the sheet, not inside a table or table cells. On iOS, tap each item individually to select it.

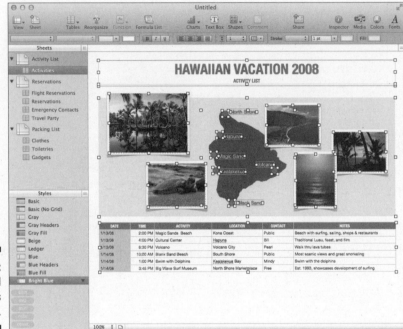

Figure 13-9:
Select all
the objects
in the sheet.

Toolbar (Mac only)

At the top of Figure 13-9, you see the Numbers toolbar. It contains buttons that are specific to Numbers as well as many that are common to other iWork applications, such as View, Charts, Text Box, Shapes, Inspector, Media, Colors, and Fonts. These buttons function as they do in the other applications. (The Inspector window has customized Numbers panes.) Tables, Functions, and Reorganize are unique to Numbers.

Format bar (Mac only)

The format bar is shown just below the toolbar. Like the toolbar, it can be shown or hidden. It has Numbers-specific features.

Sheets pane (Mac only)

At the left, you see the *Sheets pane*. It looks somewhat like the Page Thumbnails pane in Pages and the Slides pane in Keynote. Unlike those, however, you can't hide the Sheets pane, but you can resize it by dragging the divider between it and the sheet canvas to the left or right.

The Sheets pane shows the structure of the document. As you can see in Figure 13-9, there are three sheets — Activity List, Reservations, and Packing List — each of which contains tables (such as Activities, Travel Party, and Gadgets).

When you select a sheet or any table within a sheet, the sheet and all of its tables are highlighted. You can use the triangle to the left of a sheet name to collapse it, as shown in Figure 13-10.

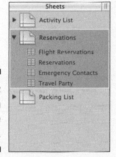

Figure 13-10: You can collapse sheets.

Sheets can contain not only tables but also charts. Tables include data shown in rows and columns; charts are graphs based on the tabular data.

At the bottom of the Sheets pane are the Styles pane and the instant calculations.

Changing table styles

Each table can have its own table style. Templates come with styles designed specifically for that template; you can add your own styles and modify the styles in your document.

Changing table styles on Mac

When you select a cell in a table, the Styles pane at the lower left of the window on Mac reflects the style for that table, as shown in Figure 13-11.

If you want to change the table's style, just click another style in the Styles pane, as shown in Figure 13-12.

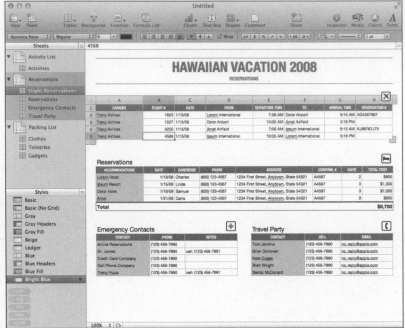

Figure 13-11:
Select a cell
in a table to
highlight the
table's style
in the Styles
pane.

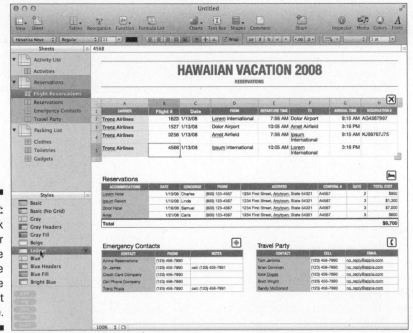

Figure 13-12:
Click
another
style in the
Styles pane
to change
the current
table's style.

Much as in the Pages Styles drawer, a triangle appears next to the selected style. You can click it to open the menu shown in Figure 13-13.

If you've modified a table's style, the Styles menu is where you can decide whether to change the style in every table that uses it or to create a new style.

Changing table styles on iOS

On iOS, you change table styles by selecting the table and using the Info pop-over, as shown in Figure 13-14. Make certain that you select Table at the top left to set the table style you want.

Figure 13-13:
Use the
Styles menu
to modify
table styles.

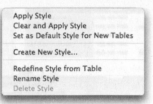

Figure 13-14:
Set table
styles
on iOS.

Instant calculation results (Mac only)

One of the most useful Numbers features on Mac is the set of instant calculation results at the bottom of the Styles pane. In Figure 13-15, a column of numbers has been selected in the second table. (To make the numbers easier to read, they've been enlarged and are shown in bold.)

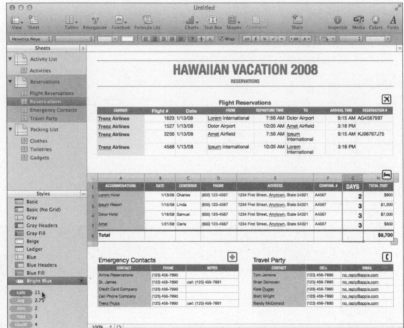

Figure 13-15:
Use instant calculations.

The instant calculation section automatically displays the results of a calculation using any selected cells. The selected cells can be a row, a column, or part of a row or column as well as noncontiguous cells selected by -clicking cells within a single table. The calculation results are sum, average, minimum value, maximum value, and count (the number of nonblank entries). You don't have to do anything for instant calculations to appear. They appear whenever your selection permits it.

Chapter 14

Creating and Editing Numbers Documents

● ●

In This Chapter

▶ Working with tables

▶ Using and formatting headers

▶ Taking advantage of cell formatting

● ●

Sometimes you can use an iWork template without any changes: Just type your text into a newsletter layout in Pages, use Keynote slides with no changes except for your text, or use a Numbers template just by typing your data. Other times, you want to customize the template in various ways, such as providing custom formatting for cells and creating your own headers for rows and columns. This chapter gets into the structure of Numbers documents, focusing on sheets and tables as well as basic formulas and common procedures such as sorting and filtering data.

As with all the iWork apps, the Mac version of Numbers has more options for customization than the iOS versions. Because many people (perhaps even most!) don't customize their spreadsheets in Numbers or any other spreadsheet program, this drawback isn't significant for them. If you do want or need the customization, you can always do it in Numbers for Mac and then work with the spreadsheets in Numbers for iOS.

Creating Sheets and Tables

Unless you're using a template without structural changes, such as adding new sheets, charts, or tables, you'll find yourself creating these objects. Chapter 15 is your resource for charts; this section shows you how to create new sheets and tables.

Creating sheets

You use sheets to organize your tables, charts, and other iWork elements, such as shapes, text boxes, and media. Sheets are often designed to be printed, so iWork provides a print view so that you can see what the sheet will look like when printed.

You can put all your charts and tables into a single sheet, or you can put one chart or table into each sheet. Most of the time, you decide which tables go into which sheets by taking into account what is most logical and how you need to print your data (if you need to print it at all). Most people make a case-by-case decision based on their way of working and the complexity of the data.

Creating a sheet on Mac

Here's how to create a sheet on Mac:

1. **Click Sheets on the toolbar to add a sheet or choose Insert⇨Sheet.**

   The sheet is named with a default name, such as Sheet 1, Sheet 2, and so on.

2. **Double-click the name of the sheet in the Sheets pane and type a descriptive name.**

   Alternatively, display Sheet inspector by opening an inspector and clicking the Sheet button (the second from the left in Figure 14-1). Figure 14-1 shows both methods of changing a sheet's name: changing the name in the Sheets pane and changing the name in Sheet inspector.

Creating a sheet on iOS

Here how to create a sheet on Numbers for iOS:

1. **Tap + at the right of the tabs, as shown in Figure 14-2.**

   A + tab always appears at the far right.

2. **Tap New Sheet in the popover.**

3. **Double-tap the tab name and type a descriptive name.**

   The name starts out as something like Sheet. If you already have named sheets (which is the case with the templates), the next one is usually Sheet 1.

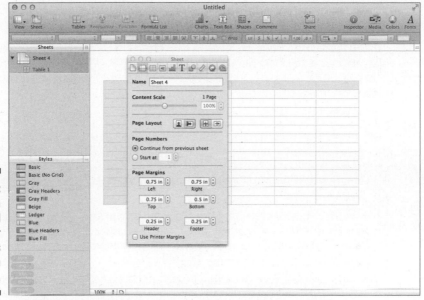

Figure 14-1:
Provide a
meaningful
name for
sheets as
soon as you
create them.

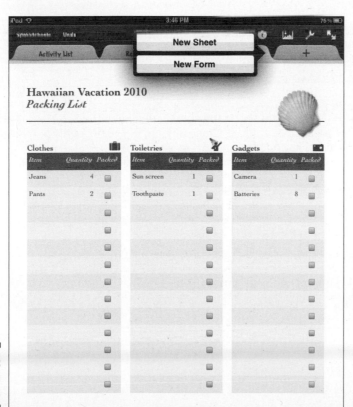

Figure 14-2:
Create a
new sheet.

Creating tables

The interface for creating tables is different on Mac and iOS, but the underlying process is basically the same. You can create six types of tables:

- **Headers:** Creates a table with headers for the rows and columns.

- **Basic:** Has headers only for the columns.

- **Sums:** A basic table that also has a row at the bottom for summary functions that add the numbers in each column. Numbers handles nonnumeric values appropriately so that text is not added in some mysterious manner to a numeric summary if you happen to type text such as *N/A* for a cell's value.

  On Mac, the formulas for the sums at the bottom are automatically inserted. You can always delete sums for any column you don't want summed. On iOS, the shaded row at the bottom is created, but it's up to you to add the formulas for the sums.

- **Plain:** The most basic table; it has no headers and no sums.

- **Checklist:** Has a header for columns and a column of check boxes at the left of the table.

- **Sums Checklist:** This combines a checklist and sums, with a header for each column, a check box at the left of each row, and a sum calculation at the bottom of each column. (This type of table is only available on Numbers for Mac.)

When you create a sheet, you automatically create a table within it. You can add charts or more tables to the sheet along with shapes, text boxes, and media. You can delete any of these objects to create an empty sheet, but by default, each new sheet contains a table.

Creating a new table on Mac

If you want to create a new table on a sheet, here's what you do:

1. **Select the sheet that the table will be placed in.**

   Select the sheet in the Sheets pane either by clicking the sheet name to select the sheet and all its contents or by clicking a chart or table within the sheet. The Sheet and all its contents are selected.

2. **Click the Tables menu on the toolbar and select the type of table you want to create, as shown in Figure 14-3.**

   You can also access this menu by choosing Insert⇨Table.

3. **Double-click the name of the table in the Sheets pane or in Table inspector, as shown in Figure 14-4, and type a meaningful name.**

   The check box to the left of the table name in Table inspector controls whether or not the table name is shown above the table on your sheet.

Figure 14-3:
Choose a
table.

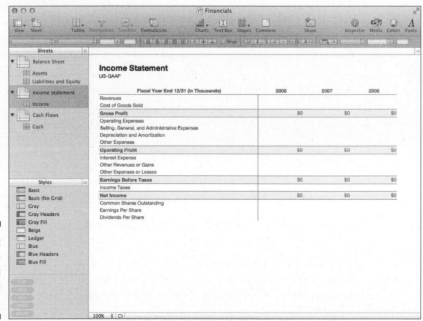

Figure 14-4:
Name the
table as
soon as you
create it.

Creating a new table on iOS

To create a new table on iOS, tap Insert and choose Tables from the top of the popover. Select the table you want to use, as shown in Figure 14-5.

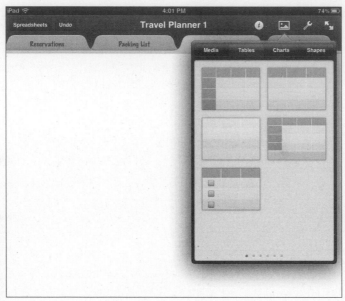

Figure 14-5:
Create a
new table
on iOS.

Modifying Tables

You can modify tables on a sheet. Just tap in any cell in the table to select the cell and the table. You see the row and column frames. In the top left, the circle is the tool you use to select the table and show its resize handles. Just as for any object, you can enlarge or shrink the circle by dragging a resize handle. The circles at the right of the column frame and the bottom of the row frame add a single column or row to the table.

Thus, you can change the size and shape of the table separately from adding rows or columns. Often, you do both.

Working with Headers

After you've created a table, you can change its headers and other settings, although you can't change one type of table (such as Sums) into another type (such as Checklist). One way around this limitation, however, is to change the separate settings for check boxes, sums, and headers.

Spreadsheets label columns with letters (A, B, C, and so on) and rows with numbers (1, 2, 3, and so on). Each cell within a table is uniquely identified with a letter and number: The cell in the upper left of a table is A1. The Financials template (part of the Business category of Numbers templates) provides an example of how headers can work. The row and column labels appear when you click in a cell to start editing the table. When you finish editing (for example, by clicking elsewhere in the sheet rather than in the table), the row and column labels disappear.

Figure 14-6 is the Income table in the Income Statement sheet for the Financials template, as shown on Mac.

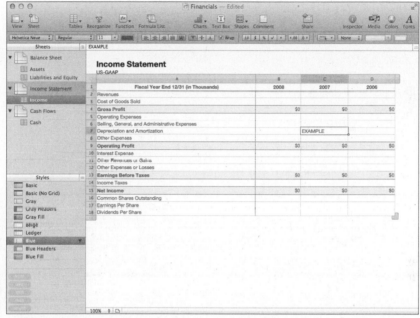

Figure 14-6:
Understand
how
Numbers
uses head-
ers on Mac.

Figure 14-7 is the same table shown on iPad. The row and column labels appear when you're editing a calculation. (You can find more on calculations in Chapter 15.) Double-tap a cell to begin editing it and then tap = to begin entering a calculation and to simultaneously show the row and column labels.

The cell containing the word *EXAMPLE* in Figure 14-6 is in column C and row 7; its identifier is C7. However, because the first row of the table is a header row and because the first column of the table is a header column, the text in those headers can also identify the cell: 2007 Depreciation and Amortization. In Numbers, you don't name cells. Instead, you name their column and row headers, and Numbers uses those to name each cell.

If Numbers can't find a header for a cell's row or column, it reverts to the old letter-and-number naming, such as C7. It also reverts to the old letter-and-number naming if you have duplicate header names. If, for example, you change the column for 2006 and type 2007 in its header, you'll have two 2007 header columns. In the case of such duplication, Numbers provides you with a reliable (but less user-friendly) letter-and-number name.

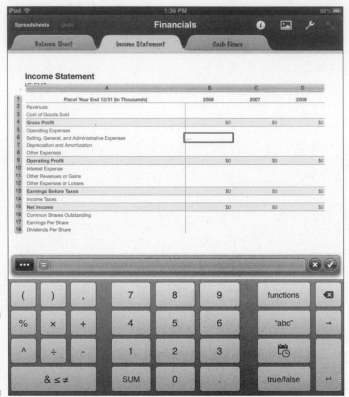

Figure 14-7:
View the same table on iPad.

Because Numbers is going to be using your header names to label cells, those names should be unique and descriptive. You only have to type them once. Numbers can handle duplicate names, but why complicate your life?

Numbers will also revert to letter-and-number naming if you don't have headers or don't have both row and column headers. Whenever possible, use both row and column headers, either by creating a table with both of them (the headers table) or by adding headers to your table.

Adjusting the number of header rows and columns in a table

Follow these steps to adjust the number of header rows and columns on Mac OS:

1. **Select the table.**

2. **Open Table inspector.**

   If you don't have an Inspector window open, open one by clicking Inspector on the toolbar. Then click the Table button (the third button from the left).

3. **In the Headers & Footer section, choose the number of rows or columns for each type of header and footer.**

   The three icons shown in Figure 14-8 let you set the number of header rows or columns for columns, headers, and footers (reading from left to right).

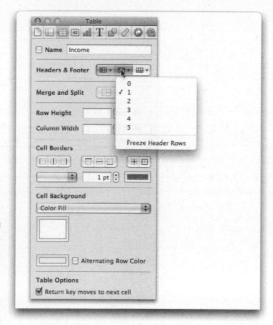

Figure 14-8: Adjust headers in a table on Mac OS.

On iOS, select a cell in the table you want to adjust and then open the Info popover, as shown in Figure 14-9. Tap Headers at the top to set headers and footers.

You can freeze header rows or columns (but not a footer row) using Table inspector on Mac OS or the Info popover on iOS. Freezing header rows or columns means that as you scroll through the table, the header rows or columns are always visible. If they're not frozen, you can scroll them out of sight.

Figure 14-9:
Adjust
headers
on iOS.

Formatting headers and creating a new style

Because headers are so important, you may want to emphasize them in your tables. Some of the templates have styles that clearly show headers in contrasting colors; others are more subtle. You may want a dramatic formatting for headers while you are entering data and a more standard formatting when you're finished.

Here's how to change heading formatting and how to save it as a new style on Mac OS X so that you can switch back and forth between the old and new styles of heading formatting:

1. **Select the header row (or rows) you want to format by clicking in the numbered label for the row at the left of the table, as shown in Figure 14-10.**

   The small triangle brings up a contextual menu that lets you add or delete header rows or columns. You don't need to worry about using it at this point.

2. **In Table inspector, make a selection in the Cell Background menu, as shown in Figure 14-11, and then select the color or image you want to use.**

   Your choices are Color Fill, Gradient Fill, Image Fill, and Tinted Image Fill.

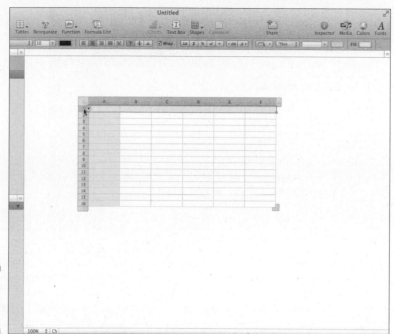

Figure 14-10:
Select a
header row.

Figure 14-11:
Use Table
inspector
to select a
cell back-
ground for
the selected
row.

3. **If you want a header column to be formatted, repeat Steps 1 and 2 with the header column.**

4. **In the Styles pane, click the arrow next to the name of the current style and choose Create New Style, as shown in Figure 14-12.**

5. **Name the new style.**

The new style appears in the Styles pane and you can use it for any table in the document.

You can switch back and forth between styles at any time. Select the object to which you want to apply a style and then click the style name from the list in the Styles pane. The style will be changed immediately for the selected object.

On iOS, you change the formatting of cells either individually or in an entire column. (See the following section for cell formatting.)

Just as using styles can improve Pages documents, style use can improve Numbers documents and save time. Instead of adjusting various table settings each time you want a new look, combine the settings into a new style that you can select with one click. Having many styles in the document is not a prob-lem as long as you give them descriptive names so that you can remember what they represent.

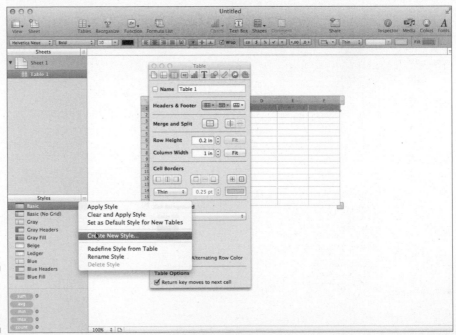

Figure 14-12:
Create a
new style.

Formatting Cells

Each cell in a table can have its own formatting. You use the format bar to set basic formatting, such as fonts and alignment. Cells inspector lets you set the way data in the cell (or range of selected cells) is displayed with decimals, currency symbols, and so forth.

Using basic formats for cells

Figure 14-13 shows the Cells inspector on Mac. The Cell Format pop-up menu (which is set to Number in Figure 14-13) determines the format. As you change its value, the middle of the Cells inspector changes to provide additional settings for that format.

On iOS, instead of the inspector, select the cell(s) you're interested in and open the Info popover, as shown in Figure 14-14. Tap Format at the top right to select a format.

On iOS, you can select all the cells in a row or column by tapping a cell in the row or column. The row and column frames appear, and you can tap the appropriate row or column to select all its cells, as shown in Figure 14-15.

Note the resize handles in the selected row or column. You can expand the selection to include several rows or columns. Also, note the two parallel lines at the top of a selected column or the bottom left of a selected row. You can drag them to resize the column or row.

Figure 14-13: Format cells with Cells inspector on Mac.

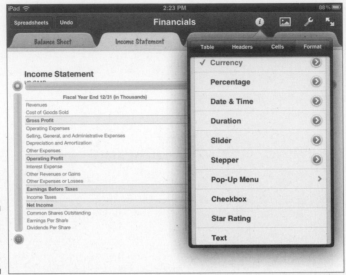

Figure 14-14:
Select a format on iOS.

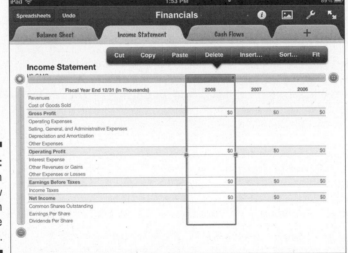

Figure 14-15:
Select an entire row or column using the frame.

If one cell is selected, the formatting affects only that cell. If you select a number of cells, the formatting you set affects all those cells. If you select a number of cells that have different formatting, the Cells inspector pop-up menu is blank. (It can't display more than a single value.) When you choose a new format from the pop-up menu, it's applied to all the selected cells.

Figure 14-16 shows the various formats built into Numbers for Mac. They are also available on iOS with the exception of

- ✔ Fraction
- ✔ Numeral System
- ✔ Scientific

Automatic and Custom are not, strictly speaking, formats; they're not available on iOS.

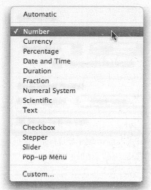

Figure 14-16:
Select a
format
on Mac.

Many of the settings for cell formats appear in more than one cell format. Here are some of the settings that are available and the formats for which you can set them:

- ✔ **Thousands separator:** Most numeric formats let you choose whether or not to use a thousands separator. (You set this in ⌘⇨System Preferences using International (Language & Text on Lion) and its Formats tab. For the United States, the thousands separator is a comma.) Available for Number, Currency, and Percentage.

- ✔ **Negative number formats:** Your choices are parentheses, the color red, a minus sign, or red in parentheses. Sometimes a check box called Accounting Style is used for the option. Available for Number, Currency, and Percentage.

- ✔ **Decimals:** The number of decimal places to be used. Available for Number, Currency, Percentage, and Scientific.

- ✔ **Currency symbol:** With Cell inspector, you can change the currency symbol for specific cells in a spreadsheet. Available for Currency.

- ✔ **Fraction:** You can specify the amount of precision; examples are given such as 7/8 (one digit), 23/24 (two digits), halves, and quarters. Available for Fraction.

Using special formats for cells

Numbers has special formats that can make your tables much easier to use. These standard controls appear in a variety of applications, such as iPhoto, Finder, and Bento on both Mac OS X and iOS:

- ✔ **Check box:** A check box is either checked or not. The first column of cells in the built-in checklist table consists of check boxes. Figure 14-17 shows a check box cell and the Cells inspector settings for it. The underlying value of the cell is either TRUE or FALSE depending on whether or not it is checked. You can prove this for yourself by formatting a cell as a check box and then using Cells inspector to change it to text or automatic formatting. The value of the cell is maintained when its formatting is changed. (This applies to all types of cells, not just check boxes.)

The figures in this section show Mac OS X, but these special formats are also available — and look the same — on iOS.

- ✔ **Stepper:** This is another quick form of data entry. As you can see in Figure 14-18, you can use Cells inspector to specify the range of values that the stepper supports. Steppers are useful for limiting input to certain values. The stepper itself is shown only when the cell is selected. When it is not selected, the value of the cell is displayed.

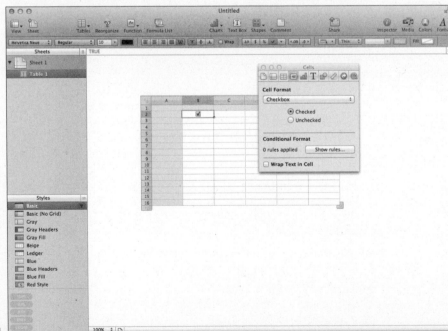

Figure 14-17:
Check boxes provide on/off or true/false settings with the click of a mouse.

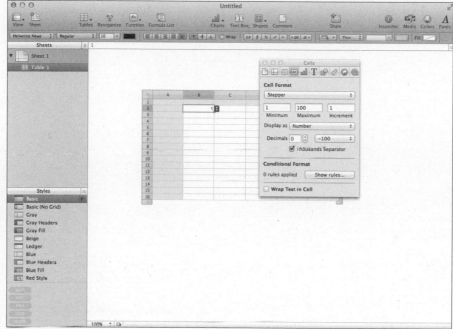

Figure 14-18:
Steppers let you move through a range of values.

✔ **Slider:** A stepper lets you increase or decrease a value by a certain amount. A slider lets you move quickly across a range of values. As shown in Figure 14-19, you can also specify the range and the intervals that a slider represents. Like a stepper, the slider is displayed only when a cell is selected. At other times, the value is shown in the cell.

✔ **Pop-Up Menu:** Pop-up menus work best for nonnumeric data, as shown in Figure 14-20. You start with three values. Double-click each row to type a new value. You can add or delete rows by using the + and – buttons at the lower left of the list of values.

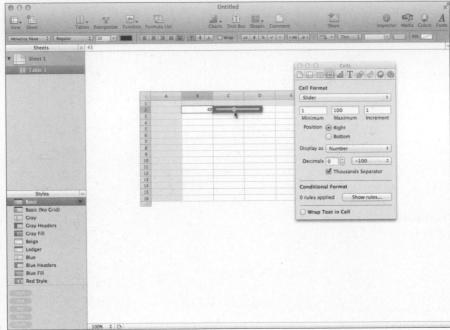

Figure 14-19:
Sliders
provide a
fast way of
changing
values.

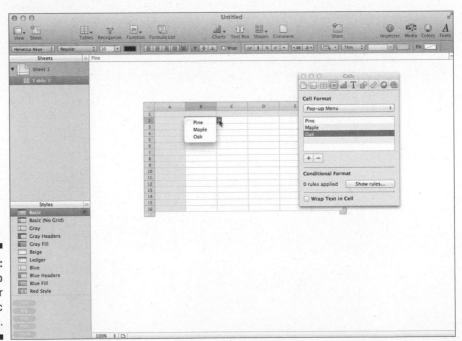

Figure 14-20:
Use pop-up
menus for
nonnumeric
data.

Formatting cells on iOS

When you select a cell and show the Info popover, you can also use Cells at the top to adjust formatting, fill color, and border styles as you see in Figure 14-21. This is how you provide the appearance produced by headers on Mac OS X.

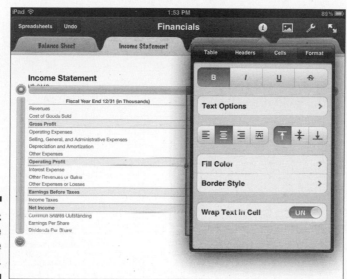

Figure 14-21:
Adjust the appearance of cells.

Chapter 15

Working with Cells and Formulas (iOS)

Numbers presents an interesting contrast between the Mac OS and iOS versions. The iOS version uses the various keyboards built into iOS, but the Mac version (no surprise here!) uses the regular Mac keyboard along with a variety of context-sensitive commands on the interface. Beneath these two distinct interfaces, the documents function the same way with minor exceptions.

The template used to illustrate the Mac features is the Financials template on Numbers for Mac. You can create a document from that template and then use iCloud, iWork.com, iTunes sharing, or e-mail to move it to an iOS device and continue with the Mac example shown in this chapter.

Because the interfaces for cell data entry and formulas are so different, the iOS and Mac versions of numbers are described separately. The iOS version is described in this chapter, and the OS X version is described in Chapter 16.

Working with Cells

You tap or double-tap a cell to work with it. If you want to add or edit data, double-tap a cell. A blue outline appears around the cell, and the keyboard appears so that you can begin entering data. Single-tap if you want to select a cell. The cell is outlined, and the table-selection elements (the column and row frames, the Cells button, the round button to the left of the column frame, and the button to the right of the column frame as well as beneath the row frame) appear.

A double-tap always makes the cell available for editing. Figure 15-1 shows how, after a double-tap in a cell, the keyboard appears.

After you've set up your spreadsheet, most of your work consists of entering and editing data of all types. That's what you'll find out about in this section.

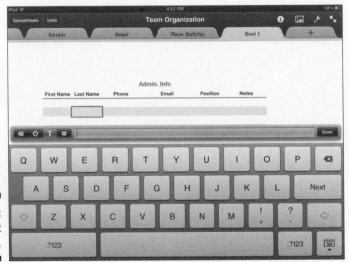

Figure 15-1: Start to edit a cell's data.

Entering and editing data

The keyboard for entering data into a Numbers cell is a powerful and flexible tool — it's actually four keyboards in one. Above the keyboard is a formula bar that lets you quickly and easily enter formulas. At the left of the formula bar are four buttons that let you switch from one keyboard to another. Starting from the left, you can choose the following keyboards:

- ✔ **42:** The first button, labeled 42, lets you use the numeric keyboard.

- ✔ **Clock:** The second button, with the image of a clock, lets you enter dates and times.

- ✔ **Text:** The letter T displays a standard text keyboard.

- ✔ **Formulas:** The = sign brings up the formula-editing keyboard.

Whichever keyboard you're using, you see what you're typing in the formula bar above the keyboard. To the right of the oblong area is a button labeled

Done (or OK, depending on which keyboard you're using) that moves your typing into the selected cell and then hides the keyboard.

You can bring up the keyboard only when you double-tap a cell or other text field (such as a tab name). That means it's selected, and it also means that the keyboard knows where the data should go when you tap OK or Done.

To the right of the keyboard area are three large buttons:

- ✔ **Delete:** This is the standard keyboard delete button located at the top right of the keyboard. As you see in Figure 15-1, it uses the left-pointing backspace character.

- ✔ **Next (adjacent):** The Next button with the right-pointing arrow inserts the typed data into the selected cell and moves to the next cell to the right.

- ✔ **Next (next line):** The Next button with the hooked arrow pointing left inserts the typed data and moves to the next line and to the left-most cell in the section of cells you are entering. For example, if you start in the third column of the fourth row, the Next (next line) button moves you to the third column of the fifth row, not the first column. (This button is not available on the text keyboard.)

Entering numeric data

The numeric keyboard (accessed by tapping the 42 button) has a typical numeric keypad along with four large buttons on the left. (Refer to Figure 15-2.) These four buttons let you choose the formatting for the cell you are editing. If you a need symbol (such as stars for ratings or a currency symbol), it will be added before or after the numeric value as is appropriate. Your formatting options are, from top to bottom:

- ✔ **Currency:** This adds the appropriate currency symbol, such as $ or € according to your settings in System Preferences.

- ✔ **Percentage:** The percent symbol follows the value.

- ✔ **Stars (rating):** This lets you display a number from one to five as a star rating. Numbers over five are displayed with five stars. To change the number of stars, type a new number or tap the star display in the cell or in the display above the keyboard. You can use stars in a spreadsheet and then sort the column of stars so that the ratings are ordered from highest to lowest or vice versa.

- ✔ **Check box:** A check box is either selected or not. Check boxes are selected and deselected by a user or as the result of a calculation.

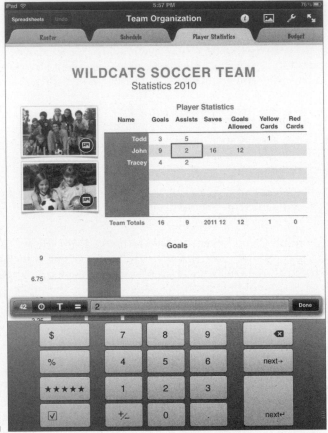

Figure 15-2:
The numeric. keyboard lets you enter currency, percentages, stars, and check boxes.

Customizing check boxes

A check box can indicate, for example, that an item is in stock or out of stock (yes/no or true/false). However, you can also use a check mark to represent numeric data. Computers and programs often represent yes/no or true/false values. That's one way you can use check boxes to track inventory. If you have the number of in-stock items in a cell, you can use a check box to indicate that none are in stock (an unchecked check box) or that there are items in stock (a checked check box). Numbers will handle the conversion for you.

Here's how that can work:

1. **Double-tap a cell to start editing it, and tap the Checkbox button as soon as the keyboard opens.**

   You see a check box in the selected cell; in the area above the keyboard, you see the word *false* in a green outline, as shown in Figure 15-3. The green outline distinguishes it from text that you type. It has the value false because before you've typed anything, its numeric value is zero.

Figure 15-3:
A check box
starts as off
and false.

2. **Type a nonzero value.**

   This value may represent the number of items in stock, for example.

3. **Tap the Checkbox button again.**

   The value you typed is changed to *true* (see Figure 15-4), and the check box is selected in the table.

   Because the formatting is separate from the data value, you can sometimes display the in-stock inventory count as a number and sometimes as the check box. All customers probably care about is the check box, but the inventory manager cares about the number.

Figure 15-4:
A nonzero
value is on
and true.

Everything in Numbers is linked, so you don't have to worry about a sequence for doing most things. If you've followed these steps, you've seen how to enter a number and have it control a check box, but that's only one of at least three ways of working with a check box.

With a cell selected and the Checkbox formatting button selected, you'll see the true/false value above the keyboard and the check box itself in the table cell. Tap the check box in the table cell: The true/false value is reversed, as is the check box itself.

Likewise, if you tap the word *true* or *false* in the display above the keyboard, the check box will flip its value, and true/false will reverse.

When you tap one of the formatting buttons, it turns blue and formats the number in the selected cell (or cells). You can tap another formatting button to switch to another format (from stars to a percentage, for example). Tapping a highlighted formatting button turns it off.

Entering date/time data

Tap the clock to enter date/time or duration data, as shown in Figure 15-5. The Date & Time button lets you specify a specific moment, and the Duration button lets you specify (or calculate) a length of time.

Figure 15-5:
Enter date
or duration
data.

Above the keyboard, the units of a date or duration are displayed. To enter or edit a date and/or time, tap Month in the formula bar and use the keypad to select the month. (The keys have both the month name abbreviations and the month numbers on them.) Similarly, tap any of the other components and enter a value. As you do so, the display changes to show the value. (Tapping AM or PM just toggles that value — you don't need to type anything.)

If you select a cell containing Date & Time or Duration data, you can use the Info button to choose the formatting to use. There's a particularly interesting user interface for the duration formatting shown in Figure 15-6. The possible components of duration are shown at the top of the view (week, day, hour, minute, second, and millisecond). Above them, a display lets you know which ones are currently selected. Drag the left or right border to display the units you want displayed. They will always be in sequence, so you can display hours, minutes, and seconds, but not hours and seconds.

Entering text data

When you tap T to enter text data, the QWERTY keyboard appears, as shown in Figure 15-7.

You can switch among letters, numbers, and special characters. Everything you type goes into the selected cell until you tap the Done button to the right of the display above the keyboard. If you enter a Return character, that's part of the text in the cell. The cell automatically grows vertically to accommodate the text you type, and you can resize the column so that the cell is the appropriate size.

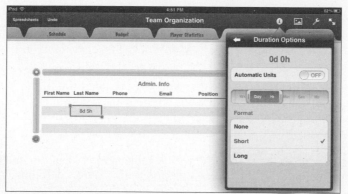

Figure 15-6:
Customize
the duration
format.

Figure 15-7:
Enter text.

Entering formulas

Tapping the = button lets you enter a formula, which automatically computes values based on the data you type in. You can display the result of the formula in a cell in any of the usual formats and then use that value in a chart.

When you're entering a formula, the four buttons controlling the date/time, text, and numeric keyboards disappear. In their place, a button with three dots appears. Tapping it returns you to the display that includes the other three keyboards. It's just a matter of Numbers saving space.

There's good news and bad news when it comes to formulas. The good news is that you don't have to type many common formulas: Almost all spreadsheets have the same built-in list of formulas. The bad news is that it's a very long list of formulas.

Formulas can consist of numbers, text, dates, durations, and true/false values. They can also include the results of formulas and the values of individual cells.

Here are the basics of creating a very simple formula in Numbers. The example in this section is about as simple as you can get. It takes the value of an existing cell, adds a number to it, and then displays it as a result in the cell that contains the formula. In this example, I'm using the Team Organization template that you see in the figures throughout this chapter.

The formula takes the starting time of a game, adds two and a half hours to it, and displays the estimated completion time in a new column. This is what you do to get there:

1. **Rename the Title column to Start.**

2. **Add a column to its right and name it End.**

3. **Select the cell into which you want to put the formula by double-tapping it.**

   I selected the End column cell next to Start, as you see in Figure 15-8.

4. **Tap the = button at the top-left side of the keyboard.**

   The keyboard changes to the formula keyboard shown in Figure 15-9.

   Note that the table's column and row frames now contain row and column identifiers. The columns are labeled A, B, C, and so on; the rows are labeled 1, 2, 3, and so on. You can identify every cell by its coordinates (such as A1 for the top-left cell).

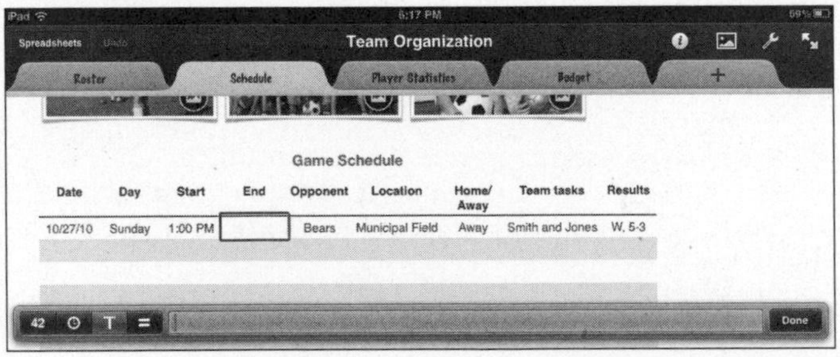

Figure 15-8:
Select the cell that will contain the formula.

Also note that, at the right of the keyboard, you have a different set of buttons than in the text, date, and number keyboards. To the immediate right of the keypad, you'll find four buttons that do the following:

- *Functions:* Brings up a list of functions, as you see in Step 3.

- *abc:* Displays the text keyboard. You can type text and tap Done, and the text is added to the formula you're constructing. You're then returned to the formula keyboard.

- *Date/Time:* The button with the calendar and clock on it takes you to the date keyboard. The date or duration that you enter uses the same interface you see in Figure 15-18. When you tap Done, the date or duration is added to the formula, and you're returned to the formula keyboard.

- *True/False:* Utilizes the same interface as check boxes; the result is added to the formula you're constructing, and you return to the formula keyboard.

5. **Add the game starting time to the formula.**

   Just tap the cell containing the game start time. The formula reflects the name of the table and the referenced cell. In this case, that reference is

   ```
   C2
   ```

   This references column C, row 2 in the Game Schedule table. You don't have to type a thing — just tap, and the correct cell is referenced.

   You now need the formula to add two and a half hours to the starting time.

6. **Tap + from the operators on the left side of the keyboard.**

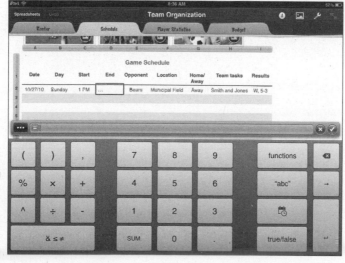

Figure 15-9: Begin to create a formula.

7. **Tap the Date/Time button to the right of the keyboard and then tap the Duration button at the left.**

8. **On the formula bar, tap Hours and enter** 2.

9. **Tap Minutes and enter** 30.

Figure 15-10 shows what the screen should look like now.

Figure 15-10: Enter the formula.

10. **Tap Done.**

This means you're done with entering the duration. You return to the formula keyboard.

11. **Finish the formula by tapping the button with a check mark on it.**

Figure 15-11 shows the formula as it is now. Note that instead of a Done button, as with the other keyboards, there's a button with a check mark and a button with an X at the right. The X cancels the formula, and the check mark completes it. If you want to modify the formula with the keys (including Delete) on the keyboard, feel free to do so.

Changing a cell's formatting

Your end time may include the date, which is probably not what you want. Here's how you change the formatting of a cell:

1. **Select the cell with a single tap.**

You can also select a cell and drag the highlighted selection to include more than one cell. Your reformatting affects all the selected cells.

2. **Tap the Info button at the top of the screen.**

3. **In the Info popover, tap Format.**

4. **Tap the format you want to use in the selected cell(s), or tap the arrow at the right of the format name to customize the format.**

Not all formats have customizations.

To properly format the end time cell, you may want to remove the date. Tap Date & Time Options and set the date option for None and the time option for the hour, as shown in Figure 15-12.

Figure 15-11: Tap the check mark to accept the formula.

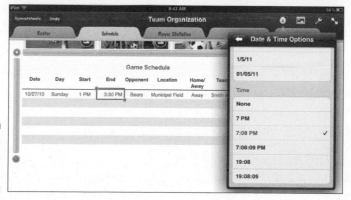

Figure 15-12: Format the result.

Utilizing Forms

A *form* is a user-friendly way of providing input to a single row of a spreadsheet. A simple form such as one you fill out on a clipboard at your doctor's office is much easier for many people to deal with. Because a form interacts with a table, you must create a table in your spreadsheet before you can create an associated form.

To create a form, tap the + tab on the far-right end of the row of tabs. You're asked whether you want to create a new sheet or a form. Choose New Form, and you see a screen similar to the one shown in Figure 15-13; I'm using my Team Organization template for the example.

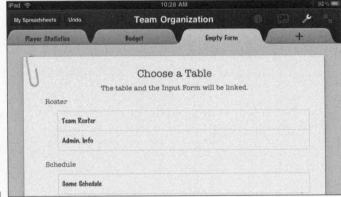

Figure 15-13:
Start to
create a
form.

You see a list of all the sheets and all the tables on them. Choose the one that the form will be used with. In this case, I'm using my Admin. Info table.

Each form is associated with one and only one table, and each table can be associated with only one form (though it doesn't have to be associated with any forms).

The form is then created automatically, as shown in Figure 15-14.

The labels for the columns on the form are drawn from the labels of the columns on the tables. You don't have to label the columns on your tables, but it makes creating forms and calculations much easier if you do so.

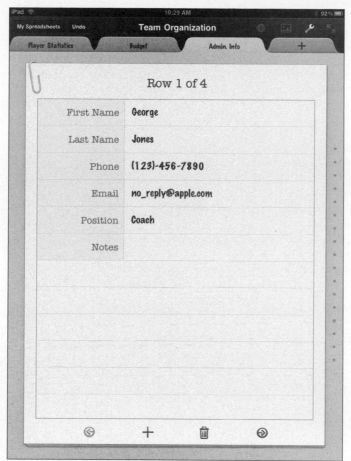

Figure 15-14:
Use a form
to browse,
enter, and
delete data.

You can use the tab to go to the form and enter data or browse through it. The four buttons at the bottom of a form let you (from left to right) go to the previous record (row), add a new row, delete the current row, or go to the next row.

Note that you can delete a form by tapping the form's tab and then tapping Delete, but you can't duplicate a form as you can duplicate a sheet tab.

Chapter 16

Working with Cells and Formulas (Mac)

*O*ne of the most important features of any spreadsheet is the ability to place formulas into cells. Other spreadsheets, such as Microsoft Excel, offer functions and formulas — often the same ones you find in Numbers. Spreadsheet users expect to find a SUM function along with a TODAY function and all the other functions that they're accustomed to, particularly if they switch back and forth between spreadsheet applications or if they're sharing their documents. What sets Numbers apart is the ease with which you can create and manage formulas along with the large number of templates that implement sophisticated uses of formulas and functions.

Starting to Use Formulas

Formulas can contain specific values (called *constants* and sometimes *literals*); they also can contain references to cells in the spreadsheet. If a formula contains a reference to a cell, every time that cell's value is updated, the formula is reevaluated. A formula can contain a reference to a cell that itself contains a formula. There is no limit to the number of formulas in the chain of formulas for a given cell. Whenever the first value in the chain is changed, every formula is reevaluated. The only limitation to this chain of formulas is that it has to be a single path. You can't create what is called a *circular reference,* a formula that relies on evaluating a previous cell that contains a formula that includes the current cell. This reference would require that each cell be evaluated before the other one is evaluated — something that is logically impossible. One of them has to be first, and one has to be second.

In addition to cell references and constants, formulas can contain *functions,* such as a function that sums a set of numbers. Formulas also can provide information that doesn't rely on values in the spreadsheet. For example, the TODAY function in most spreadsheets returns today's date. If you're working late and the clock strikes midnight, the TODAY function will return the date for the new day.

Using a formula to summarize data

Perhaps the most common formula is a summary at the bottom of a column, which is where most people place a summary when they work with paper and pencil. Summaries can also appear at the top of a column or on the right or left of a row. Spreadsheets also make it easy to place a row or column summary in another location on the spreadsheet (perhaps a section of summary data in which all sums are shown for all relevant columns or rows). The built-in tables have built-in summary formats; the Sums and Sums Checklist tables have built-in summaries at the bottom of each column. (You can find out more about summaries in "Working with Functions," later in this chapter.)

The example in this section uses the Financials template in the Business section of the Numbers templates, as shown in Figure 16-1. I've entered some test data for the figures in this section.

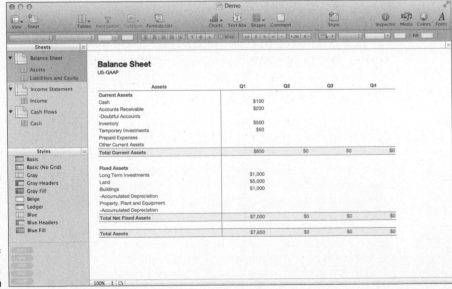

Figure 16-1:
Summarize
data in col-
umns and
sections of
columns.

If you experiment with the template, you'll see that the summary at the bottom of the table is not the sum of all the numbers in a column. Rather, the column has several sections, each of which is summed:

- ✔ **Total Current Assets ($850):** This is the sum of rows 3 through 9. It has distinct formatting to separate it from the detail lines above it.

- ✔ **Total Net Fixed Assets ($7,000):** This is the sum of rows 13 through 18.

- ✔ **Total Assets ($7,850):** This is the sum of Total Current Assets and Total Net Fixed Assets. If you added all the numbers in the column, you would get a column total that is exactly twice what it should be because it would include both the detail rows (3 through 9 and 13 through 18) and their subtotals.

Summarizing data that already includes subsummaries is one of the most frequent spreadsheet errors. Always do a reality check on your formulas. The arithmetic total of all numbers in the Q1 column in Figure 16-1 is $23,550. The total of all the detail lines is $7,850, which is the real total not including subsummaries.

In the Financials template, the correct summarization has been done for you. If you had to work from scratch, here's how to do subsummaries, such as Total Current Assets and Total Net Fixed Assets, as well as the grand summary, Total Assets:

1. **Remove the formulas from the Financials template.**

   This step lets you practice implementing the formulas for yourself. Select the cells that summarize data (B10 through E10 for Total Current Assets, B19 through E19 for Total Net Fixed Assets, and B21 through E21 for Total Assets). Then choose Edit⇨Delete. This deletes data values and formulas but leaves the formatting intact.

2. **Check that all formulas have been removed.**

   After you delete the formulas, the summary cells will be blank. If any cell displays $0, it means that a subsummary cell (such as Total Current Assets) has been cleared, but the grand total (Total Assets) retains its formula. Except for the cells in which data is typed, you should not have any numbers in the main part of the table.

Creating formulas using the SUM function and a range of cells

The first summary to create is the Q1 summary of Total Current Assets. Then you can copy it to Q2, Q3, and Q4. Follow these steps:

1. **Begin to build the formula.**

   In cell B10 (Q1 Total Current Assets), type =. Typing = at the beginning of a cell starts to build a formula. Formula Editor opens, as shown in Figure 16-2.

2. **Select the cells you want to summarize.**

   In this case, select cells B3 through B9 (Cash, Accounts Receivable, Doubtful Accounts, Inventory, Temporary Investments, Prepaid Expenses, and Other Current Assets). Formula Editor displays the cells you're summarizing, as shown in Figure 16-3. By default, it uses the SUM function.

3. **Click the check mark to accept the formula and close Formula Editor.**

   The calculation is performed, as shown in Figure 16-4.

   Verify that the formula is working correctly by changing various numbers in the cells that are part of the formula; the result will change.

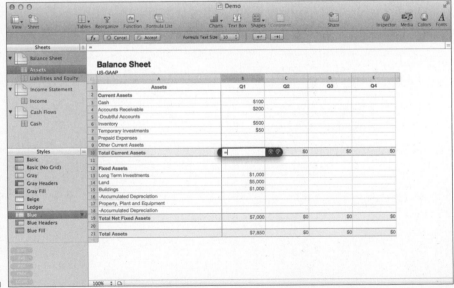

Figure 16-2: Open Formula Editor by typing = in the cell.

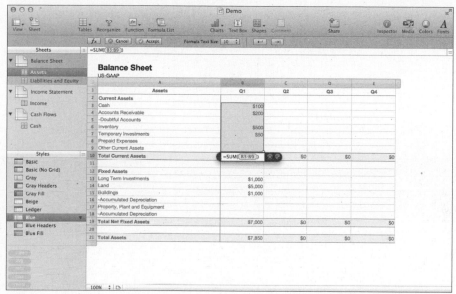

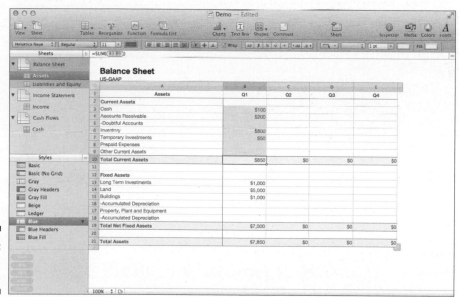

4. Copy the formula from Q1 to the Q2, Q3, and Q4 cells.

The simplest way is to select the Q1 cell, where you've created the formula, and drag to add Q2, Q3, and Q4 to the selection. Choose Insert⇨Fill⇨Fill Right to fill the formula into the other selected cells.

Note that you can fill right or down. The first cell in the selection must contain the formula you want to fill to the adjoining cells. If a formula uses other cells in its calculation, the filled formula cells will use the appropriate numbers. In other words, the Total Current Assets formula that is filled into Q2 will use the Q2 data values, not the Q1 data values.

Create the subsummary formulas for Total Net Fixed Assets in the same way. SUM is the default function, but there are 250 built-in functions. The most commonly used functions are available from the Function menu on the toolbar. Select the cells you want to use in the function, click Function on the toolbar, and then choose the function, as shown in Figure 16-5.

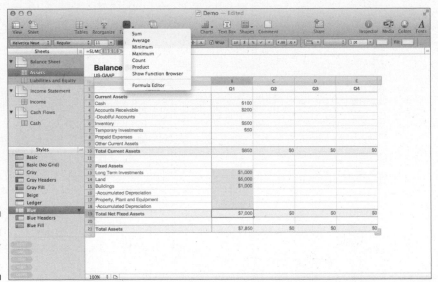

Figure 16-5:
Use other functions.

Creating formulas by selecting individual cells

Sometimes you don't want to use a range of cells in a formula. That's the case for the Total Assets formulas for the bottom row in the sample table. It should summarize just two cells: the values for Total Current Assets and Total Net Fixed Assets.

Here's how to add the subtotals for Total Assets:

1. **Open Formula Editor by typing = in the Q1 Total Assets cell.**

2. **Click in the cells you want to include in the formula.**

   Click Q1 Total Current Assets and Q1 Total Net Fixed Assets. The cells are added to the formula, separated by + signs, as shown in Figure 16-6.

   If you've specified headers, Numbers attempts to use the cell names it generates from the headers. If it can't use them, it uses the cell letter and cell number names.

Editing formulas

When you select a cell that contains a formula, the *formula bar* appears. It's just below the toolbar in Figure 16-6. If you've chosen to show the format bar, it appears between the toolbar and the formula bar.

As you build a formula, it appears in both the formula bar and Formula Editor. You can click in the formula in either place and type additional text. If you select a cell or a range of cells, the cell or cells are added to the formula. You can also type the name of a cell by using the letter-and-number notation. By default, the + sign separates items in the formula.

You can use parentheses in complex formulas to indicate the order in which calculations should be carried out. Parentheses have the same meaning that they do in programming languages or algebra: Items within parentheses are evaluated first. Then the result of that evaluation is used to continue the formula.

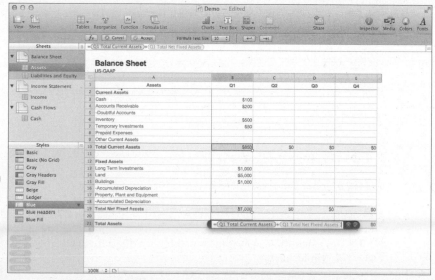

Figure 16-6:
Build a formula by clicking the cells to use.

Refining cell references

When you add a cell to a formula, either by typing its letter and number or by clicking it, that cell is referenced relative to the cell of the formula that is being built. For example, in building the subsummary for Q1 Total Current Assets, the range of cells above the Q1 Total Current Assets cell is selected. When you fill that formula to the right, the formulas in the cells for Q2, Q3, and Q4 Total Current Assets use the corresponding cells above them. This is also true if you copy and paste a formula. For example, if you copy and paste the formula from Q1 Total Current Assets anywhere else, it summarizes the seven cells above it — whatever the values of those cells may be — just as it does in the original Q1 Total Current Assets formula.

Sometimes you don't want this behavior. When you want to refine a cell reference in a formula, using the formula bar or Formula Editor, place the mouse over the formula. When the small arrow in a circle appears, click to open the contextual menu shown in Figure 16-7.

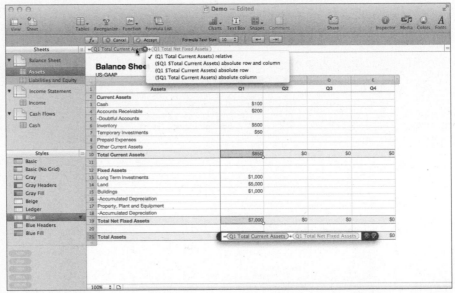

Figure 16-7:
Refine cell
references.

For each of the cell references in a formula, you can choose one of four options:

- ✔ **Relative:** This is the default setting. The cell reference is relative to the cell in which the formula is located. This is how the formula for cell Q1 Total Current Assets can be pasted or filled into Q2 Total Current Assets and still work.

- ✔ **Absolute:** By preceding the row and/or column indicators with a dollar sign, the reference is to that cell at all times. If you copy the formula to another cell, the reference to cell B10 or Q1 Total Current Assets always references that cell. The format you can choose is $B$10 or $Q1 $Total Current Assets.

- ✔ **Absolute row:** The reference for the cell is always in the chosen row, but the column reference varies depending on the formula cell.

- ✔ **Absolute column:** The reference for the cell is always in the chosen column, but the row reference varies depending on the formula cell.

If you're creating a what-if formula in which each row (or column) of data represents a different assumption, you may want to use absolute references for the items that don't change. You can also use unchanging values with absolute references for sales tax rates and the like.

Creating a multisheet and multitable summary

As is the case with all financial statements that follow Generally Accepted Accounting Principles (GAAP), the financial statement has three distinct sections:

- ✔ **Balance Sheet:** Summarizes assets and liabilities. A Balance Sheet contains separate tables for assets and liabilities.

- ✔ **Income Statement:** Combines income and expenses.

- ✔ **Cash Flow:** Shows the amount of money coming in and going out.

Each statement provides a different view on the operation of a business, and each has its own summaries. It can be convenient to have a single overall summary of the summaries, such as the one shown in Figure 16-8.

In this case, the summary simply brings together information from several sheets and tables; that information has itself been summarized, so you need to collect only the sums. Here's how to do it:

1. **Begin by creating a new sheet and table for the summary.**

   Click the Tables button on the toolbar and select the Headers built-in table. Name both the sheet and the table Summary.

2. **Set the header columns to the years you want to track.**

   Copy and paste (or type) the names of the rows you want to collect, such as Total Assets.

3. **Start to create a formula by typing = in a cell.**

   Format Editor opens, as shown in Figure 16-9.

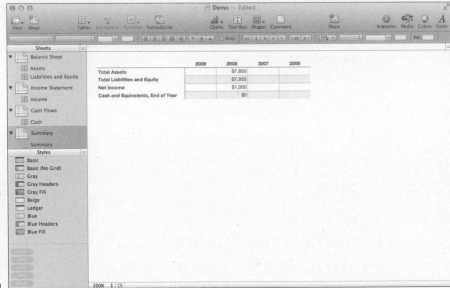

Figure 16-8:
Summarize data across sheets and tables.

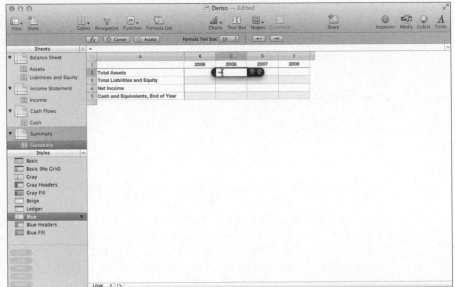

Figure 16-9:
Begin the formula.

4. **Navigate to the cell you want to reference (in this case, Q1 Total Assets in the Assets table).**

   As you move to other sheets and tables using the Sheets pane, notice that Formula Editor stays in place. The sheets and tables appear to move beneath it. You can drag Formula Editor to a new location if you want to.

Also at this time, the cursor changes to a function cursor, as shown in Figure 16-10.

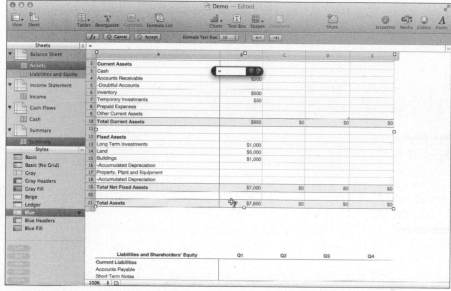

5. **Click the cell you want.**

6. **Click the check mark to accept the summary.**

   Formula Editor closes, and you return to the table where you started entering the formula. Repeat with any other cells you want to place on your one-page summary.

Using the format bar with formulas

If you show the format bar, you can use it as you're building a formula. When you start to edit a formula, the format bar changes, as shown in Figure 16-11. You have Cancel and Accept buttons, you can change the font size, and the buttons on the right insert a line break or a tab in the formula. At the left, you can click to open Function Browser.

Using Formula List

You can show Formula List by clicking the View menu on the toolbar or by choosing View➪Show/Hide Formula List. When Formula List is displayed, it appears at the bottom of each sheet, as shown in Figure 16-12.

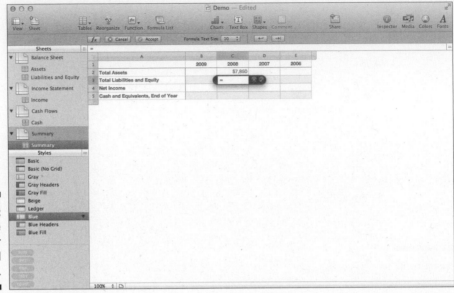

Figure 16-11:
Use the
format bar
as you build
formulas.

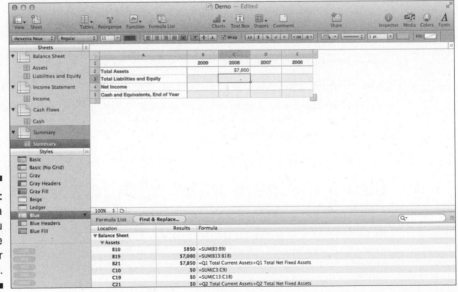

Figure 16-12:
Formula
List lets you
manage
your
formulas.

Formula List shows your sheets and tables; you can collapse or expand each sheet and table by using the disclosure triangle next to its name. If you click a formula, you immediately go to the cell in which it is defined.

The Find & Replace button opens a dialog that lets you search for parts of formulas, such as a cell reference name, an operator, or a function. You can replace them if you want (for example, replace all references to 2010 with 2011). If you rename a header row or column, you don't have to worry: Numbers propagates the change appropriately. But if you want a wholesale replacement in various formulas, Find & Replace will do the trick.

Working with Functions

Numbers has 250 built-in functions, and you can even create your own functions. Click Function on the toolbar to open a menu from which you can select the most common functions — SUM, AVERAGE, MAXIMUM, MINIMUM, COUNT, and PRODUCT (the multiplied results of the items in the formula). You use the same menu to open Formula Editor in the selected cell and to open Function Browser.

Function Browser has the full list of Numbers functions. (The Function menu on the toolbar contains only the most common functions, but it also lets you open Function Browser.)

The vast majority of Numbers functions are common to most spreadsheets and, in fact, to many other applications. Most of these functions were around long before computers. You'll probably use a small set of these functions, and that set will depend on the kind of work that you do.

The functions are divided into categories. You can open Function Browser, shown in Figure 16-13, in any of these ways:

- ✓ Choose View➪Show Function Browser.
- ✓ Click Function on the toolbar and choose Show Function Browser.
- ✓ If you're editing a formula and the format bar is displayed, during the edit the format bar will change (refer to Figure 16-11). Click the *fx* button at the left to show or hide Function Browser.

At the left are the categories of functions. Selecting a category shows the functions within it at the right. At the top of the left pane, you can choose to see all functions or just the ones you've used recently. Functions in the right pane are always displayed alphabetically.

Click a function to see its full description, as shown in Figure 16-14.

Figure 16-13:
Use
Function
Browser
to get
complete
function
documenta-
tion and
examples.

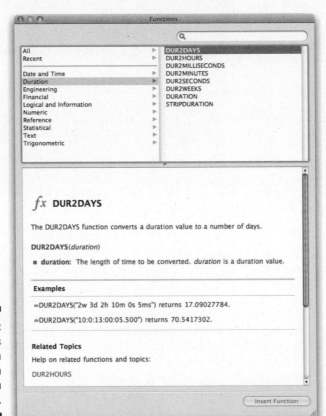

Figure 16-14:
Find details
of each
function in
Function
Browser.

The format for these descriptions is always the same:

- **Function name.**

- **Brief description.** This tells you what the function does.

- **Syntax:** This shows you how the function should be used. The name of the function is shown in dark gray. It is followed with parentheses that contain the *parameters,* or *arguments,* of the function. All functions have parentheses following the function name. The arguments must be in the same order in which they are shown in Function Browser. Some functions — such as TODAY() — do not have arguments.

  Each argument is described. If an argument is optional, the description identifies it as such, and it appears at the end of the list of arguments.

  Arguments can be cell references or constants. Sometimes constants are numeric or text values with their own values (such as the number of months in a loan). Other times, the constants are specific instructions to the function about how it should operate. These arguments typically have values such as TRUE, FALSE, 1 (true), or 0 (false).

- **Usage Notes:** Sometimes there will be usage notes with suggestions and comments about how to use the function.

- **Example:** Finally, you see an annotated example of the use of the function.

You can use the Insert Function button at the lower right of Function Browser to insert the function in the current formula. The function is inserted with the placeholder arguments shown in the syntax section. If you don't replace them or if you make another mistake in the function, you see a red triangle and an error message, as shown in Figure 16-15. A yellow triangle is displayed for a warning. In either case, the formula containing the function is invalid, but in both cases, you can still save the Numbers document so that you can come back later and correct the problem.

Function Browser uses styled text with colors, italics, and various font sizes. None of this matters in the use of the function in your formula. Function names are often shown in CAPITAL LETTERS as they are in this book.

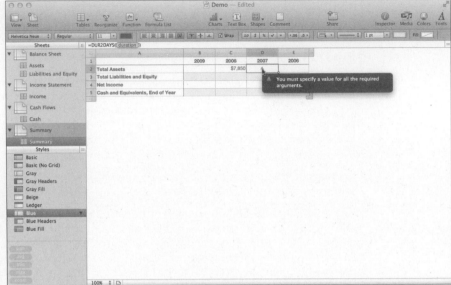

Figure 16-15:
Numbers
checks your
function
syntax.

Using Lookup Functions

Formulas and functions are not just about numbers. Some of the most impressive uses of formulas and functions have nothing at all to do with numbers. In this section, you look at an example of the VLOOKUP function that is taken from the Grade Book template in the Education section.

Although this example is from a Grade Book, the basic principle here — looking up data from another table based on a value the user has typed — applies to many applications.

As shown in Figure 16-16, the first sheet is Student Data. It contains raw grade scores as well as grades that are scaled using a curve. Everything in this sheet is data.

A separate sheet, shown in Figure 16-17, contains reports. This division between data in one sheet and reports in another means you can change the reports and the way in which data is displayed without any fear of corrupting the data.

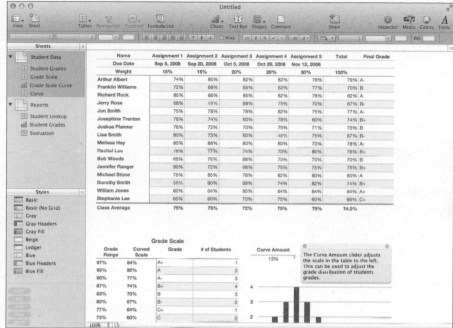

Figure 16-16: Student Data contains the data.

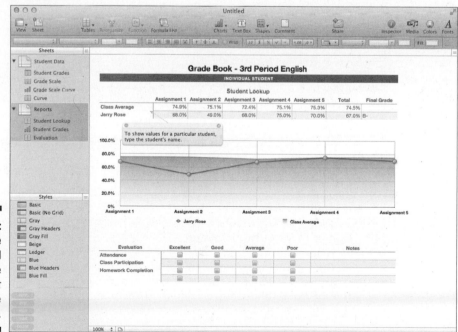

Figure 16-17: Reports are separated from the sheet that contains the raw data.

As the comment in Figure 16-17 suggests, you can type a student's name into cell A3, and Numbers will retrieve that student's data. Try it with the Grade Book example to see how it works. What happens here is created with the VLOOKUP function.

When you type a student's name in cell A3, data from Student Grades is shown in cells B3 through H3 of the Student Lookup table in the Reports sheet. The chart, Student Grades, is created from the data in Student Lookup. That means if the data in Student Lookup changes — for example, if you type another student's name, that student's data is placed in Student Lookup — the chart is automatically redrawn with the new student's data.

This mechanism works as long as cells B3 through H3 in Student Lookup are picked up from Student Grades. So, all you need is a formula to take the student name typed into cell A3 and retrieve the corresponding data from Student Grades.

The VLOOKUP function is the answer. It searches a range of cells for a matching value and then retrieves specific data in the row or column of that matching data. Here is the function as described in Function Browser:

```
VLOOKUP (search-for, columns-range,
         return-column, close-match)
```

The formula for cell B3, which contains the Assignment 1 grade, is

```
=VLOOKUP($A3,Student Grades :: $A$1:$H$20,COLUMN(),FALSE)
```

This function uses four arguments:

- ✔ **search-for:** This is what should be searched for. In this case, it's the value the user types into cell A3.

- ✔ **columns-range:** This is where VLOOKUP will look for the search-for value. In this case, it's the Student Grades table and the range of columns from A1 to H20. Refer to Figure 16-16, and you see that the range A1 through H20 is the entire Student Grades table.

- ✔ **return-column:** This argument tells Numbers which column from the selected row will be returned. In the example, the return-column argument itself is a function call: COLUMN(). COLUMN() returns the column number of the current column — that is, the column in Student Lookup. Because the columns in Student Lookup and Student Grades are identical, the formula in column 2 of Student Lookup will return the value of column 2 of Student Grades that matches the value of column 1 — the student name that has been typed into Student Lookup. For a mechanism like this to work, the columns must match.

✔ **close-match:** This argument takes a constant value that controls whether close matches are acceptable. If the value of close-match is TRUE (1) or if it is omitted, Numbers finds the row with the largest value that is less than or equal to search-for. For exact matches, you use FALSE (0) for this argument.

If you explore the cells in Student Lookup, you see that each cell from B3 to H3 has the same formula. Each includes the COLUMN() function, and each formula picks up the right data. Because you want each formula to search the entire Student Grades table, the rows and columns in Student Grades ($A$1:$H$20) are given absolute addresses. In that way, the entire table is always searched.

Because the entire table is always searched for a value that matches A3, you can type Class Average for the student name and retrieve the class average. If you do so, you'll have Class Average with identical data in the two rows of Student Lookup.

Now it's time to explain why the address for the first argument to VLOOKUP is column-absolute. Column A is always the name of the student to look up. If you add another row to the bottom of Student Lookup, you can copy the data from row 3 to row 4 and everything will work perfectly. The formula still searches the entire Student Grades table, and it still uses COLUMN() to select the column value based on the column in Student Lookup. And if you do copy row 3 to row 4, the first argument to VLOOKUP in row 4 is now $A4. That's because the column is absolute, and when you copied and pasted row 3's data into row 4, the label for column A stayed the same, but the row number changed.

The chart still displays data only from the first two rows.

Chapter 17

Working with Charts

Some people have no problem looking at a table of numbers that fills an entire page and seeing the patterns right away. For other people, a chart can clarify data, making it much easier to understand. If you're preparing information for several people to understand, you probably need to present both the raw data and a visual representation in a chart.

The same rules that apply to numeric data apply to visual data: Be clear and don't mislead.

For many people, using charts is a matter of trial and error. You usually start with the data, and then you prepare the chart and try it out on a test subject (yourself, to begin with). Does it clarify things? Does it help you understand? Numbers is a great tool to use for this experimentation because it makes it easy to both create charts and change their attributes.

The interfaces to cells and formulas differ between iOS and OS X (see Chapters 15 and 16). Charts, the subject of this chapter, are the opposite case. Although iOS and OS X have minor differences, the interfaces are very similar. In fact, in this chapter, the screenshots switch between the iOS and Mac versions.

You can create charts in Keynote and Pages. Those charts are almost as powerful as Numbers charts, and they look very much the same. You can paste Numbers charts into Keynote and Pages documents, and they retain their relationship to your Numbers document where possible, unless you choose to unlink them. (If the chart and the data are in separate files, you may encounter difficulties when you move to another computer.)

Creating a Chart

You create a chart in Numbers in two basic ways:

- ✔ **Start from the chart:** Create a chart. Numbers automatically creates an associated table with sample data in it. You can then modify, paste, or retype that data so that it flows into the chart.

- ✔ **Start from the data table:** Create a table that contains the data for your chart. Select the table or specific cells from that table and then create a chart.

Every chart must have a table associated with it, whether it is a Numbers placeholder table or one that you've created.

Describing a chart

All spreadsheet tables can serve as the basis for charts. Figure 17-1 shows a basic table. This table has row and column headers. The column headers are 2007, 2008, 2009, and 2010. The row headers are Region 1 and Region 2.

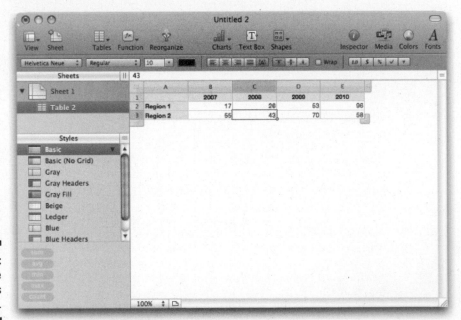

Figure 17-1:
Use a table as the basis for a chart.

Each type of chart has its own way of representing data, but the basic parts of a chart remain the same regardless of the chart type. Each value on a chart has three components:

- ✔ **Value:** This is the numeric value, such as a number of people, a temperature, or miles per gallon. Numeric values are usually plotted against the y-axis of a chart (the vertical line at the left). By convention, numeric values increase as you go up the y-axis. The selected cell in Figure 17-1 has a value of 43.

- ✔ **Category:** Each value is associated with a *category*. A category can be a date, a location, or any other attribute that applies to all values. Charts let you easily compare values for one category against another — for example, the temperature at one location with the temperature at another location. Categories can be text (such as place names) or numeric (such as dates, times, or altitudes). Categories are usually placed along the x-axis of a chart (the horizontal bottom line of the chart). If they are numeric (including dates and times), they are usually plotted so that they increase as you go to the right along the x-axis. The selected cell in Figure 17-1 is in category 2008.

- ✔ **Data series:** Each value is also associated with a *data series*. Like a category, a data series can be a piece of data, a region, or any other attribute that applies to all its values. You can compare values for one data series against another — for example, the temperature on one day with the temperature on another day. The selected cell in Figure 1-7 is part of data series Region 2.

Numbers makes it easy for you to switch a chart's orientation. In the scenario described here, the categories are years, and the data series are temperatures. As you can see in the following section, you can click a button to change the categories to temperatures and the data series to years. Depending on your purpose and the data you're dealing with, one format rather than another will often make more sense.

Creating a chart from scratch on OS X

On OS X, you can either start from a chart or from a table; you then create the table or chart. On iOS, you always start from a table, as described in the following section.

Follow these steps when you want to create a chart starting from a Numbers document:

1. **Create the Numbers document for the chart and its data.**

   Alternatively, open an existing Numbers document and select the sheet you want to use for the chart.

2. If necessary, delete the table from Sheet 1.

A new Numbers document has a single sheet and a single table. Most of the time, you work inside a Numbers document that may have other tables or sheets in it, but by deleting any existing table, you can isolate the charting process to make it easier to see.

3. Click Charts on the toolbar and select a chart to create.

In this example, I chose a line chart. Numbers automatically creates the chart and an associated table. You can modify the table as you would any other table. Experiment with changing values and watch the chart change.

4. Change the chart's series orientation.

Select the chart by clicking it. The table now has a dark frame, as shown in Figure 17-2. At the upper left, you can click the icon to change the chart's data series; in other words, the chart uses the table's rows instead of the table's columns as categories.

When you change a chart's series orientation, you switch the categories with the data series. The values, which are plotted against the y-axis (the vertical axis at the left), are the same, but their representation (the color of their line, their dots, or their bars) changes.

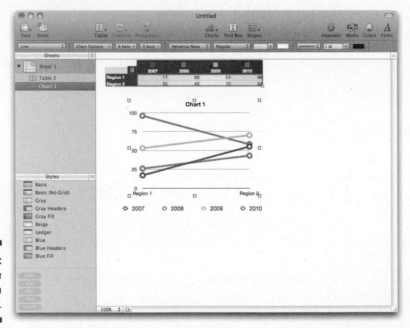

Figure 17-2:
Change the chart's data series.

Creating a chart from a table on iOS

Many times you create a chart from an existing table. It can be an entire table or part of a table. Figure 17-3 shows a table that lists reservations for a theater. Each cell in the table contains the number of reservations for a specific performance on a specific day. Many of the cells are empty: Not every type of performance is presented on every day.

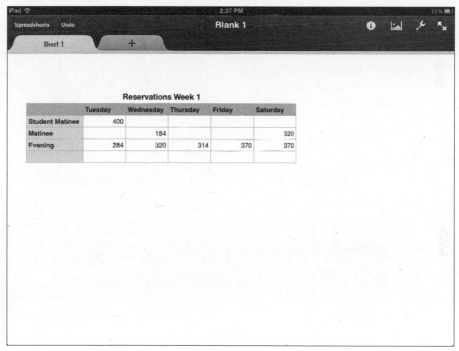

Figure 17-3: Start from a table of data.

Here's how to turn the table shown in Figure 17-3 into a chart:

1. **Select the table.**

   Make certain that you select the table and not an individual cell. If you select a single cell by just clicking in the table, you'll chart that cell: a single value.

2. **Tap Insert and choose a chart to create (see Figure 17-4).**

   A chart is created for the selected table. In this example, I chose a stacked horizontal bar chart. Numbers begins to create the chart (see Figure 17-5).

3. Select the cells from the table you want to chart.

As you select the cells, you see the chart being built.

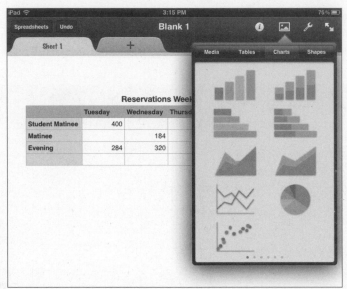

Figure 17-4:
Select the chart type.

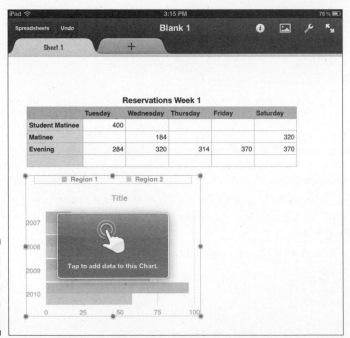

Figure 17-5:
Numbers creates the chart from the table.

4. **Change the chart's series orientation.**

   Just as when you create a chart first and let Numbers create the associated table, you can change the chart's series orientation.

   Use the actions button at the top right of the screen, as shown in Figure 17-6.

5. **Tap Done.**

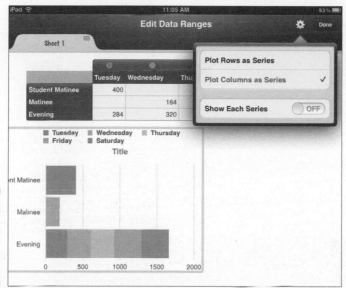

Figure 17-6:
Change the chart's series orientation.

Modifying the cells in a table or chart

Depending on which rows you've selected, you may have a number of blank cells in the chart. You also may have categories that aren't used (that is the case if an entire row is blank and not even labeled). On OS X, select the chart. This highlights the table with a dark frame around the selected cells. Drag the corner of the frame up or down or to the left or right until the correct cells are shown.

On iOS, a very similar interface is presented. The only difference is that buttons let you hide a column.

To modify the cells in a chart:

1. **On iOS, tap the chart to bring up the command bar.**

2. **Tap Edit References to bring up the controls, shown in Figure 17-7.**

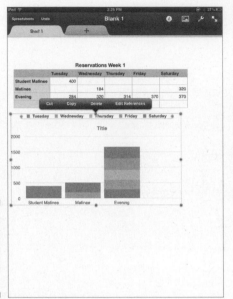 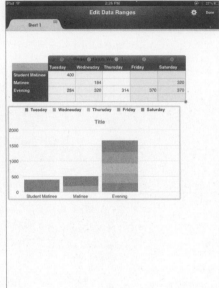

Figure 17-7:
Manage
the cells
included in
the chart.

Moving charts and tables

Whether you start from a chart or start from a table, you'll wind up with the chart and table next to one another on a single sheet. Once both are created and Numbers has created the link between them, you can move either one or both to other sheets — the connections remain. Just copy and paste the tables or charts to the sheets where you want them to be.

Using Chart Inspector on OS X

You can change the chart type and many other attributes of a chart using Chart inspector in the Inspector window on OS X. Select Chart inspector by clicking the Chart button at the top of an Inspector window. Click to select the chart to inspect and adjust.

You can customize a chart just as you want with the Chart inspector, but for many people and many charts, you don't need to ever use Chart inspector. The default settings are often just fine. (Numbers even matches the colors to your template's colors.) You may find that just experimenting with switching the data series orientation is sufficient customization.

Changing chart types

To change a chart's type, you can always delete the chart and create a new one. But it's much easier to use Chart inspector. Select the chart you want to change and use the menu at the upper left of Chart inspector to open the same menu of chart types you see in Charts on the toolbar or choose Insert⇨ Charts. Figure 17-8 shows Chart inspector with the chart types menu.

In addition to changing the data series orientation, changing the chart type gives you the widest range of major changes. As you change the chart type, the size and shape of the chart can change, so you may have to rearrange objects on your sheet, such as graphics, titles, tables, and even other charts.

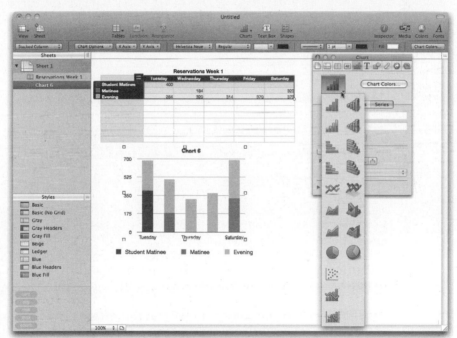

Figure 17-8: Change the chart type.

Changing chart colors

The Chart Colors button at the top of Chart inspector opens the window shown in Figure 17-9.

Select the set of colors you want to use for your chart. Drag each color to the color on the chart you're replacing. You see a small color swatch and a plus sign on the pointer as you move the new color into place. That color will replace the previous color everywhere it's used on the chart.

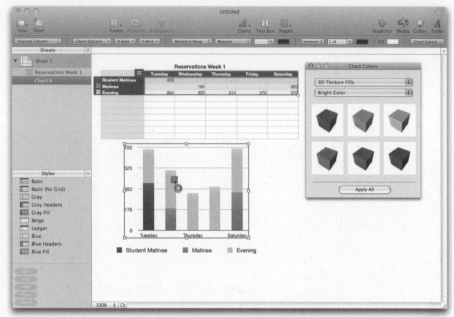

Figure 17-9:
Change
chart colors.

Formatting chart titles, legends, and bar formats

The Chart tab in Chart inspector lets you show or hide legends, titles, and hidden data. The legend, which identifies categories by name and color, is shown at the bottom of the chart.

The chart title, if it's shown, appears above the chart. To change it, simply double-click and type a new name.

If your table has hidden data, you can control whether or not it's shown in the chart. You probably will choose not to show the hidden data; if it's hidden in the table, it usually should be hidden in the chart.

Be careful about hiding data. If you're hiding it for reasons of confidentiality, it may make sense to hide identifiable data in the table and chart. If you're hiding data because it's distracting and the chart is clearer without it, make certain that you're not misleading the viewer.

Finally, in bar charts, you can adjust the width of individual bars as well as the space between sets of bars, as shown in Figure 17-10. A stacked bar chart stacks all the bars for a given category on top of one another, with no space between sets of bars.

The category legend names and color codes are in their own section. You can move it and adjust its width (and therefore its height), as shown in Figure 17-11.

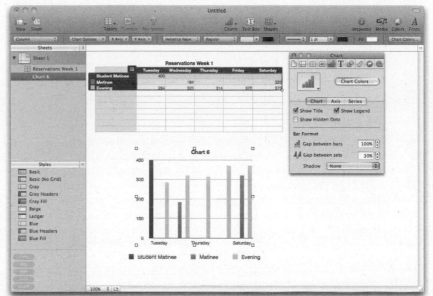

Figure 17-10:
Format titles, legends, and bars.

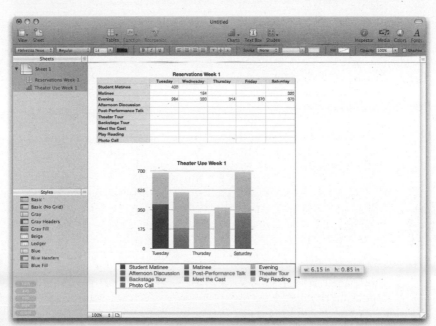

Figure 17-11:
Format legends.

Setting axes, labels, ticks, and grids

You use the Axis tab in Chart inspector to control axes, labels, ticks, and grids. The x- and y-axes have separate settings, which depend on the chart type. In Figure 17-12, you can see the settings for the y-axis on OS X. These are the default settings for a stacked bar chart. Notice that the axis pop-up menu is where you set ticks and grids — the marks on the axes that provide a scaled reference for numbers and categories of an axis.

You can choose the maximum and minimum values for the y-axis, as shown in Figure 17-13. If you don't choose your own values, Numbers will choose appropriate settings.

If you're preparing charts that will be compared to one another, you usually want to set the same minimum and maximum values for the y-axis for like data. In other words, if you have several charts that are plotting grades, they might all be scaled from 0 to 100. A separate set of charts plotting audience attendance in the 400-seat theater might all be scaled from 0 to 410 (to allow for standing room). If you present like information with different scales, the result is misleading. This is a common mistake in preparing charts. Unfortunately, it's also a deliberate step that some unscrupulous chart designers take.

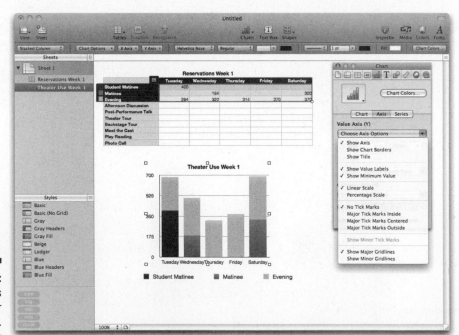

Figure 17-12:
Use y-axis settings for a chart.

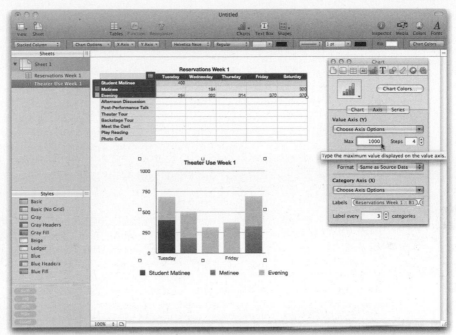

Figure 17-13:
Set maxi-
mum and
minimum
settings for
the y-axis.

At the bottom of the Axis tab of Chart inspector, you can set the intervals between category names. In Figure 17-12, labels are shown for every category. In Figure 17-14, labels are shown for every third category, and the bottom of the chart is much cleaner. This approach works very well when the categories have some obvious sequence. Most people can guess that the two categories between Tuesday and Friday are Wednesday and Thursday. On the other hand, if your categories are Plumbing, Haberdashery, Gifts, and Accounting, showing the labels for only Plumbing and Accounting won't give people a clue as to what those other two categories are.

Adjusting series in Chart inspector

The Series tab in Chart inspector lets you adjust and inspect the data series in your chart. Select a series in the chart (not the chart itself) by clicking any of the bars or data points in the series. In Figure 17-14, you can see that the Matinee series is selected: Round dots appear at the top and bottom of each bar that applies to that series. In addition, the corresponding row in the table is highlighted.

You can also see that a data series is a formula. You can edit it just as you would any other formula. In addition to the data series data, the labels are also taken from a range in the table; you can change this range as well so that the labels will change.

Perhaps most important, you can change the order of each data series. You don't have to rearrange the data in your tables to put one series on top of another in your stacked bar chart. Just as with the minimum and maximum values on the y-axis, keeping your data series in the same order across several charts can make it easier for people to compare one chart with another.

You can turn value labels on and off as well as change their location and formatting, as shown in Figure 17-15.

The chart in Figure 17-15 is a stacked bar chart, so the final label position option (placing it above the bar) is not available. If you choose to place the value labels in a specific position, remember that the chart will usually look best if you use the same position for all data series.

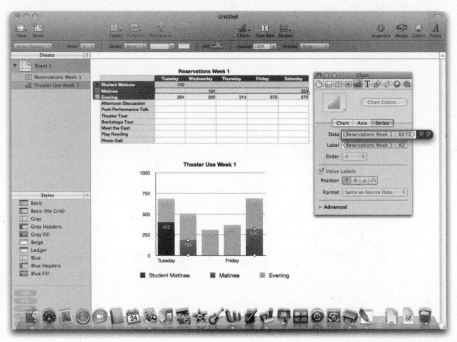

Figure 17-14:
Select a
data series.

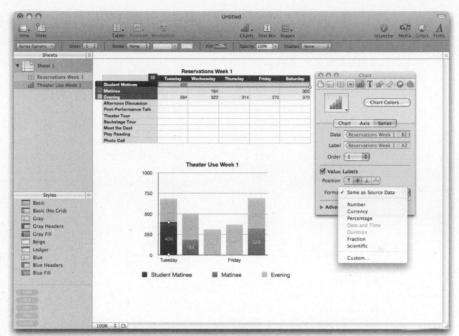

Figure 17-15:
Set label
positions
and formats.

Inspecting Charts on iOS

Although the interface on iOS is different from Chart inspector on OS, the functionality is basically the same.

To change chart types on iOS, select the chart and open the popover with the actions button.

To set axes, labels, ticks, and grids on iOS, select the chart and open the inspector. Choose X Axis or Y Axis, as shown in Figure 17-16, to adjust the settings.

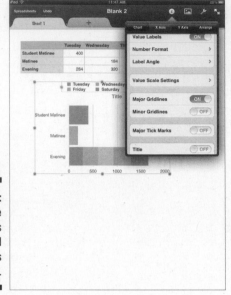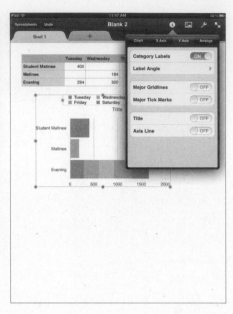

Figure 17-16:
Change
settings
for x- and
y-axes
on iOS.

Chapter 18

Formatting and Printing Numbers Documents

In This Chapter

▶ Displaying charts and tables effectively on paper

▶ Reorganizing, sorting, and categorizing data

▶ Searching for data values

▶ Printing on mobile devices

*E*ach iWork app has its own settings for its documents and their major subdivisions (sections for Pages documents, slides for Keynote documents, and sheets for Numbers documents). For Keynote presentations and Pages documents, the size of the canvas you're working with is set for the document. In the case of Numbers documents, each sheet can have a different size; it's only when it comes time to print a sheet that you need to worry about its actual size. That's one of the reasons why the procedures for formatting and printing Numbers documents are somewhat different from the procedures for formatting and printing other iWork documents.

Many people use their Mac rather than an iOS device to manage large documents, particularly for printing. Accordingly, this chapter focuses on Numbers for Mac. As you can see at the end of the chapter, Numbers for iOS doesn't support several formatting features, but the data is just fine. In fact, the printing process can be simpler than on Mac OS.

Formatting Multiple Charts on a Single Sheet

Creating multiple tables and charts on multiple sheets in Numbers so that you can track data is simple. Figure 18-1 shows a multiple-sheet solution. (It's one used previously in Chapter 17.)

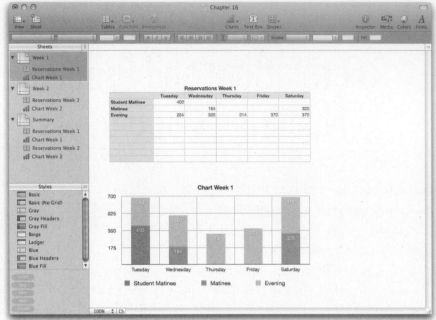

Figure 18-1:
Create mul-
tiple sheets,
each with
its own
tables and
charts.

Keeping each sheet focused on one set of data (a single week in this case) makes it easy to manage just the information you care about.

But you can also create a new sheet to provide a summary so that you can see all the data together. This section shows you how to combine the tables and charts and how to reorganize and reformat them so that they look their best.

The sequence of steps depends on your charts and tables as well as your preferences. As you're rearranging and reformatting your own tables and charts, you may notice something that appears wrong to you. Feel free to refer to the appropriate section in this chapter to fix that issue.

Here's how you make charts placed together on a single sheet look as good as possible:

1. **Create a new sheet and name it Summary.**

   Click Sheet on the toolbar and double-click to rename it in the Sheets pane.

2. **Copy and paste each chart from its own sheet into the Summary sheet.**

   Don't worry what the sheet looks like as you proceed — you'll clean it up in this section.

Be careful that you copy only the charts (not the accompanying tables). Do this by clicking once in the center of each chart so that the chart's eight handles are visible. Then copy and paste each chart to the Summary sheet. In this way, the chart on the Summary page and the chart on the original sheet page will both reference the same table.

3. Rearrange the charts so that they look the way you want them to look.

As you move the charts, guide lines appear, as shown in Figure 18-2. In this case, the charts are aligned on their horizontal centers. Experiment with different types of alignment, which will help you uncover errors. For example, if you place the charts next to one another, you'll see a mistake.

4. Check the axes to make certain that they're consistent.

In Figure 18-2, the y-axis goes from 0 to 700 in the Week 1 chart; in the Week 2 chart, it goes from 0 to 800. Two charts displaying the same type of data that are placed next to one another should have the same values on their axes. If you take out a ruler and measure the height of bars with similar values, you'll see that they are different heights. This height discrepancy becomes increasingly apparent if you place them next to one another. (Using inconsistent axes is a common mistake and, in some unfortunate cases, an attempt to deliberately mislead people.)

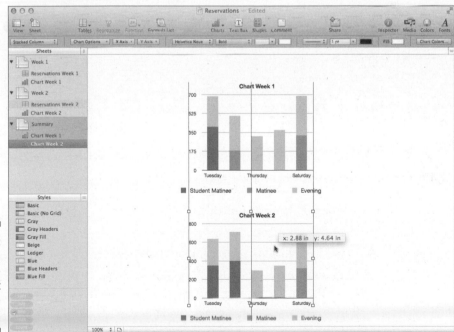

Figure 18-2:
Create a single summary sheet with all the charts.

5. Change the axis minimum or maximum value to make them consistent.

Usually, you want the values from the larger range of values. Use Chart inspector to change the values of the y-axis, as shown in Figure 18-3.

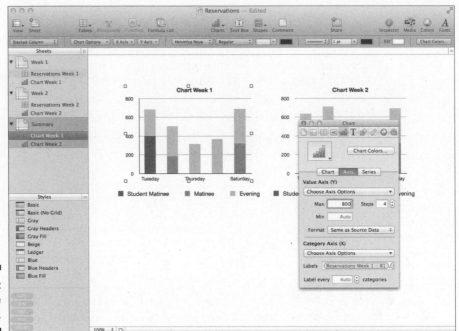

Figure 18-3:
Adjust the axes scales.

Printing Charts on a Single Sheet

After your charts look good onscreen, you're ready to make them look good when they're printed. Here's how:

1. Switch to Print view to see how your sheet will look when it's printed.

Use any of these commands:

- Choose View⇨Show Print View.
- Click View on the toolbar and choose Show Print View.
- At the bottom of the window, choose Show Print View (see Figure 18-4).

When Print view is displayed, the Sheets pane shows the number of pages it will take to print that sheet, as shown in Figure 18-4.

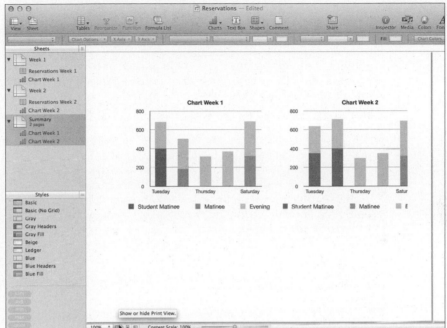

Figure 18-4:
Show Print
view.

2. **Scroll to make certain that the page breaks are appropriate.**

   In this case, a page break toward the right side of the Week 2 chart looks terrible.

3. **If necessary, fix the page breaks.**

   Here's where judgment comes in. You have a variety of options:

   • Rearrange the sheet so that one table or chart appears on each page. This approach, however, is usually overkill.

   • Use the Content Scale slider in the center of the bottom of the window to change the size of the sheet's content. If almost every thing fits on a single page, this option may work for you. If you reduce the content size, though, print it to check it for readability before distributing the chart.

   • Use the controls in the bottom of the window to switch between portrait (vertical) and landscape (horizontal) orientations.

   • Manually adjust the content. Instead of scaling all the content, make informed judgments about specific rescaling choices. For example, in this case, you may want to reduce the size of the charts while leaving the legends the same size.

Sorting and Reorganizing Data

Like other spreadsheets, Numbers can sort and reorganize data quickly. As you think about how to print data, you may want to consider not just the layout but also the way in which the data is organized and selected. This section provides an example of how to do that. Both sorting and reorganizing data help people focus on the points you're trying to make.

Many of the examples in this book and the Numbers documentation focus on small problems because it is usually easier to see the basic principles. But I chose the example in this section to show you the power of Numbers. The data used here is from the United Status 2000 census. The complete data file is a quarter of a million records; several thousand are enough to demonstrate Numbers in action. You see how to display the data, format it, and create subtotals by category.

Sorting data with the Reorganize dialog

Here's how to sort data using iWork's Reorganize dialog:

1. **Download the `censususa` data file as described in the Introduction.**

   Open the file in Numbers.

2. **Use Table inspector to set headers for each column.**

   Type names for each header (Age, Count, Sex, and State). The spreadsheet should appear as shown in Figure 18-5.

3. **Select the entire table and click Reorganize on the toolbar to open the Reorganize dialog, as shown in Figure 18-6.**

   Sort the table based on ascending age, as shown in Figure 18-6. Note how quickly the sort is performed: Numbers is fast. Also note that by supplying header values for the columns, you've made it easier to use the Reorganize dialog. There's no question that you're sorting by age because that's the name of that column.

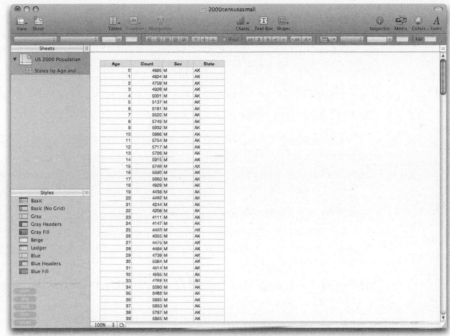

Figure 18-5:
Open the census file in Numbers and set headers for the columns.

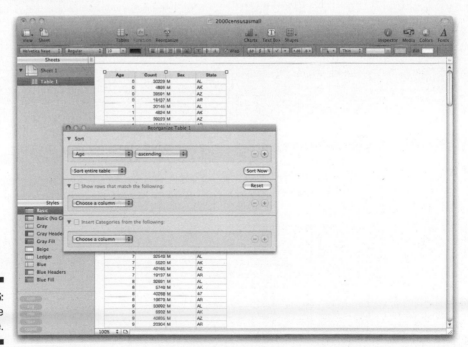

Figure 18-6:
Sort the table by age.

Using data categories

Numbers makes categorizing data easy. Just follow these steps to categorize the census data by state and age:

1. **Download the censususa data file as described in the Introduction.**

2. **Use Table inspector to set headers for each column.**

   You also may want to use Cell inspector to format the data values as numbers with thousands delimiters.

3. **Select the entire table and click Reorganize on the toolbar to open the Reorganize dialog.**

4. **Select the State category, as shown in Figure 18-7.**

   (Use the Insert Categories From the Following check box to turn categories on and off.) You can collapse or expand any category by using its disclosure triangle.

5. **Use the plus sign at the right to add a category to the Reorganize dialog.**

   Add the Age category below the State category. The display changes, as shown in Figure 18-8.

6. **Clean up the display.**

   You can hide the columns for State and Age — they're shown as categories. The table that results is shown in Figure 18-9.

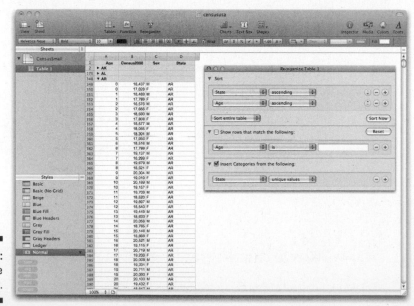

Figure 18-7:
Use
categories.

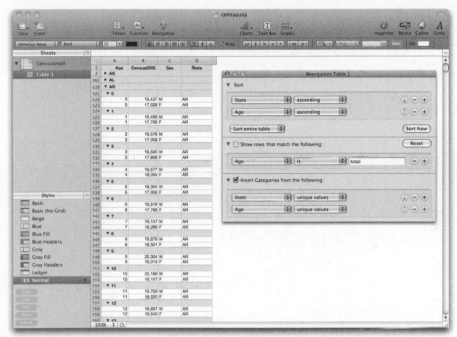

Figure 18-8:
Use subcat-
egories.

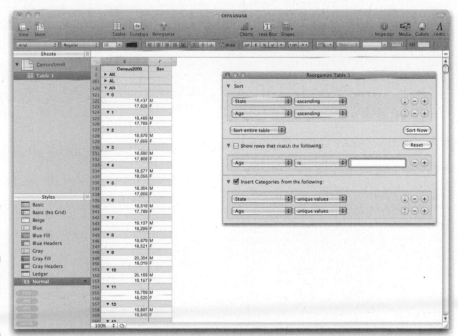

Figure 18-9:
Clean up
the spread-
sheet.

7. **Add a summary function for the categories.**

Click any summary cell (such as a state) and use the disclosure triangle that appears at the right to open the menu shown in Figure 18-10. Choose a summary function for that category and the column you've clicked in. For example, if you click in the Age column and the State category, you can create subtotals for all ages and all states as shown in Figure 18-11. There's nothing more to click: Numbers just goes to work.

Subtotals in large tables can take a while to calculate. Some people are tempted to go wild with summaries. Consider what it is you're trying to communicate. Perhaps separate smaller tables with fewer summary fields (or a chart!) can make your point more simply.

Finding data

When you have a small table, you can look at it and understand the data at a glance (particularly if you've used charts). But when you have a large table with hundreds or thousands of cells, you need help to find the data you're looking for.

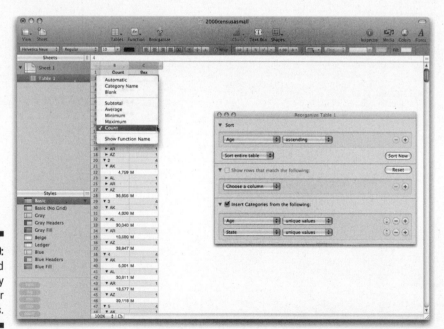

Figure 18-10:
Add
summary
functions for
categories.

Here's how to search a table for data on Mac OS:

1. **Select the table or part of a table you want to search.**

2. **Select the column you want to search.**

3. **Provide the condition you are looking for, as shown in Figure 18-12.**

   In addition to Is Greater Than, you can choose other standard comparisons from the pop-up menu.

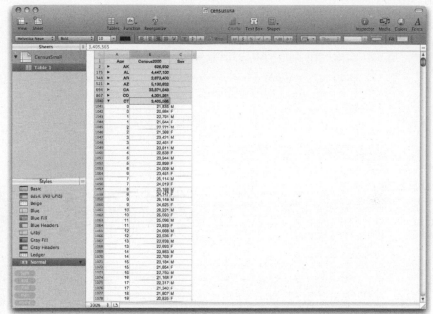

Figure 18-11:
Numbers
performs
the sum-
maries
automati-
cally.

Figure 18-12:
Select the
operator for
the search.

4. **Enter the value to search for.**

   You can click the + sign to add another condition to the search.

5. **Show the data.**

   When you select the Show Rows That Match the Following check box, Numbers performs the search. The search is very fast because Numbers has been working on it while you've been specifying the search terms.

Here's how to search for data on iOS:

1. **Tap Tools (the wrench at the right of the toolbar).**

2. **Tap Find.**

3. **Enter the text you want to search for.**

   Depending upon whether you also want to replace the found text, use the triangle in the upper left to show or hide the replace field (see Figure 18-13).

Figure 18-13: Enter text to find.

4. **Tap Search in the lower right to perform the search.**

   Tapping Done in the upper right means that you're done with the find — it doesn't perform the search.

   The results appear (see Figure 18-14).

5. **Use the arrows at the bottom left and right to find next and previous instances of the search string.**

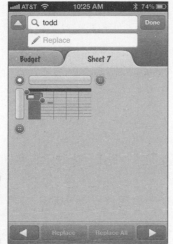

Figure 18-14:
View the
results.

Printing on iOS

If you've created a heavily formatted document on your Mac, when you first open it on an iOS device, you may be a bit alarmed. Some of the formatting features aren't supported, as shown in Figure 18-15.

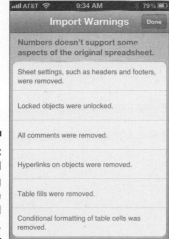

Figure 18-15:
Not all
formatting
features are
implemented
on iOS.

Never fear: The data is there. You can print it in the same basic way you print from almost any iOS app:

1. **Open the sheet you want to print.**

2. **Tap Tools (the wrench) at the right of the toolbar.**

3. **Tap Share and Print.**

4. **Tap Print.**

   The print screen opens, as shown in Figure 18-16.

5. **If you want, tap Actions (the gear wheel) to set options, as shown in Figure 18-17.**

6. **After you've set any options, tap Done to return to the screen shown previously in Figure 18-16.**

7. **Tap Print to open the standard iOS print controls shown in Figure 18-18.**

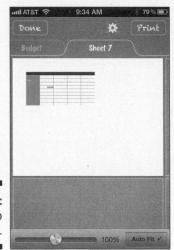

Figure 18-16:
Start to
print.

Figure 18-17:
Set printing
options.

Figure 18-18:
Choose a
printer and
the number
of copies.

Part IV
Presenting Keynote

The 5th Wave   By Rich Tennant

In this part . . .

Keynote started as a project for Steve Jobs, for his presentations at MacWorld and Apple's World Wide Developer Conference. Well-known for his attention to detail, he didn't like the existing presentation software. When you're the head of a company like Apple, you can address the issue by having software written to your specifications.

Over time, Keynote was refined and became the first component of iWork. It's possible to create ugly and boring presentations with Keynote, but it's a lot harder to do so than with some other software.

Although Keynote has great graphics and terrific transitions, its strength is that its features are all focused on the main purpose of the presentation: presenting and clarifying information rather than drawing attention to gee-whiz effects.

Keynote was the first iWork app to venture into the world of iOS apps: Keynote Remote has been available for some time now so that you can use your iPhone as a controller for your Mac and its Keynote presentation. Today, you can present from your Mac or from your iPad. The ability to run Keynote on an iPad has given rise to a new type of presentation: a *nanopresentation* presented around a table or even on a sofa with a colleague or two. You can use all the trappings of traditional presentations, but you can also bring all those tools to bear in an informal and small presentation.

Chapter 19

Creating a Keynote Presentation

Keynote was the first component of iWork. It was originally written for Steve Jobs to use when he gave presentations at conferences and trade shows, including Apple's World Wide Developers Conference and the Macworld conferences. After these "trials by fire," Keynote and Pages became the first two components of iWork.

Word-processing programs and page layout programs, such as Microsoft Word and Pages, focus on preparing paper-based documents. They often are viewed on a computer display, but generally they are tied to paper. Spreadsheets, such as Microsoft Excel and Numbers, have a different pattern. Spreadsheets are sometimes printed; other times, they're designed for interactivity and what-if analyses in which a person uses the spreadsheet's ability to rapidly calculate and recalculate data.

Presentation software is a different type of product. It's really not paper-based like word-processing or page layout software, and it's not designed for the kind of interactivity provided by a spreadsheet. Presentation software uses the capabilities of a graphics-based personal computer to let people create effective presentations.

This chapter is the overview of the basic Keynote tools that help you create and present your Keynote presentations.

Creating Effective Presentations

When you prepare a presentation well, you bring together the information to be presented along with visuals and slides of text. The presentation can involve notes for yourself as well as a structured sequence of slides. By organizing the presentation in this way, you provide the most interesting and useful presentation.

Perhaps you've had the experience of sitting through a presentation in which the speaker reads every word on every slide: It quickly becomes tedious. Organizing your presentation into separate components of visuals, speaker's notes, planned discussion topics, and time for questions can provide a useful and interesting presentation for your audience — and for yourself.

A lot of confusion and misinformation about presentations exists, creating a bad reputation for presentations and presentation software. By looking at these issues, however, you can find out how to avoid problems and how to make your own Keynote presentations more effective and productive.

Making your presentations effective

Presentations differ from other types of documents in that they're often not designed for a person to use on their own. A presenter (usually you) controls the pace of the presentation. And, what's more, because presentations are often given in a darkened room, you can't always tell whether you're losing your audience. Here are some tips for avoiding problems in this area:

- **Avoid the dark:** Use the least amount of room-darkening you can for your presentation. Make certain you can see your audience.

- **Use Q&A sections:** Use more (and shorter) Q&A sections in your presentations to involve your audience as much as possible. Don't just ask for questions — you'll probably get no response. For each Q&A section, have one or two questions ready that you can ask the audience in case they have no questions of their own. (These questions fit nicely into the speaker's notes section of Keynote.)

- **Use a roadmap:** Let people know where you're going in your presentation and where they are at any moment. When you're reading a book, the heft of the unread pages gives you an idea of how far you've come. With a presentation, one slide after another can come out of the dark without any clue as to how it fits into the presentation.

✔ **Time and rehearse your presentation:** Fortunately, Keynote has excellent presentation tools so that you can make your presentation as efficient as possible. Depending on your topic, your experience with presentations, and who you are, you may find it more important to work on timing or to rehearse your presentation. Some presenters need no more than a few minutes' rehearsal, but many others need hours to come up with a 15-minute presentation.

Those are the traditional characteristics of presentations. Increasingly, people are creating presentations to be used by one person viewing the presentation on a computer screen (and that includes mobile devices, such as iPad and iPhone).

If you're creating a presentation, think about whether it fits into the darkened room/group audience or the device/individual user model. It is a rare presentation that works well in both environments. For example, a Q&A slide that works well to stimulate discussion in a group audience just wastes time for an individual user.

Using documents that move

What you use for a presentation is a sequence of slides displayed on a large projection screen or sometimes directly on a computer display if the audience is small (or a single person). You have options for movement that you don't have with a printed document. You can add effects to the transition from one slide to another along with moving elements, including QuickTime movies.

These tools, however, are among the most misused of presentation features. In fact, some time ago, one presentation application (not Keynote) even had a feature that allowed you to select a different random animated transition from one slide to the next. The audience had no idea why one transition was used rather than another.

Experiment with the Keynote transitions and use them to help people understand where in the presentation you are. For example, you can use a certain type of transition to go from one slide to another slide that provides details on the first slide. You can use yet another transition to introduce a new topic.

Your audience is sitting there in the dark trying to figure out what all this means: Give them a helping hand.

Working on a small scale

The last point to remember when working on a presentation is that you're using a very small canvas. Although your slides may be blown up to large sizes on a screen so that a roomful of people can see them, each slide has much less space than a piece of paper (or a spreadsheet page) for information.

Given the relatively small size of your slides, you may decide to break up text into multiple slides, such as Strategies (1), Strategies (2), and Strategies (3). This is a time-tested way to antagonize your audience. You're asking them to remember too much. For each slide, make its title clear and its subject understandable. Instead of Strategies (1), try New Customer Strategies. Instead of Strategies (2), try Returning Customer Strategies.

You may think that you have to do more organization for a large document than for a 20-slide presentation, but the opposite may be true. In part, that's because with a large printed document, your readers can always flip a few pages back or forward if they lose the sequence of what you've been writing about. With a slide presentation, they have to remember where they are in the presentation.

Working on a personal scale

With iPad, there's another aspect to the scale of your presentation. You can create a one-to-one presentation that's designed for you to show to someone across a table or sitting next to you. Never underestimate the impact of a presentation that's this simple and direct. A projector, wires, and even a wireless remote, such as an iPhone, are all barriers between you and the person you are talking to. iPad is a terrific presentation tool for this reason because you can talk to someone directly.

Think about these issues as you explore Keynote. Fortunately, with the built-in themes, you'll find plenty of tools. The folks at Apple have used presentations for years, and they're very good at them. Keynote isn't just presentation software; like Pages and Numbers, it's a hands-on training seminar in the nuts and bolts of communicating.

Come back to these issues as you work with Keynote.

Exploring the Keynote Window on Mac OS X

Everyone prepares a Keynote presentation differently. There is no one right way — not for a specific topic, not for a specific audience, and not for a specific speaker. The Keynote window is flexible enough to let you work in the way that's easiest for you.

The Keynote window has six major areas that you can show or hide. If you hide an area, however, the information in that area remains in the presentation. If you hide the presenter notes, for example, that's all you've done: hidden them. Want to see them again (perhaps during your presentation)? Just display them. You don't lose anything. (And no one in your audience sees the presenter notes at any time.)

The Keynote window lets you work on a presentation. When it comes time to present the presentation, you can use the techniques in Chapter 20.

As with other iWork apps, an area to the left of the window provides quick access to the structure of your document. This area, called the Navigator, is shown in Figure 19-1.

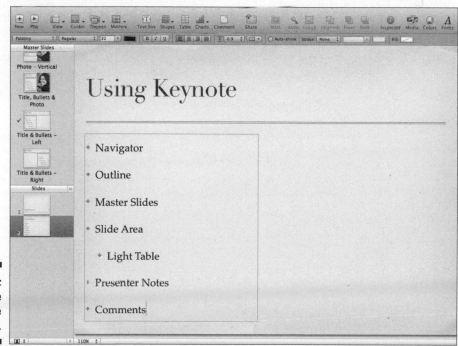

Figure 19-1:
Use the
Keynote
window.

The Navigator

The Navigator has two components: master slides and slides. Slides are always displayed, but the display of master slides is optional.

You create the slides for your presentation using the New button on the toolbar or by choosing Slide⇨New Slide. As you add information to the slides, you can rearrange them by dragging them up or down in the Navigator.

The structure of a slide is part of Keynote, so you can select a slide and switch its master slide to another format. You may have to do some reformatting, but you won't lose any data.

You can show master slides using the View menu on the toolbar (or the View menu in the menu bar). If you've shown them, the appropriate master slide appears with a check mark next to it when you select a slide that uses that master slide.

Slide outlines

If you choose to show slide outlines, the Keynote view changes, as shown in Figure 19-2. You can show slides and master slides together, but neither of them can be shown with slide outlines. Compare the slide in the main section of the window in Figure 19-2 with the outline shown at the left. The outline is generated automatically from the slide's total text, including bullets.

This automatic synchronization between slides and outlines works in both directions. For example, in Figure 19-3, a new inner bullet is being typed (*Basic Sli* is all that has been typed so far). As you type in the slide outline area, the appropriate text and bullet appear in the main slide.

Bullets in Keynote presentations, like outlines and bullets in Pages documents, rely on the tab key. To indent some text for an outline or bullet, just tab to the indented position. To outdent (that is, move a bullet to the left), use Shift-tab. With bulleted or outlined text selected, use the Bullets tab of Text inspector to choose the image for the bullet and to verify the indent level.

When you're creating slides, sometimes it makes sense to bounce between typing in a slide and typing in a slide outline. The outline helps to show you the structure of the slide, and that outline sometimes makes gaps and omissions easier to see and quickly repair.

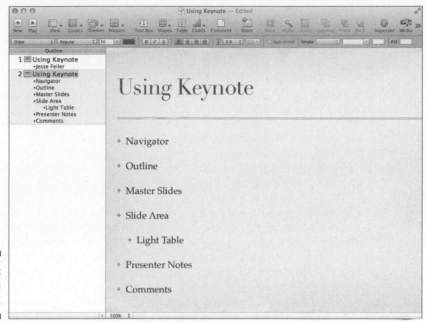

Figure 19-2:
View slide
outlines.

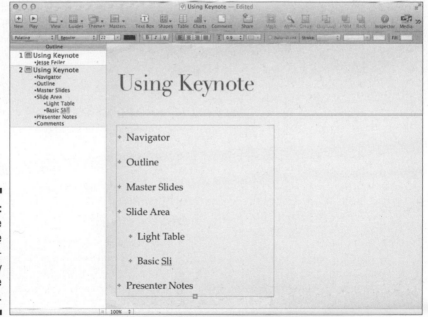

Figure 19-3:
Type the
slide outline
and auto-
matically
update the
slide.

Master slides

Each Keynote theme has its own master slides, and many themes have variations on some of the master slides (usually marked with *Alt* for *alternate*). To make your Keynote presentation consistent, display the master slides and then scroll through them, deleting the ones you won't be using. That way, you'll limit your master slides to a smaller and consistent set. The master slide can be shown from View in the toolbar, as shown in Figure 19-4. You can also use View⇨Show Master Slides.

Not every theme supports every master slide structure, but by and large, you'll find that most master slide structures are available.

If you enter text or photos on master slides, you can change the theme of your presentation. Do not do so without checking: Sometimes there are slight differences in fonts and spacing, so you'll need to make manual adjustments to text on the master slide. In general, if you've left a little bit of space around a master slide's text or title, you'll be safer than if you've used every pixel.

The standard suite of master slides provides the basics for an excellent presentation. You can create your own slides from blank master slides, but if you use the built-in master slides, you'll give your presentation not only a consistent look but also a logical structure.

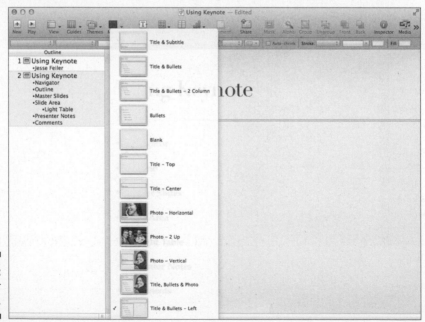

Figure 19-4:
Use master slides.

With Keynote for iOS, you choose a master slide as soon as you create a new slide, as you see in Figure 19-5.

You can find out more about using, modifying, and creating master slides in Chapter 21.

The light table

If you're used to arranging slides, you may have used a light table — either an actual light table lit from below or one generated by software. In Keynote, you can move slides around, as shown in Figure 19-6. Reorganizing your slides is also another way of doing a consistency check. As you organize your slides into a logical sequence, you'll quickly be able to see if something about the sequence is distracting (perhaps a repeated graphic or too many bulleted slides in a row).

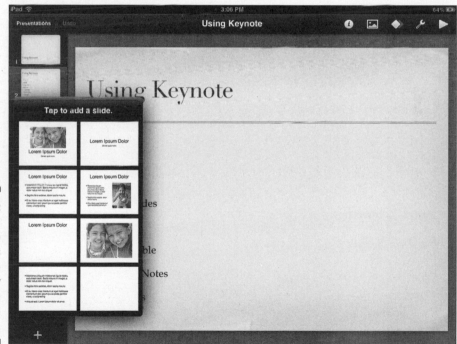

Figure 19-5:
Choose a master slide as soon as you create a new slide with Keynote for iOS.

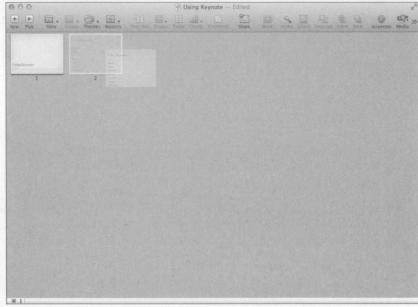

Figure 19-6:
Use a light
table to
organize
your slides.

Presenter notes

One technique that skilled presenters use is presenter notes, as shown in Figure 19-7. Presenter notes can provide you with reminders of questions to ask as well as issues to mention. Don't bother providing a preview of the next slide. In most cases, you can use Keynote's presenter's display (see Chapter 20) so that you can see where you're going next.

If you have good speaker's notes, your presentation is a combination of the slides and your talk. If you rely on your memory, you may find that you're putting everything onto a slide so that you don't forget it; that means you will have little to add and will soon bore your audience.

Your speaker's notes shouldn't be too long; otherwise you'll spend too much time reading them and not talking to your audience. You can enlarge the speaker's notes pane at the bottom of the window so that there's more room. This is useful as you're preparing your presentation. When you're actually presenting it, if you use the speaker's display as described in Chapter 20, there's plenty of room for speaker's notes alongside the full image of each slide.

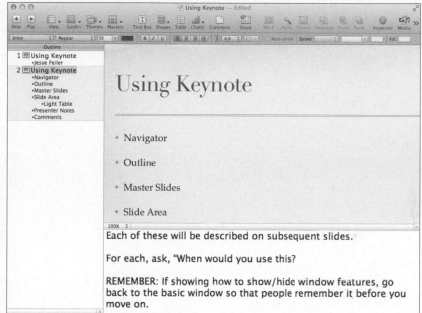

Figure 19-7:
Use pre-
senter
notes.

 There's a special case for speaker's notes: a presentation that's designed for use by several people. You may want to try out your speaker's notes with several speakers to make certain that the resulting presentations are more or less what you had in mind. Striking a balance between each speaker's spontaneous words, the text on the slides, and the speaker's notes is a difficult task, but after you've learned it, you're ready to entrust your presentation to a variety of speakers.

Comments

Each iWork application allows you to add comments; those for Keynote appear much like sticky notes, as shown in Figure 19-8.

 Comments are free-format; you can place them anywhere on a slide. The best use for them in a Keynote presentation is as a reminder of something still to be done to prepare the presentation. Don't use comments for speaker's notes; they won't show up with other speaker's notes on the speaker's display and can easily be overlooked.

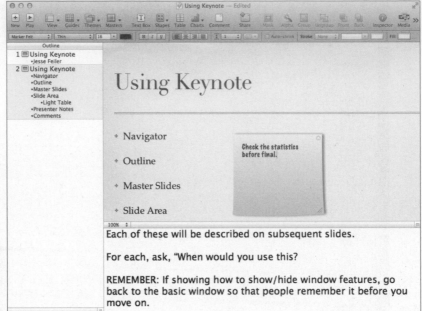

Figure 19-8:
Use
comments.

Exploring Keynote on iOS

When you open (or create) a Keynote document on iPad, the basic Keynote screen appears, as shown in Figure 19-9. The name of the document is centered in the toolbar at the top. At the left, a Presentations button functions exactly as the Spreadsheets button does in Numbers and as the Documents button does in Pages — small images represent the first page of each of your saved files. And for good measure, the Undo button behaves the same as it does in the other apps — it lets you undo your last action.

One difference between Keynote and the other iWork apps is that it always appears in landscape (horizontal) orientation; as you rotate the iPad, the image does not rotate. This is because the slides are all designed to be shown horizontally. It's not really a Keynote limitation but rather a nod to the realities of projectors and displays. On the left side of the screen are thumbnail views of the slides in your presentation. (This is the *navigator.*) To go to any slide in your presentation, just tap the thumbnail.

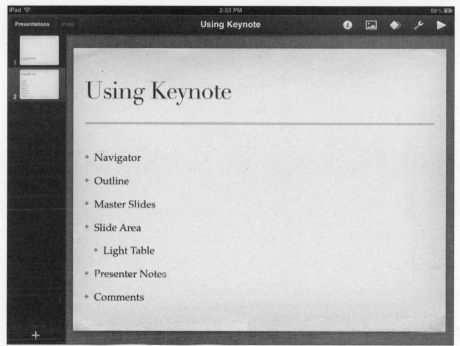

If you move a Keynote presentation from your Mac to an iOS device, you may get some messages such as the ones shown in Figure 19-10. Not all features available on Mac OS X are supported on iOS. Some of the changes will be made permanently in the presentation so that when it is moved back to the Mac, they will remain. When you are back on the Mac, if you want to undo the changes (such as relocking unlocked objects), you can do so. But there's one very important point to note about the changes shown in Figure 19-9: They don't affect the content. No slides are deleted or added, and no text is changed. Formats and fonts may change, but your presentation is intact as it moves from an iOS device to a Mac and back again.

Because some features, such as fonts, don't convert from one platform to another, it's a good idea to move a few slides back and forth as you start to design your presentation to see whether you've chosen a font or other feature that doesn't convert.

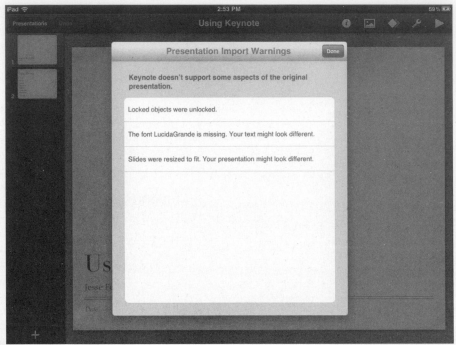

Figure 19-10:
Review any conversion messages.

On the right side of the toolbar, you have the usual buttons with two additions. The buttons, from left to right, are

- ✔ **Info:** As always, this button lets you modify the selected object or objects. The choices depend on what type of object is selected. (If nothing on the slide is selected, the button is grayed out.)

- ✔ **Insert:** This button, which looks like a landscape, lets you insert media, such as photos, tables, charts, and shapes, just as in the other iWork apps.

- ✔ **Transitions on a single slide:** You've probably never seen some of these effects, such as slide and zoom, and transitions. I describe them in Chapter 21.

- ✔ **Tools:** Tapping the Tools button gives you the popover shown in Figure 19-11. You can select share and print your presentation, use Find to search the Keynote document, show presenter notes (even if they are to yourself), and get help.

  Use Advanced for even more tools.

  - • **Advanced:** These tools let you turn slide numbers on and off, set the presentation type, and use guides and remotes as you see in Figure 19-12.

- **Presentation Type:** This is where you can set a presentation to loop or to autoplay (see Figure 19-13).

  Guides for alignment guidelines can appear as you move an object toward the center of the slide or other objects, at the edges of the slide, or at 10 percent increments horizontally and vertically along the slide. You can turn automatic slide numbering on and off. Just as with pages of a Pages document, it's best to let the app handle the numbering so that the slide (or page) numbers are correct even if you move things around, delete slides, or add slides. You don't need a special spell-check option because it's now built into iOS.

- **Remote:** You can enable a remote device to control the presentation. The remote device (such as an iPhone) communicates wirelessly with your iPad or Mac, which then plays your presentation as if you were tapping the screen or clicking the mouse. This setting means that you can put your iPad or Mac next to a projector and avoid a tangle of wires while you speak from the front of a room.

✔ **Play:** This starts the presentation playing; if you have an external display adapter, the slides appear on the display while the iPad screen shows the controls.

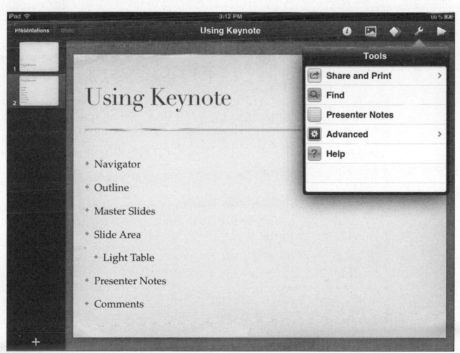

Figure 19-11:
Use the
Keynote
tools.

Figure 19-12:
Use the
Keynote
advanced
tools.

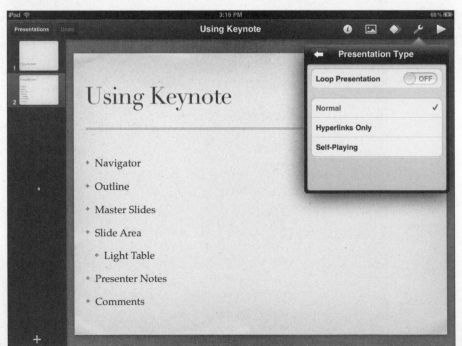

Figure 19-13:
Set the
presentation
type.

Introducing the Keynote Themes

When you launch Keynote or create a new document on Mac OS X, you're prompted to choose a theme, as shown in Figure 19-14. As always on iOS, you pick up from the last thing you were doing when you reopen Keynote, but when you create a new document, you can choose from one of the iOS Keynote themes. (Note that the size of each theme's slides is shown in the lower right of the window. With some themes, you can choose from alternate sizes.)

Theme Chooser looks very much like Template Chooser for Pages and Numbers. One immediate difference is the pop-up menu in the lower right: You can select the size of your presentation slides when you select a theme.

Another difference between Theme Chooser and Template Chooser is that the themes are not divided into categories, such as Education or Business.

But the biggest difference between themes and templates is that themes are interchangeable. With a template, you normally create a document from the template and go on to customize it. You can modify colors and patterns in the template, but your document has its own logic and structure. If you want to switch to a new template, you can do so by starting a new document, or you can modify the existing document.

Figure 19-14:
Choose a
theme on
Mac OS X.

With a theme (rather than a template), you can switch back and forth from one theme to another. You can do this because the structure of the underlying document is independent of the theme, so the theme can always be replaced.

Just as a Numbers document can contain a number of sheets, each with its own tables and charts, and a Pages document can contain a number of pages or sections, each with its own formatted elements, a Keynote document consists of a number of slides, each of which has its own formatted elements. Unlike Pages and Numbers, the structure of those slides is specific, and you'll see that the slide structures — called *master slides* — allow you to switch from one theme to another. In addition, these structures help you implement the type of roadmaps and structures cited previously as ways to improve your presentations.

On iOS, you will notice two differences. As I already noted, unlike the other iWork apps, Keynote works only in the horizontal or landscape orientation. The second is that you have a limited number of themes available. Compare the iOS themes shown in Figure 19-15 with the Mac OS X themes shown in Figure 19-14.

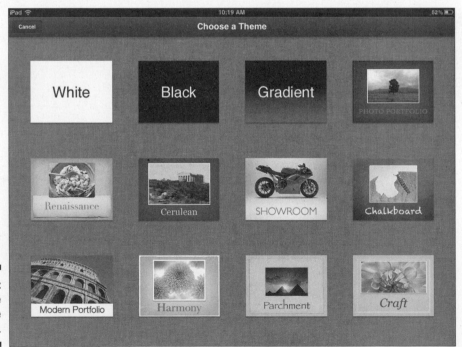

Figure 19-15:
Review the iOS Keynote themes.

Chapter 20

Presenting a Keynote Presentation

*U*nlike Numbers spreadsheets and Pages documents, Keynote presentations aren't designed to be given to someone to read or study: You're a key component of your Keynote presentation. Sometimes you prepare a presentation for someone else to use or vice versa. But most of the time, you run the show, stage center. Fortunately, Keynote has a host of tools that make it easy for you to fulfill the dual roles of presentation author and presenter. This chapter gives you an overview of those tools.

Choosing Your Presentation Options

The earliest presentation software tools used the computer monitor to display slides. Often, a second monitor, frequently a projection TV, was connected. Keynote for Mac lets you select your primary display (usually the projection TV) and configure the other one with timers and presenter's notes.

With iWork, you have another way of working with Keynote for Mac. You can download Keynote Remote, an app for iPhone and iPod touch. It's available from the App Store in iTunes and currently costs $0.99. You can use the iPhone or iPod touch, both of which communicate wirelessly with the computer running Keynote, to control the slides. Another wrinkle in this scenario is that speaker's notes can be visible along with the slide on your iPhone or iPod touch. This means you have two displays for presenter's notes and other nonslide information: the presenter's display on a computer as well as your iPhone or iPod touch.

Setting Presentation Preferences with Keynote for Mac

You can set preferences for how Keynote handles multiple displays, for how the slide show will be managed, for the presenter's display (if you have multiple displays), and for using a remote (if you have one). In most cases, the default preferences for iWork apps are fine. However, when it comes to customizing your environment — particularly if you're using multiple displays — you need to pay attention to these settings.

Setting preferences for two displays

Laptops and iMacs have built-in displays; desktop Macs do not. All Macs have a plug for another display in addition to the built-in display or the main display for a desktop Mac. You use System Preferences⇨Displays to manage the displays on your computer. Three basic display configurations are available:

✔ **Single display:** You have a single display, built-in or not. All windows you open with any program on your Mac are shown on this display. You can move them around, but you can't totally move a window off a single display. (You can minimize it in the dock, but it remains part of the main window.)

✔ **Mirrored display:** This configuration allows you to have two displays connected to your computer. In the Displays section of System Preferences, use the Mirror Displays check box to ensure that the same image appears on both displays. When it comes to presentations, many times the second display for a computer is a projector. By mirroring the displays, you can work with the computer's display as you normally would, and the mirrored display (the projector) displays that image in an enlarged version.

✔ **Separate displays:** The Displays section of System Preferences shows all screens attached to your computer. (Some people have more than two!) Only one of them shows a menu bar at the top of the screen. Drag that menu bar to the primary screen. Often the primary screen will be your desktop or laptop screen; you can use the secondary screen (without the menu bar) for other windows that you can use for your work.

If you're going to be giving a Keynote presentation that uses two screens, try to use Displays in System Preferences before you're ready to begin. If you can get to the presentation area ten minutes before the audience arrives, you can arrange screens so that they see what's important. If you can't do this, temporarily create a new user account on your computer and copy your presentation and any other needed files to that user's Public folder. Do this without connecting to any publicly visible screen. Then, log on as the new user. The desktop will be empty, and the only visible files will be your presentation. If you need to move files around and adjust the screen layout, you can do this without everyone looking at the files you have on your computer. Still, the better choice is to use your actual account and set things up before the waudience arrives.

Regardless of how you arrange the screens, use Energy Saver to prevent the screen from dimming. If you're using a laptop, plug it in. You'll use a bit more power, but you won't have to jiggle the mouse to prevent the computer from going to sleep.

Like all iWork applications, you can set preferences for Keynote for Mac. Begin by choosing Keynote⇨Preferences to open the Preferences window shown in Figure 20-1.

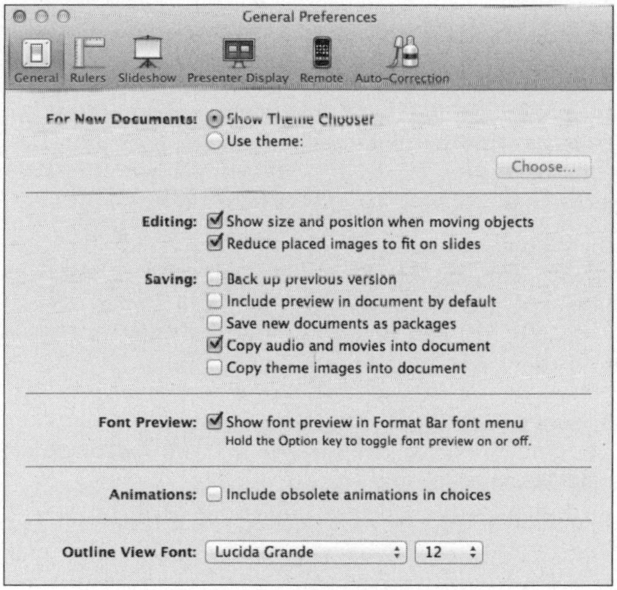

Figure 20-1:
Set Keynote
preferences.

The General, Rulers, and Auto-Correction preferences are standard for all iWork apps. The ones that matter for your presentations are Slideshow, Presenter Display, and Remote. I go over each in this section.

Slideshow preferences

Here are the choices for you to consider about Slideshow preferences:

✔ **Scale slides up:** This option *scales* (that is, enlarges) the slides to fill the display. Particularly on a projector, you have plenty of space to play with, so you might as well use it. However, if your presentation will be made at different times on different size displays, you may want to reset this preference for the display just before you give your presentation.

✔ **Exit presentation after last slide:** Consider what will happen at the end of your presentation. If you exit the presentation, there you'll be (along with your audience), looking at your desktop and the files on it. Consider placing a special slide at the end of the presentation. It can be a simple "The End" slide, but you can also make it more useful. "For more info, contact XXX" provides a neutral final slide that can remain visible until the last person has left the room.

✔ **Minimize distractions from transitions and other applications:** That's the idea behind reducing Cube transitions, reducing Flip transitions, and not allowing Exposé, Mission Control, Dashboard, and other apps to intrude on your Keynote presentation.

✔ **Set pointer preferences:** You have three pointer preferences. If you're used to pointing with the pointer, use the option to show the pointer when the mouse moves. (The alternative is to have a separate pointer for your presentation, which seems like overkill.)

✔ **Choose the display for slides:** If you have more than one display, choose the one for slides to appear on. If you have a single display or a mirrored display, you don't have a choice. Otherwise, choose the display that is connected to a projector. It doesn't matter if it's a primary or secondary display: Keynote will do the right thing.

Also consider a special introductory slide that can play as a movie before your presentation begins. Create a movie or an iPhoto slide show from relevant photos and images. You can add music. If you watch various presentations, you'll see that such introductory movies or slide shows can consist of excerpts from previous presentations, promotional materials, or even advertisements. Your goal is to provide a lead-in to your presentation.

Presenter Display preferences

Figure 20-2 shows the Presenter Display preferences. The Presenter Display is available only if you have two displays connected to your computer or if you're using Keynote Remote on an iPhone (or iPod touch), but the Presenter Display preferences are available even if you only have one display at the time you're setting the preferences. This means you can configure your

Presenter Display preferences before you get to the auditorium with the big projection display.

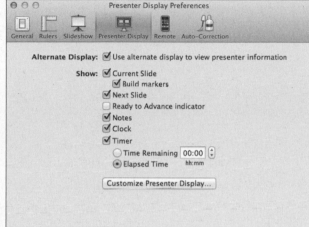

Figure 20-2: Set Presenter Display preferences.

In addition to customizing the Presenter Display preferences, you can format the presenter's display by using the Customize Presenter Display button at the bottom of the Presenter Display Preferences screen. Click that button to open the window shown in Figure 20-3; drag items to rearrange them on the presenter's display.

If you're accustomed to giving presentations, two features are absolute gifts. The first is the time. Elapsed time for a slide is useful, but if your presentation is scheduled from, say, 2:00 to 2:45, knowing the exact time can help you speed up as needed or stop for a Q&A period if you see that there's time to spare. Of course, you don't need Keynote to do this: You can step up to the podium and take your watch off so that you can keep track of time. There is a technical word for this frequently repeated gesture: tacky. It's almost as bad as a speaker rifling through the remaining pages of a speech to see how much material is left. Keynote hides what should be hidden and shows it to you if and when you need it.

Equally valuable is the ability to see the next slide. Transitions from one slide to another are often left to the speaker, as in "But how does that work in practice?" or "What's a good example of this?" If you see the next slide cued up, you can make the appropriate transition.

Another feature of the Presenter Display is shown in Figure 20-3: You can add presenter's notes to the display. By being able to see the current slide and the next slide along with notes you've prepared, everything you need for your presentation is in front of you without distracting the audience.

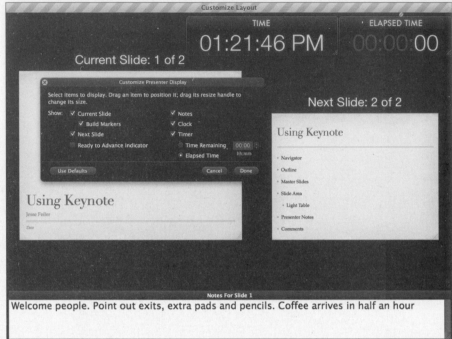

Figure 20-3:
Rearrange items on the presenter's display.

You enter presenter's notes for a slide by choosing View➪Show Presenter Notes or clicking View on the toolbar. This preference controls where and if the presenter's notes you've entered for slides are shown on the presenter's display.

Presenting with iPad

You have dotted every *i* and crossed every *t* in your presentation, added all the great ideas you've been storing in your brain, and tweaked the animations, and you're happy with what you have. Now you need to prepare for a captivating presentation.

The cable known as the Apple iPad Dock Connector to VGA Adapter ($29 from the Apple Store at the time of this writing) connects your iPad to any VGA device, such as a projector. With it, you can use Keynote to give your presentation.

The Digital AV Adapter cable accessory is available for $39. You can use it to connect to devices enabled with Thunderbolt high-definition media technology or to devices such as HDTVs that have HDMI connectors. With iPad 2 and later, you can set the adaptor to mirror the iPad screen or to project from it as you want to do with Keynote. Note, too, that the issue of connecting projectors to iPads is an area that changes rapidly with new technology. A visit to the Apple Store (online or in a bricks-and-mortar store) can be very useful).

When you connect a projector (or any other type of display) to your iPad with the iPad Dock Connector to VGA Adapter, the Keynote app can sense that it has a second display. It uses this display when you start a slide show in the Keynote app. While it's sending the presentation to the external display, it lets you control it from your iPad. Figure 20-4 shows what you see on the iPad as it plays a presentation on an external display.

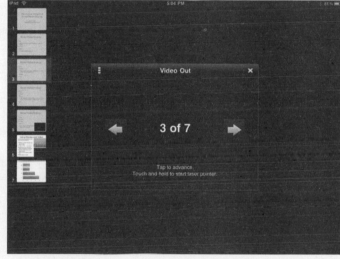

Figure 20-4:
Control a presentation on an external display.

The slides are displayed on the external display, but you can control the presentation using your iPad. On the left side of the screen, a navigator shows thumbnail images of your slides. Being able to see the next slide helps you transition to it elegantly without shuffling papers and distracting your audience and yourself. You can tap the arrows in the center of the iPad screen to move forward and backward among slides.

Presenting with Your iPhone and the Keynote Remote App

With iWork for Mac you can control presentations and view presenter's notes by downloading the Keynote Remote app from iTunes and installing it on your iPhone, iPad, or iPod touch.

To pair your iPhone and Mac with Keynote Remote:

1. **Launch a Keynote presentation on your Mac and then launch Keynote Remote on your iPhone.**

   The iPhone locates a nearby computer running Keynote, and Keynote asks you to confirm the connection, as shown in Figure 20-5.

2. **If you want to connect to that iPhone, click the Link button at the right.**

   When you click Link, a code is displayed on Keynote Remote on your iPhone.

3. **Type that code displayed on Keynote Remote, as shown in Figure 20-6.**

   The connection between iPhone and Keynote is now complete.

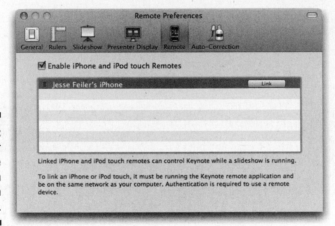

Figure 20-5:
Accept (or decline) the invitation to link to an iPhone.

Figure 20-6:
Accept the pairing.

To set Keynote remote options, you see the first slide of the current presentation on your iPhone (see Figure 20-7).

Options in the upper left of the screen let you move to the view you see in Figure 20-8.

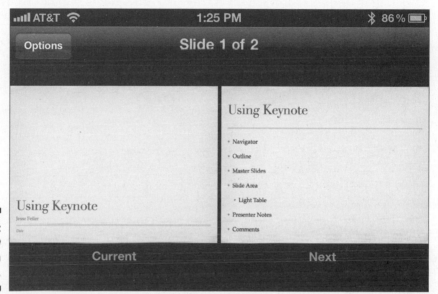

Figure 20-7: Preview slides on your iPhone.

Figure 20-8: Swipe to move to the next or previous slide.

Buttons on the screen let you skip to the beginning or end of the presentation. For standard movement, just use your finger to swipe the current slide aside on your iPhone. You don't need to touch your computer.

Settings lets you show presenter notes below the slides on your iPhone (see Figure 20-9). This means you now have two places for presenter notes: on the computer or on an iPhone. You can also use Settings to choose among several versions of Keynote on a Wi-Fi network. (This is a great tool for a class in which each student is working on a presentation and you want to switch from one to the other as you comment.)

Figure 20-9:
Use Settings to control presenter notes and switch Keynote computers.

Using your iPhone means that you can wander around more: The computer with its projection TV output doesn't need hands-on attention from you because you're driving the slides from your iPhone. However, now that you're untethered from the computer, you can no longer use the mouse to point to parts of a slide. (You could use a laser pointer or a wooden pointer.)

Chapter 21

Improving Your Keynote Presentation

In This Chapter

▶ Adding a personal touch to themes and master slides

▶ Working with motion in movies, transitions, and builds

▶ Using sound

When it comes to Numbers and Pages, you have a variety of choices for sharing your documents. But those choices are insignificant next to the choices for sharing and automating Keynote presentations. This chapter shows you some features you can add to your presentations. Because presentations involve text, images, and a variety of media components, you can export them to any of the movie and DVD formats available on your Mac. You can also share them through the web — using the various iLife apps as well as web-sharing sites, such as YouTube.

In general, the features you can add using Keynote transfer without effort to these other formats and platforms. In this chapter, I show you how to add Keynote features for motion, sound, and automation to your presentation.

Creating Different Types of Presentations

The Keynote themes are interchangeable, and each has certain basic slides that suggest the types of presentations you can create. You can easily fall into a trap of thinking that these presentations are the only types you can create with Keynote. This section gives you some additional ideas.

Reviewing the master slides

You don't have to use all the master slides in a given theme. Here are some of the types of presentations you can create with the various themes and master slides:

✔ **Basic structured presentations:** These presentations emphasize content and organization. They typically use bulleted lists of information. Keynote's organizing tools help people follow your presentation without getting lost.

✔ **Catalogs, albums, and event presentations:** These tend to use master slides with space for photos. Whereas basic structured presentations tend to use bulleted lists to create a hierarchical structure, these presentations have a less hierarchical structure. Their organizing structure can be chronological (a wedding day, for example) or informational (a product catalog is a good example).

✔ **Creative presentations:** Keynote is part of iWork, but that doesn't mean you can't use it to explore your creative side. You can merge the structure of bulleted slides with images for an art appreciation presentation. You can also use a Keynote presentation to tell a story or create a scrapbook. Depending on your resources and your audience, it may be easier to construct your story as a Keynote presentation than as an iPhoto slide show. One deciding factor may be whether you have photos and video that you can use in telling your story. If you don't, Keynote, with its excellent handling of text, can be more effective than iPhoto.

Planning your presentation

Different types of presentations lend themselves to different types of interactions with their audiences. Keynote lets you package and automate your presentation. Most people find that self-running presentations work well for catalogs and albums; they can stand on their own, like advertisements or magazine articles.

Complex structured presentations, such as those used at trade shows or in classrooms, often don't work well as self-running presentations. Instead, having someone (probably you) control the presentation and stop for questions and discussions can help get the message across.

The choices are built into Keynote, mostly through its themes, so it's just a matter of experimenting with your options to find the most effective method for your own presentation.

One way to improve your Keynote presentations is to watch other presentations. What interests you? What do you like? If there's a live audience, watch them and see what they like. There are no hard-and-fast rules. A presentation designed for a college class is different from one designed for a Bridal Faire (and not just in spelling of the title). Some presentations benefit from a serious approach, while others work well with humor and added features.

Customizing Themes and Master Slides with Keynote for Mac

Themes and master slides save you time and help you create better presentations. With Keynote for Mac, you can go further by creating your own customized themes and master slides.

Creating a customized theme is simple. Create a presentation with Keynote as you normally do. Make any customizations you want to fonts, background colors, and the like. Then choose File⇨Save Theme and name the theme. The theme is automatically stored with that name and appears in the list of themes in Keynote for Mac.

If you will want to use your theme on both Mac OS and iOS, test it out on both to make certain that the fonts and other selections you've made work well on both platforms.

Actually, the theme is stored in `~/Library/Application Support/ iWork/Keynote/Themes/<the name you choose>`. After you've saved your theme, you can remove it if you want by removing that file. (This doesn't affect presentations built on it.) On Mac OS X 10.7 (Lion) or later, if you don't see the Library folder, hold down Option while you open the Go menu in the Finder. But if you need this little tidbit, maybe you shouldn't be poking around there. Whatever you do, don't touch anything outside the Keynote/Themes folder. The Library folder is hidden for a good reason. It's there for super-powered power users.

Customizing master slides

You can customize master slides and save them in your own theme. Customizing master slides is the heart of building your own themes. First, create a copy of a theme and give it a meaningful name. That way, if things don't work out, you won't have messed up anything that matters because you can start over again.

Here is how to get started customizing master slides:

1. **Because you'll be working with master slides, show the navigator (View⇨Navigator) as well as the master slides (View⇨Master Slides).**

    You can achieve the same result with View in the toolbar.

2. **Show the Master Slide inspector (see Figure 21-1).**

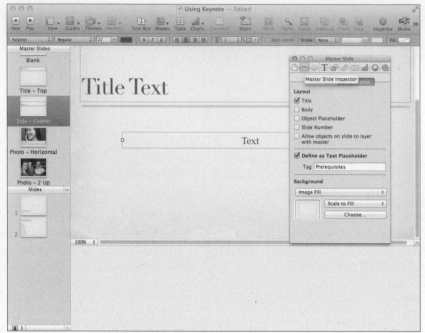

Figure 21-1:
Use the
Master
Slide
inspector.

3. **Select Appearance at the top right.**

   In Figure 21-1, Appearance is slightly hidden by the help tag identifying the Master Slide inspector.

4. **After you have the Master Slide inspector open, you can select any of the check boxes and options shown in Figure 21-1.**

   The first three items (Title, Body, and Object Placeholder) create objects with hints of what you should place in them. For example, Figure 21-2 shows a customized master slide.

Creating a new master slide

In addition to customizing an existing master slide, you can create a new one. Just show the master slides as in Step 1 of the previous section. Then select any master slide and create a new one with Slide⇨New Master Slide.

If the command is New Slide or if the result of the keyboard shortcut is that you create a new slide (not a master slide), you did not have a master slide selected in the navigator.

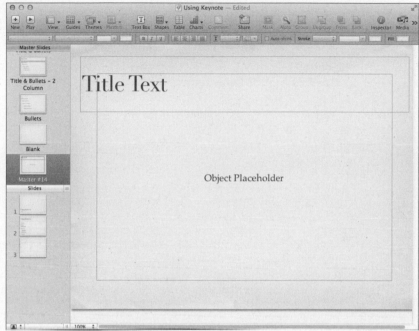

Figure 21-2:
Customize
a master
slide

Adding Motion to Your Presentation

Motion can make a slide show more interesting and keep people's attention. (Or it can be distracting: Use your judgment.) Your Keynote slide shows can use motion in three ways:

- ✔ **Insert a QuickTime movie onto a slide:** Movies enliven your presentations. With the editing tools you have on Mac OS X and on iOS, you can customize your presentations as much as you want.

- ✔ **Add transitions between slides:** Transitions provide animated effects between slides.

- ✔ **Add builds within slides:** Builds provide animated effects within a slide such as when bullet points appear one by one.

Adding a movie to a slide with Keynote for Mac

The most basic way of adding movement to your presentation is to add a QuickTime movie to a slide. Here's how you do it:

1. **Click Media on the toolbar to open Media Browser, from which you can choose movies, photos, and audio, as shown in Figure 21-3.**

2. **Drag the movie into the slide where you want it.**

   Remember that in Media Browser, the movie is shown as a single-frame thumbnail image. When you drag it into a slide, it appears either as a shape with the typical eight handles or as the movie itself (not the thumbnail). That's why you see the FlorenceMovie.mov thumbnail in Figure 21-3, and part of the movie itself in Figure 21-4.

3. **Select the QuickTime movie on the slide and use QuickTime inspector to set up the movie.**

   Depending on the movie, you may want to vary the settings shown in Figure 21-5. If the movie is to start with a click, most likely you'll want to set a poster frame so that a still image is visible on your slide before the movie starts playing. If you're using the movie for an introductory or final slide, you may want to set the Repeat options so that the movie loops over and over or loops back and forth. If you're using the movie as part of your presentation (that is, as a movie to be played from start to finish with the click of a mouse), you probably don't want any looping.

Adding a movie to a slide with Keynote for iOS

Themes provide some slide layouts with image placeholders in them. To change a placeholder image, simply double-tap it. A dialog opens, showing media sources, such as your Photo Albums. Locate an item and tap to insert it.

Figure 21-3:
Add a movie to your presentation.

Figure 21-4:
Position the
movie on
the slide.

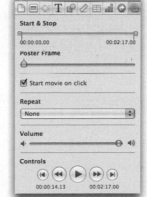

Figure 21-5:
Use
QuickTime
inspector to
set up the
movie.

If you want to add an image outside of a placeholder, make sure that no placeholder is selected and then tap the Insert button. Tap any of the four tabs: Media, Tables, Charts, or Shapes. Choose the item you want to insert, and it appears on your slide.

You can now move the object around with your finger. You select an object on a slide with a single tap (the same as in Numbers and Pages). You can drag the object around; Keynote provides the coordinates for precise positioning, and also provides you with guidelines as you align the object with the center of the screen or the edge of other objects. To resize an object, drag a corner handle until it's the size you want and then let it go.

Adding a transition between slides with Keynote for Mac

Another way to add motion to your presentation is to use one of the transition effects between two adjacent slides. Here's how to do that:

1. **Select the slide for the transition.**

   The transition will come into play when you move from this slide to the next one.

2. **Click the Slide button in Slide inspector and then click the Transition tab, as shown in Figure 21-6.**

3. **Select the transition you want from the list of effects shown in Figure 21-7.**

   Try to avoid turning your presentation into a presentation about transitions. If you limit your transitions to a few, and if you choose consistent directions, you'll find that your transitions serve your presentation rather than the other way around.

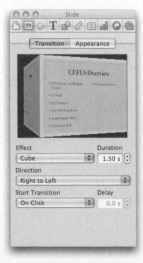

Figure 21-6: Use Slide inspector and the Transition tab to set up a transition.

Figure 21-7:
Select the
transition
and its
direction.

Onc tcchnique many presenters use is to home in on two or three transitions, cach of which plays a distinct role. For example, if your presentation is highly structured, you may want to use a dramatic transition, such as a 3-D effect, to introduce each major section of the presentation. Then, within each major section, use simpler 2-D effects for minor transitions. If you're consistent with the use of transitions, they add to your presentation.

As you can see from Figure 21-5, transitions are available that use text and graphics so that you can move from one slide to another without causing distraction. One interesting transition is Magic Move, which you use when you have the same object, such as a text box, on both slides that are part of the transition. If the same object appears on both slides in different locations, Keynote performs a transition that appears to move the object from its location on the first slide to its location on the second slide. This transition is powerful when you're discussing the object and its text or graphics.

Adding a transition between slides with Keynote for iOS

Use the Transitions button at the right end of the toolbar, at the top of the Keynote screen, to begin setting a transition. When you tap the button, you move to the transition editor. Notice the Done button in the top-right corner of the screen — until you tap the Done button, you're working on a transition.

Transitions can work on slides as a whole or work on parts of slides; when they work on parts of slides, they're often called *builds*. Note that a transition consists of two parts:

- ✔ **Effect:** This is the visual effect that's displayed.
- ✔ **Options:** Options include the direction in which the animation moves as well as whether it starts in response to a tap or after a previous transition is finished. Options also include the duration of the transition.

Though a transition may appear to happen *between* two slides, it happens *after* you tap a slide to go to the next one. The transition is attached to the first slide in the sequence of two adjacent slides.

Here's how to build a transition:

1. **Tap the Transitions button to enter the transition editor.**

2. **In the navigator on the left side of the screen, tap the slide for which you want to build a transition (see Figure 21-8).**

   The current transition (if any) is shown.

3. **Tap + in the transition to see the list of effects, shown in Figure 21-9.**

   A number of transition effects are available; swipe up and down to see them all. (The list of transitions is controlled by the Effects button at the bottom-left corner of the popover.)

4. **When you find a transition effect that interests you, tap the name to select it and see a preview.**

   You can tap the triangle in the top-right corner of the popover to repeat the preview.

   After you apply a transition effect to a slide, it appears whenever you select that slide in the navigator while using Transitions, as shown in Figure 21-10.

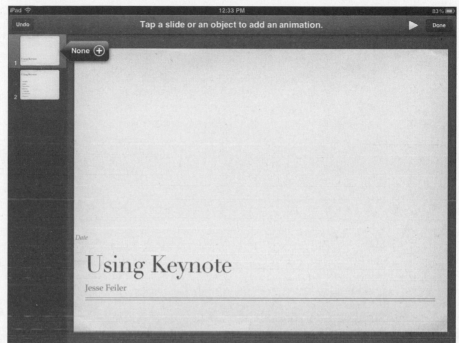

Figure 21-8:
Begin
building a
transition.

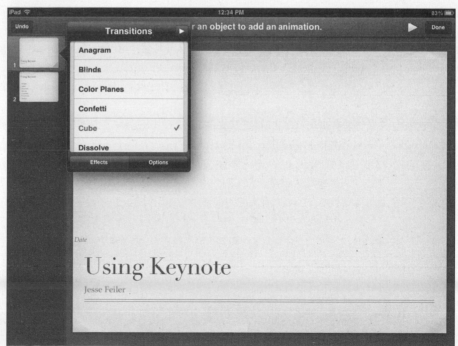

Figure 21-9:
Choose an
effect.

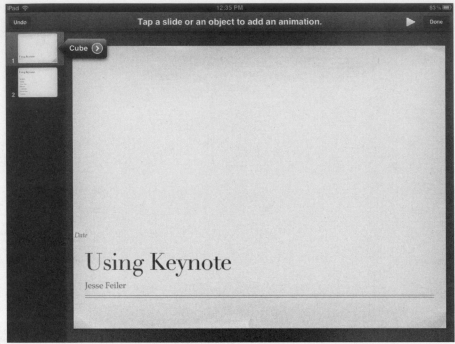

Figure 21-10:
The effect
is shown on
the slide
in the
navigator.

5. **Tap the Options button in the bottom-right corner of the popover to set the effect options.**

   Use the big circle in the middle of the popover to select the direction the animation moves, as you see in Figure 21-11.

6. **Swipe up on the popover to see the remaining options (see Figure 21-12).**

7. **Continue to change the effects and options until you're satisfied.**

   You'll probably want to try out the combinations with the triangle in the upper-right side of the popover several times.

Adding builds within slides with Keynote for Mac

Builds can also work within a single slide; they let you bring slide items, such as bullets, onto the slide with animation effects.

Builds have three aspects: Build In (for items appearing on the slide), Build Out (for items disappearing from the slide), and Action.

Figure 21-11:
Set the
direction
option.

Figure 21-12:
Set the
duration and
start.

You set the builds as follows:

1. **Begin with the complete slide.**

   Make certain that all bullets, titles, and graphics are visible.

2. **Open Build inspector, as shown in Figure 21-13.**

3. **On the slide itself, select the first item to build.**

   It doesn't matter if it's built in or out.

   With the item (such as a bullet) selected, choose Build In or Build Out and then choose an effect, a direction, an order, and a color. The order determines the sequence in which builds are performed.

   The Delivery option lets you set items within a group: all at once, by bullet, by bullet group (such as a subgroup), and by highlighted bullet.

   Watch out, because this is an area where you can obscure the content of your presentation with too many and too varied builds.

4. **Using the same process, select all the build ins and build outs you want.**

   You don't need to have both build ins and build outs. In many cases, a single style of build is more than enough.

5. **Use effects for movement that may be less structured than the sliding in and out of a build.**

   The available effects include Blast, Convergence, Cube, Fly In, and Shimmer. Try them to see what they look like.

Figure 21-13:
Build
inspector.

Adding builds within slides with Keynote for iOS

Here's how to set a build within a slide:

1. **Tap the Transitions button.**

   Until you tap the Done button, you're creating a transition. Because builds are done within a slide, you work on the slide itself (not on the navigator).

2. **In the display portion of the screen, tap the object you want to build, as shown in Figure 21-14.**

   Each object can have two sets of builds: effects to build it *into* the slide (when the slide is shown) and effects to build it *out* of the slide (when the slide is closed).

3. **Tap the appropriate button for the type of build you want to apply — either a build-in or a build-out.**

   In Figure 21-14, both Build In (on the left) and Build Out (on the right) are set to the default — None.

4. **Select the build effect you want to use, as shown in Figure 21-15.**

   As with slide-to-slide transitions, as soon as you select an effect, it's previewed for you. You can repeat the preview with the triangle in the upper-right corner.

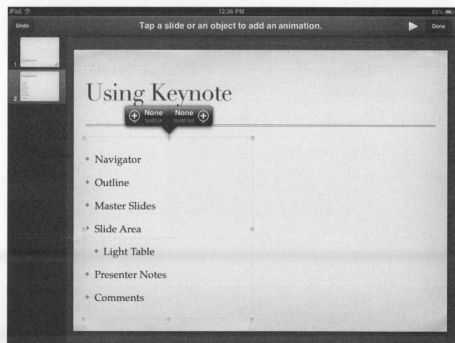

Figure 21-14: Set builds for an object.

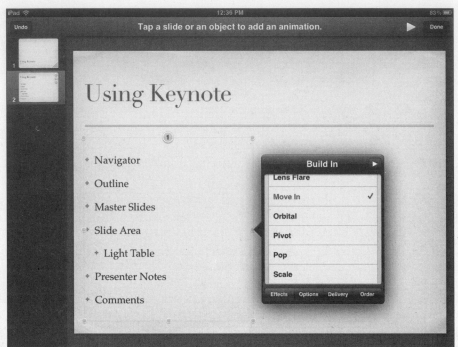

Figure 21-15:
Select the
build effect.

5. **As soon as you select a build effect, you can set options, as shown in Figure 21-16.**

   Note that a number in a yellow circle is created on the object you're applying the build to; you can tap the number later to go back and change the effect or options.

6. **Tap the Delivery button at the bottom of the popover to select whether the build happens all at one time or with the addition of each component, as shown in Figure 21-17.**

   Depending on what the selected object is, this step can build each item in a bulleted list separately or each wedge in a pie chart in sequence. (Delivery options may not be available if they don't apply.)

Managing multiple builds on a single slide

As you create builds, each one is numbered. The numbers appear in small, yellow circles as soon as you have chosen an effect. You can manage the sequence of these builds. To do so, follow these steps:

1. **Select the appropriate slide and tap the Transitions button.**

   You see the yellow circles around the numbers of the builds on that slide.

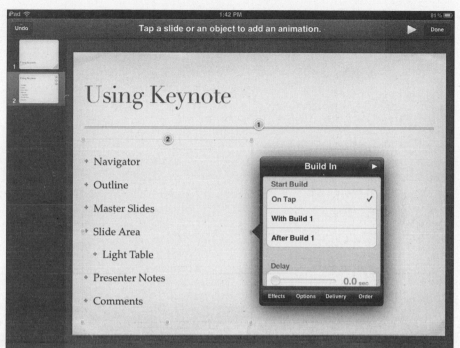

Figure 21-16:
Choose an
option.

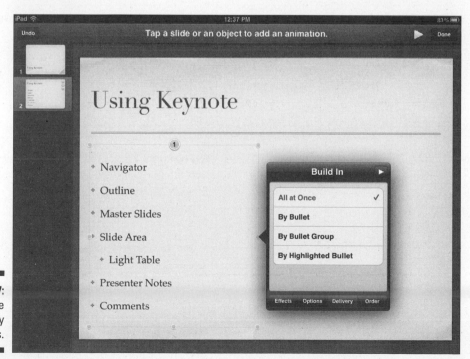

Figure 21-17:
Set the
delivery
options.

2. **Tap any build to edit it using the techniques you used to create the build.**

The yellow circles, by default, represent the order in which you created the builds. You often want to rearrange them.

3. **To reorder the builds, tap the Order button in the bottom-right corner of the popover.**

Using the horizontal bars at the right of each build (see Figure 21-18), drag them to the order you want them to be executed. The numbers automatically change. Keynote picks up identifying text, such as the title, so that you can keep them straight.

4. **When you're finished, tap Options again to review the reordered builds.**

You can use the arrow in the top-right corner of the popover to test the builds.

5. **When you're satisfied, click Done.**

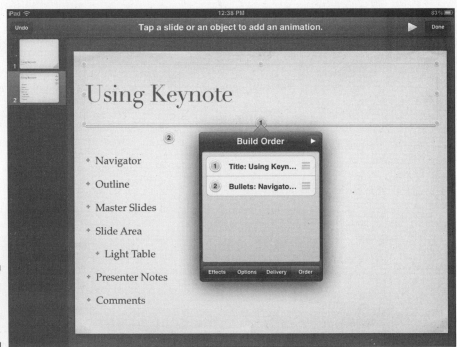

Figure 21-18:
Edit an existing build.

Adding Sound to Your Presentation on Mac OS X

You can add sound to your presentation in three ways:

- ✔ **QuickTime movies:** If you're adding a movie to your presentation, that movie can have a soundtrack, and you can play it with the movie.

- ✔ **Voice-over slide show recording:** You can prerecord your narration of a presentation. This prerecording adds a soundtrack; it also automatically saves the timing of slides so that they're synchronized with your soundtrack. By adding a soundtrack like this, your presentation is playable automatically.

- ✔ **iTunes music for a soundtrack:** You can add iTunes music to your presentation.

Recording a slide show

To add a voice-over soundtrack, begin with the Audio tab of Document inspector, as shown in Figure 21-19.

Click the Record button in the Slideshow Recording section at the bottom of the window. You walk through the presentation; in the upper left, a sound level appears as you speak. Keynote keeps track of when you have advanced to the next slide so that the presentation and the soundtrack are both recorded.

Figure 21-19: Use Keynote's Document inspector.

Use the Sound pane in System Preferences to adjust the volume and to choose whether to use the computer's built-in microphone or an external USB or other microphone. Note that if you're recording a slide show for others, you should use the best quality microphone you can find.

Using the recorded slide show

Figure 21-20 shows how you can use Document inspector with a recorded presentation. The Presentation pop-up menu includes a Recorded option and a Self-Playing option after you have recorded the presentation. Together with the option to automatically play when the Keynote document is opened, you have a powerful self-running presentation.

Figure 21-20: Take advantage of your prerecorded presentation.

Adding an iTunes song

You can add an iTunes track to your presentation. You can use the looping feature to repeat it behind all the slides. Note that adding an iTunes song is in addition to the ability to use Media Browser's Audio tab (click Media on the toolbar and then click the Audio tab) to add an iTunes track to an individual slide.

Part V
The Part of Tens

In this part . . .

The chapters in this part are top ten lists. They provide you with ways to share content, ways to let iWork do the work for you with Automator and AppleScript on Mac OS X, and ways to make your documents more effective using writing tools (such as spell checking).

The features described in this part of the book apply to all iWork applications. It makes for a full circle with Part I, which also applies to all iWork applications.

If you come away with the impression that iWork has a powerful set of commands and features available in any of its apps, that's good. The differences between Numbers, Pages, and Keynote reflect their specific objectives, but what you have in iWork is perhaps the most robust and full-featured user interface for productivity tools that has yet been created.

Chapter 22

Ten Ways to Share Content

In This Chapter

▶ Sharing content with others

▶ Working with photos, music, movies, PDF files, and more

▶ Transferring info into iWork

*Y*ou don't have to start from scratch every time you create an iWork document. You can build on other documents you've created, and you can build on the templates that are part of iWork. You can also include content that has been created with other applications. iWork and Mac OS X make it easy to reuse your work. This chapter provides you with ten ways to accomplish that goal.

Sharing Content by Copying and Enabling Access

You can share content in two basic ways:

✔ **Copying content:** You can copy content to a flash drive, iWork.com, or other place from which you and others can retrieve it.

✔ **Accessing content:** You can provide a mechanism that lets people access the data. You don't copy the data: There is one file, and everyone accesses it. This eliminates problems with data synchronization because there are no copies.

Sharing content means sharing content with other people. *Synchronizing* refers to the tools that make your documents available on all your own devices (usually through iCloud). Sharing means with others; syncing means on your own devices.

Sharing Content with People on Your Network

If you're working on a local network, letting people access your Public folder is handled differently than when you're using MobileMe on the web.

If you want to allow other people on your network to access your Public folder, choose System Preferences➪Sharing to open the pane shown in Figure 22-1. (This is set up for you with a clean install of the operating system.)

The settings in Figure 22-1 determine what other people can see when they navigate to your public folder. Figure 22-2 shows the view of your home directory that you can see yourself.

With the settings shown in Figure 22-2 in place, other users can see the folders but aren't able to see inside them. The Public folder's sharing preferences are set as shown in Figure 22-1. The result is shown in Figure 22-3. Users can see only a drop box folder inside the Public folder. A special icon next to Jesse Feiler's Public Folder indicates that it's a drop box. Anyone can drop files and folders into the drop box, but they can't see the contents — even if the contents consist of files and folders that they have dropped into the drop box. For a drop box, no users (except the owner) can see inside the folder. That includes all information, including the modification date, which isn't shown in Figure 22-3.

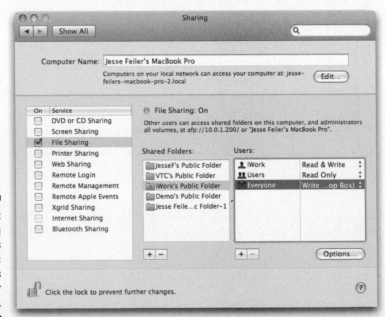

Figure 22-1:
Set sharing privileges for public folders on your computer.

Figure 22-2:
Set privi-
leges for
folders.

The settings on your computer are set during the installation of the operating system. Many times, those settings are brought forward from a previous install (and those, in turn, may have been brought forward from an even earlier install). Unless you've done a clean install and not touched anything, it is usually worth checking your settings.

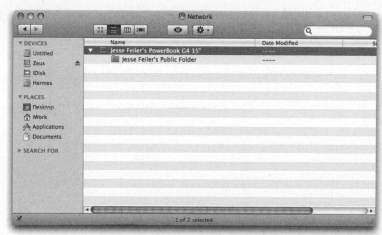

Figure 22-3:
View
access to
a drop box
folder inside
someone's
Public
folder;
there's
nothing to
see if you're
not the
owner.

Sometimes you need to log on to another user's folder on your network with a different user ID than the one you are currently logged in with. (This could happen if you have saved settings in KeyChain and now want to log on with a different ID.) Here's how you do it:

1. **Log out from the remote server.**

   In the Finder, drag the remote server to the Trash. (The Trash may change to an Eject icon when you're dragging a server or disc rather than a file or folder.) Or select the remote server on the desktop, ⌘-click to open the contextual menu, and choose Eject. A third method is to click the eject button next to the remote server's name in the Finder sidebar.

2. **Log on again with the new ID you want to use.**

   Click the Network icon, as shown in Figure 22-4.

3. **Make certain that you log on as a registered user instead of a guest.**

Figure 22-4:
Connect
again.

Sharing Content Using Send To

Choosing Share⇨Send via Mail lets you send documents via e-mail. The Send To command lets you send a PDF file or a native iWork file. In addition, you can send the corresponding Microsoft Office file type (Word, Excel, or PowerPoint).

Using Media from iPhoto, iTunes, and iMovie

All the iWork applications let you insert media from iPhoto, iTunes, GarageBand, or iMovie. Begin by clicking Media on the toolbar to open Media Browser, shown in Figure 22-5.

Figure 22-5:
Use Media
Browser
to insert
media.

The iWork apps have tools to adjust inserted media. These adjustments don't affect the basic media file itself, so you don't have to worry about accidentally making changes to your valued photos, music, and movies.

Using PDF Files as Images

PDF files can serve as images for your iWork documents. Remember that you can save almost any type of document as a PDF file. After the document has been saved as a PDF file, you can insert it in an iWork app. This is a backup strategy for sharing files; iWork apps can open many types of files directly. For example, the standard File⇨Open command in Pages lets you open a Microsoft Word document; Pages takes care of the conversion for you. The PDF strategy works well for any type of document that you can print as a PDF file and that you're not able to open directly in an iWork app (although you may not be able to make changes in it).

Adding Hyperlinks to iWork Documents

You can add hyperlinks to iWork documents so that you can click the hyperlink and see the hyperlink's data on the screen. Here's how to add a hyperlink to an iWork document:

1. **In an iWork document, select the text that will become the hyperlink.**

2. **Open Link inspector, as shown in Figure 22-6.**

3. **Select the type of link and then type the link's URL in the inspector.**

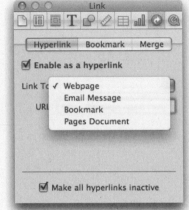

Figure 22-6:
Use Link inspector to create a hyperlink in an iWork document.

Moving Data from Other Applications into iWork

The all-purpose method for moving data from other applications into iWork is Insert⇨Choose. This opens the standard file dialog shown in Figure 22-7. Among the types of files you can open are standard GIF and JPEG files, Photoshop files (.psd), HTML files, and PDF files.

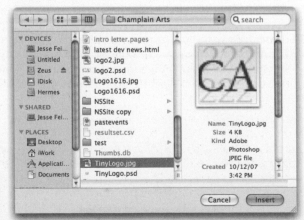

Figure 22-7:
Import a variety of file types.

Chapter 23

Ten Ways to Let iWork for Mac Do the Work for You

Are you pointing and clicking your way through the tasks at hand? With the Mac OS X automation tools, you can specify what you want to do and then have Mac OS X and apps such as the iWork apps carry out your wishes.

A wide variety of automation tools are available. Some construct scripts using scripting languages found not only in Mac OS X but also in other operating systems. Two of the most important Mac OS X–only tools are AppleScript and Automator. They're the jumping-off point for this chapter. After you see the basics of AppleScript and Automator, you find specific ways to use them to automate your iWork projects.

AppleScript's syntax is built into Mac OS X and many applications, including the iWork applications. AppleScript has two major components:

✔ **AppleScript Editor:** This is the primary application that you use to create scripts for AppleScript. It is within the Utilities folder, which is inside the Applications folder on your hard drive. You don't have to do anything to turn on AppleScript Editor; it's part of the normal Mac OS X installation.

✔ **AppleScript dictionaries:** Every AppleScript-aware application has its own AppleScript dictionary. The AppleScript dictionary for an application is built automatically from the AppleScript commands that the developer supports in the application; no external documentation is required. If AppleScript is supported by the app, the AppleScript dictionary is visible in the File➪Open Dictionary command of AppleScript Editor.

Letting iWork do your work

A host of timesaving features are built into the iWork apps. The most obvious are the built-in themes and templates. Instead of starting from a blank document, you can start from a document with built-in pages, sheets, and sections. You don't have to worry about laying out your documents. You can perform the much simpler task of modifying existing documents.

There's a second way to save time with the iWork apps. Rather than retype content, you can copy and paste it from other documents (not just from iWork documents) or drag it over to your new document. This reuse of material

helps you get the most out of your previous analysis and keystrokes (not to mention movies and graphics you've already stored in your media libraries on Mac OS X).

With AppleScript, you have yet another way of saving time. You can construct scripts that create and format sections of iWork applications. These can work together with the built-in themes and templates. To get the most out of iWork (and the most out of your time!), you'll probably want to explore all these ways of working. Use whatever feels most convenient at any given time.

Finding and Browsing the Keynote AppleScript Dictionary

The first step in using AppleScript is to browse the dictionary for the appropriate application. Browsing the dictionary is the first step to scripting the creation of an iWork (or any other app) document. Here's how to browse the Keynote dictionary:

1. **Launch Script Editor.**

   Choose Applications⇨Utilities⇨AppleScript Editor (on pre-Lion versions choose Applications⇨AppleScript⇨Script Editor). By default, you see the basic window shown in Figure 23-1.

2. **Open the script dictionary by choosing File⇨Open Dictionary.**

   Locate the application you're looking for, as shown in Figure 23-2. Note that each application has its own version number. You'll probably find a number of previous versions of your various software products.

3. **View the suites.**

   AppleScript dictionaries are divided into suites, as shown in Figure 23-3. Each suite can have commands (a C in a circle) as well as components (a C in a square). Each has a syntax description.

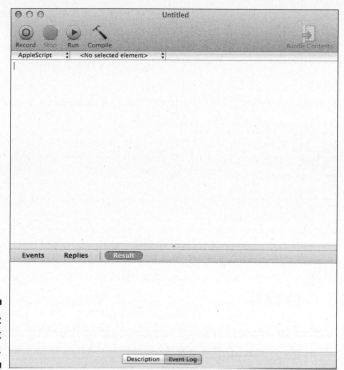

Figure 23-1:
Open Script
Editor.

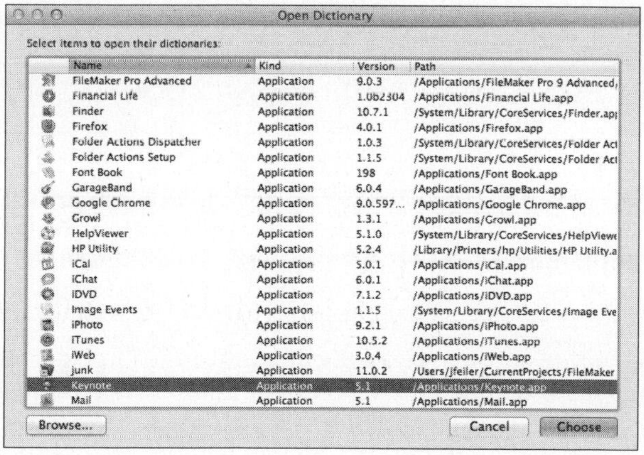

Figure 23-2:
Open the
appropriate
dictionary.

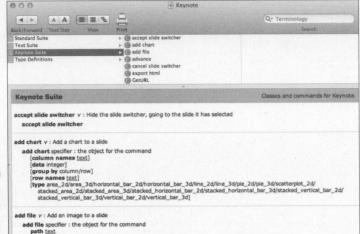

Figure 23-3:
Look at the
suites.

Creating a Script

If you've used any programming languages, you'll find using the syntax for a script even simpler because AppleScript Editor has the full syntax and examples in its Help menu.

Scripts are usually addressed to specific AppleScript objects: These can be applications or objects within applications. (The dictionary tells you what objects are addressable.) Figure 23-4 provides a basic script for use with Keynote.

Counting slides in a slide show

Commands are addressed to scriptable items. Spacing is generated automatically in Script Editor when you click either Run or Compile. If there are syntax errors, the text coloring or spacing (or both) clearly indicates that there's a problem.

The script shown in Figure 23-4 is simple. Here's what's happening:

✔ `tell application "Keynote":` All commands within this section (called a `tell` *block*) are sent to Pages.

✔ `tell slideshow 1:` Within Keynote, each opened document is given a number automatically when it is opened. Document 1 is the frontmost document, and Keynote makes certain that it receives the next line of code.

✔ `count slides:` Document 1 is asked to count the number of tables it has.

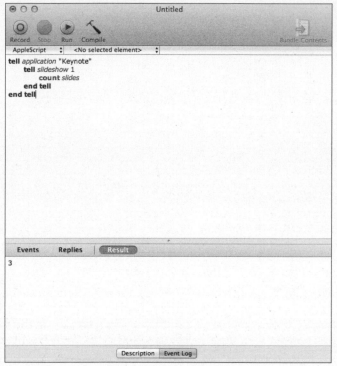

Figure 23-4:
Create a
script for
Keynote.

The dictionary for Keynote includes the count command in the Standard
Suite, as shown in Figure 23-5. As soon as you've spent some time with
AppleScript, you'll become familiar with the basic suites, such as the
Standard Suite. Developers are encouraged to implement the basic parts of
AppleScript in the same way for each application. This task is made easier
because the Mac OS X development framework (Cocoa) handles a lot of this
implementation so neither user nor developer needs to worry much about
the implementation of the count command.

The syntax is similar for each iWork app. With Pages, use tell document
1 to count pages; with Numbers, use tell document 1 to count
sheets. The dictionary for each one tells you what the document or other
object is and what it can contain.

Adding a slide to a slide show

The script shown in Figure 23-6 is a variation on the previous script. It tells
the current slide show to add a slide and then to count the resulting number
of slide. The code to add the slide is part of the Keynote application suite.

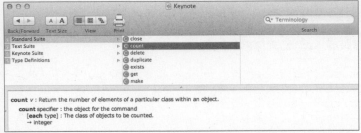

Figure 23-5:
The count
command is
described
in the
dictionary.

This is a fairly typical structure of suites for an AppleScript-enabled application. Suites such as the Standard Suite are implemented by almost all AppleScript-enabled applications. Then a specific application such as Pages, Numbers, or Keynote is likely to have its own application suite that can act on objects within the application. Further focused suites, such as the Pages Graphics Suite and Pages Text Suite, handle specific types of operations.

Figure 23-6 shows the script that adds the slide.

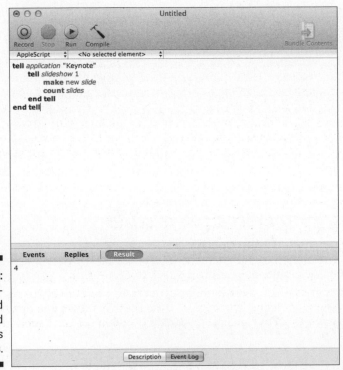

Figure 23-6:
Tell a document to add a table and count its tables.

Retrieving properties about a slide in Keynote

You can always get properties for objects that are addressable in AppleScript. Figure 23-7 shows you how you can get the properties for the slide you just created.

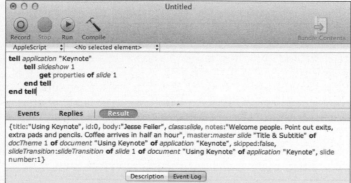

Figure 23-7: Tell a document to get the properties for a table.

Compare the properties of a slide as retrieved through AppleScript with the properties for the same table as shown in Slide inspector in Keynote. If you really want to get into the nuts-and-bolts of an application like Keynote (or any other iWork app), you can get used to this cross-referencing of settings. Often a slightly different terminology is used for an Inspector window than for AppleScript properties. Sometimes the difference in terminology reflects different audiences for interactive users of the software and people who are writing scripts.

Setting properties for a slide in Keynote (version 1)

As you can see in Figure 23-7, you can get the properties for a slide (or any other iWork object). You can set those properties interactively using the Inspector window or using AppleScript. This section shows you one way of setting preferences. (You can find another method in the next section.)

In previous scripts, you've seen how you can get or set information through AppleScript. In general, you create a *tell block* to send information to Keynote (or whatever app you're dealing with). Within that `tell` block, you ask the app to send one or more commands to a specific document (or slide show in the case of Keynote), and the app then asks slide show to reference the slide or other object you need to handle. In the previous examples, you ask the app to tell Slideshow 1 to get information about Slide 1.

To set properties, you can use the structure shown in Figure 23-8. Here, the same `tell` block sends commands to Keynote; within that `tell` block, messages are sent not to Slideshow 1, but instead to Slide 1 of Slideshow 1.

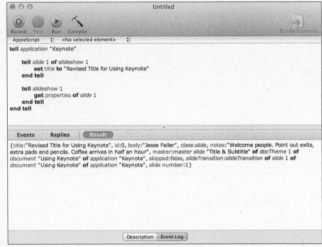

Figure 23-8:
Set preferences
(version 1).

A final `tell` block is addressed to Slideshow 1, not to Slide 1 of Slideshow 1, because the document needs to retrieve the properties for the table it contains.

The section that sets properties is based on the output shown previously in Figure 23-7. Although you can look up properties in the AppleScript dictionary, the fastest way to find the correct names and spelling of properties is to get the properties for a similar object (such as a table) and use the names and spellings such as those shown in Figure 23-7 as the basis for setting properties as shown in Figure 23-8.

Setting properties for a slide in Keynote (version 2)

This version of setting properties uses a `tell` block that goes directly to the appropriate slide show. Instead of dispatching commands to Slide 1 of Slideshow 1, the commands are dispatched to Slideshow 1, and those commands reference Slide 1, as shown in Figure 23-9.

Neither of these two versions is better than the other; you can use whichever one seems easiest to you at the time.

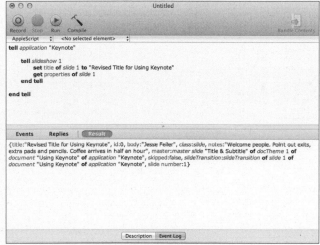

Figure 23-9:
Set pref-
erences
(version 2).

Using Automator with Keynote

One of the other major components of Mac OS X automation is Automator. Like AppleScript, it's installed automatically as part of your operating system. You can find Automator in your Applications folder.

Figure 23-10 shows you the basics of Automator. With Script Editor, you can create scripted code for operations you want to perform. With Automator, you're developing a workflow that brings together sequences of events.

At the left side of the Automator window are various actions that you can use to build a workflow at the right. When you select an action at the left, its description is shown at the bottom of the window. As you drag it into the workflow area, the actions are added, one to the other. The arrows between the actions indicate that output from one action can flow into the next action as input.

The sample Automator workflow shown in Figure 23-10 lets you select Finder items. It then automatically creates new Keynote slides from each image you've selected.

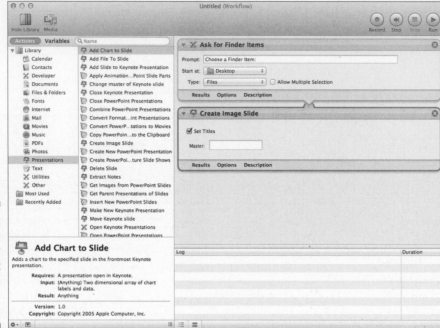

Figure 23-10:
Use
Automator
to import
images to
Keynote
slides.

Using Automator with Images

Automator comes with a number of actions that you can assemble into workflows to handle images. Figure 23-11 shows how you can use three actions in a workflow to prepare images for use in any application (including the iWork applications).

Simply drag these three actions into the workflow. As you drag the scaling and rotating actions, you'll be warned that these actions will permanently affect the files you've selected. Automator not only warns you but also offers to add actions to the workflow to copy the files before they're adjusted. Those steps have been omitted from Figure 23-11 for simplicity.

This type of workflow can make your use of images more consistent so that they are scaled appropriately.

Using Automator with Multiple Files

Many of your Automator workflows start with the Ask for Finder Items action. You set up the workflow you want to perform, and everything is automatic once you start it running and select the files.

Instead of selecting an individual file, create a folder into which you put a number of files that you want to process. You can put those files into the folder whenever you feel like it — possibly over a period of days. Then, when it comes time to carry out the workflow, start with the Ask for Finder Items action as usual to select the folder, but then insert one of the two actions that can automatically select the individual files:

✔ Get Folder Contents starts from the folder you select in Ask for Finder Items and then takes each file within it and sends the whole set of files into the next action. An option lets you repeat this action for subfolders (*recursively*, as programmers would say).

✔ Filter Finder Items selects all the files within a folder based on criteria you specify, such as the filename (or part of a name) or the type of file.

You can combine both actions so that you get the contents of a folder (and possibly its subfolders), then filter only the JPEG files, and pass them on to image manipulation or to another action, such as `Create Image Slide`.

The Finder handles alias files just as it does actual files. This means you can create a folder into which you place aliases of files you want to process in Automator. (To create an alias, select the file and choose File⇨Make Alias or ⌘-L.) You can keep the actual files wherever you would normally store them on your computer. When you've finished with the Automator action, you can trash the folder with the aliases.

Looping Around Automator

Automator excels at combining actions and sending the output from one action into the next one as input. It easily picks up all the items in a folder, possibly filtering them. "All" is an important part of Automator. It means you don't have to write code that is repeated for each folder or other object.

But sometimes that's important. A recent addition to Automator is the `Loop` action. Along with the `Run Workflow` action, you can create powerful workflows that can help you with iWork and other applications.

The `Loop` action lets you run the following action a certain number of times. You can take any action you have already created and run it with `Run Workflow`. This means that you could modify the workflows suggested previously so that you can make slides from the first 10 JPEG images in a folder. That's a handy workflow to use to test if your slide layout is going to work with those images. When you're satisfied, take out the loop and let the workflow run overnight with all your images.

You can use `Loop` and `Run Workflow` to create handouts for a meeting. Create a workflow that prints several documents. You can use `Ask for Finder Items`, but you have to interact with it (so it can't run unattended). Use `Get Specified Finder Items` so that you can specify the items you want in advance and the workflow can then run unattended.

For each document that you want to print for the handout, use `Get Specified Finder Items` to select that one document. In the workflow, place `Print Finder Items` below it so that document will be printed. Then repeat the process with each document you want for the handout. The workflow will then print them in the order you have specified. Add the `Loop` action to run that workflow, and you'll have an automated way to print and collate as many copies of your handouts as you specify (provided you don't run out of paper).

Index

• E •

• G •

• H •

• Q •

• R •

• S •